Books by Philip C. Beam

THE LANGUAGE OF ART

WINSLOW HOMER AT PROUT'S NECK

Winslow Homer
at Prout's Neck

Fig. 1. WINSLOW HOMER IN HIS MIDDLE FORTIES.
Photograph taken about 1880. Homer Collection, Bowdoin College Museum of Art.

Winslow Homer
at Prout's Neck

by PHILIP C. BEAM

With a foreword by Charles Lowell Homer

ILLUSTRATED

LITTLE, BROWN AND COMPANY · BOSTON · TORONTO

Published simultaneously in Canada
by Little, Brown & Company (Canada) Limited

PRINTED IN THE UNITED STATES OF AMERICA

TO CHARLES LOWELL HOMER,
WHOSE UNTIRING HELP AND
INTEREST MADE THIS BOOK
POSSIBLE

Foreword

THIS new study of the life, character, and methods of work of my uncle Winslow Homer has had from its beginning my full approval and cooperation.

When Philip Beam, who has always expressed intense enthusiasm for the art of Winslow Homer, suggested that he wished to write a new biography, I asked only that the truth, good and bad, be presented in sufficient detail to reconstruct a living personality.

I have placed at his disposal all records, old letters, maps, genealogies, drawings, and paintings in my possession. I have explained their significance to him. I have welcomed him to live and work in Winslow Homer's old studio, to walk the cliffs and study the rocks and the sea, just as Uncle Winslow painted them. I have given him my recollections of my uncle as well as my wife's. And I have introduced him to residents of Prout's Neck who knew and walked with Winslow Homer, in order that he might get all available information to make this a true and authentic record of the character of Winslow Homer the man.

The art of Winslow Homer is best epitomized by the lines on the memorial tablet in the sanctuary at Prout's Neck: ". . . Winslow Homer who with his brush gave Prout's Neck to the world."

CHARLES L. HOMER

Prout's Neck, Maine

[ix]

Preface

THE writing of this book has been from beginning to end a fascinating task, primarily because the first time I saw one of Winslow Homer's paintings I was attracted to his art and have never ceased to enjoy it. Through this book I hope to communicate something of that pleasure to others.

I have also been motivated by a desire to further scholarly and critical understanding of Homer's work. I wanted especially to make available information about the artist which was given to me over many years by his nephew, the late Charles Lowell Homer, and by other residents of Prout's Neck, Maine, who knew Homer intimately, as well as information in the family archives and memorabilia given to Bowdoin College by Doris Piper Homer (Mrs. Charles L. Homer) and known as the Homer Collection. In order to give this material its fullest meaning, I have presented it in relation to the chronology of Homer's life, drawing background data from the excellent biographies by William Howe Downes (1911) and Lloyd Goodrich (1944) and from numerous other books and periodicals (see the Selected Bibliography following the text). The factual material in this book thus derives from both personal interviews and printed sources.

In addition I have tried to contribute something original to appreciation of Homer's character and art through interpretation based on the facts at my disposal and upon internal evidence in his pictures as I have come to know them during twenty years of study. I wanted to provide in this way a pair of eyes for those less familiar with his work.

In seeking to enhance understanding of Homer's art I have stressed two main avenues of inquiry: one pointing toward refinement of our critical evaluation of Homer's art; the other toward fuller understanding of his historical position in relation to American and European art of his time and to Western and Oriental traditions in art. These, I believe, are the directions that studies of Homer will take for a number of years to come, and that is why I have been at pains to include in the following pages as much material as possible on Homer's personality and on activities that bore subtly and indirectly, as well as obviously, upon his career.

The difficulty of placing Homer within a tradition stems in part from his working through much of his life in isolation and his singular taciturnity about his artistic practices. Hence he gives the impression of being extraordinarily independent, an artist owing little to anyone else — a view he himself tended to encourage. That this impression is erroneous is one of the things I have tried to prove. Homer had neither the provincialism nor the retarded development that complete isolation usually means; his mind and art developed tremendously during his long career. How much of that growth was due to innate capacity and how much to the ability to learn from others is one of the questions I have weighed. My aim is to do credit to Homer's undoubted originality and at the same time to give him his rightful place in the history of European and American art. For to be great in art does not mean to tower alone, but to excel within a strong tradition.

Where both documentary evidence and testimony from the artist were lacking, I have sought to establish his roots and ties by stylistic, or circumstantial, evidence. In art as in legal procedure, it is often the surest kind. I have devoted the main body of the text primarily to a running critical analysis and appraisal of Homer's work as it developed from 1883 to 1910, when his principal residence and base of operations was Prout's Neck, Maine. The introductory chapter and the Tynemouth chapter are intended only to provide a summary of his activities prior to 1883. In trying to define both his intrinsic distinguishing characteristics of style and his comparative merits, I have striven to be as objective as my enthusiasm permits. I have no fear of appearing to debunk or belittle, because Homer's limitations are an integral and complementary part of his character and art as a whole.

The crucial critical questions, as I see them, are two: Was Homer, visually speaking, primarily a naïve naturalist who only recorded what he saw in the limited physical sense, or an interpretive realist who imposed an abstract rhythm of his own creation upon everything he depicted? To put the question another way: Did he produce merely recognizable relationships or create a style founded upon organized relationships? And, second, was he intellectually only an illustrator of incidents or a profound observer of nature and human life? In the answer to these questions lies his stature as a man and an artist.

P.C.B.

Bowdoin College
Brunswick, Maine

Acknowledgments

I<small>T</small> is a pleasure to acknowledge here the help given me by many people, and especially by Charles Lowell Homer. Hundreds of footnotes would be needed to qualify precisely the extent to which he aided me. In addition I received assistance and encouragement over a period of many years from other members of his family: his first wife Mary George Clark Homer, his daughter Alice (Mrs. A. Osborne Willauer), and his widow Doris Piper Homer.

I wish also to mention my obligation to the following residents of Prout's Neck and Scarboro, Maine, who helped me generously: Miss Sadie Ellis, Miss Emily H. Everett, Dr. Charles Farr, Mr. Joseph Foss, Mr. Roswell Googins, Mrs. Charles Harding (Ida Meserve), Mr. Harry Kaler, Mrs. Howard C. Larrabee (Marie Annie Seavey), Mrs. Allen Libby (Maude Googins), Mr. Leonard Libby, Mrs. William H. Munroe (Annie Jane Fearns), Mrs. George Putnam (Lucy Holland), Mrs. Loring C. Richardson (Sadie Sylvester), Mrs. Maxwell Savage (Marguerite Downing), Mrs. Albert Stevens (Charlotte Googins), Mr. Harvey Urquahart, and Mrs. Edward G. Vaill (Addie Kaler).

Professor William Witherle Lawrence and Mr. John Howard Stevens of Portland, and Mr. Alexander Bower, formerly Director of the Portland Art Museum, furnished me with information and recollections of Winslow Homer for which I am grateful. I was assisted too in the clarification and development of a number of troublesome points by the late Harold Trowbridge Pulsifer of Cundy's Harbor, Maine, whose family knew Homer intimately.

Several members of the faculty of Bowdoin College — Dr. Edward Kirkland, Dr. Norman Munn, Dr. Thomas A. Riley, and Dr. Carl N. Schmalz, Jr. — gave me the benefit of expert knowledge in their fields for which I stand in their debt. James S. Coles, President of Bowdoin College, gave me valuable encouragement and practical help, as did Marvin S. Sadik, Director of the Bowdoin College Museum of Art, and Miss Gertrude Plaisted and Mrs. Dee Hiebert, former Secretaries of the Museum. I wish also to express my thanks for a grant from the Shell Oil Company which provided the extensive secretarial work and typing necessary for any research project.

Chandler Rathfon Post, late Professor Emeritus of the Fine Arts Department of Harvard University, read the first draft of the text and advised me on many matters of organization and revision, giving me throughout the benefit of his vast experience in orientation and emphasis and his encyclopedic knowledge of the history of art. The longtime interest and encouragement of Professor Benjamin Rowland of the Fine Arts Department of Harvard University was also greatly appreciated.

I can hardly thank sufficiently another close friend, Stephen E. Merrill, a brilliant raconteur, lecturer, photographer, and poet, who aided me through hundreds of hours in the revision, organization, phrasing and styling of the completed text.

I am grateful to the private collectors and public museums which own works of art by Winslow Homer for cooperating with me by sending photographs with permission to use them, and information about them. I wish also to thank the Macbeth, Babcock, and Knoedler Galleries of New York for supplying me with photographs and lending me negatives of pictures which would otherwise have been inaccessible. All of them illustrate the extent to which a book of this sort is a cooperative venture.

In that respect, I wish particularly to acknowledge my indebtedness to Little, Brown and Company of Boston for their fine and unstinting cooperation throughout the process of publication.

P.C.B.

Bowdoin College
Brunswick, Maine

Contents

Foreword by Charles L. Homer   ix

Preface   x

Acknowledgments   xiii

List of Illustrations   xvii

I.   THE YEARS OF PREPARATION, 1836–1881
An Introduction   3

II.   AN ARTIST AT THE CROSSROADS
Tynemouth, 1881–1882   15

III.   MATURITY AT PROUT'S NECK, 1883–1889   25

IV.   THE NINETIES
The Peak of a Career   85

V.   THE MAN AND THE ARTIST   174

VI.   THE FINAL DECADE, 1900–1910   209

Appendix   259

Selected Bibliography   265

Index   273

Illustrations

(All dimensions are in inches; height precedes width.)

1. WINSLOW HOMER IN HIS MIDDLE FORTIES. Photograph taken about 1880. Homer Collection, Bowdoin College Museum of Art, Brunswick, Maine.   *frontispiece*

2. WATCHING THE TEMPEST. 1881. Watercolor. 14 x 20. Fogg Art Museum, Harvard University, Cambridge, Massachusetts. Grenville L. Winthrop Bequest.   22

3. THE OCEAN FRONT AT PROUT'S NECK. Photograph taken about 1883. Homer Collection, Bowdoin College Museum of Art, Brunswick, Maine.   30

4. WINSLOW HOMER'S STUDIO AT PROUT'S NECK. Photograph taken in 1936 by Charles L. Homer. Homer Collection, Bowdoin College Museum of Art, Brunswick, Maine.   31

5. LIVING ROOM OF WINSLOW HOMER'S STUDIO. Photograph taken in 1936 by Charles L. Homer. Homer Collection, Bowdoin College Museum of Art, Brunswick, Maine.   32

6. WINSLOW HOMER'S MOTHER. Homer Collection, Bowdoin College Museum of Art, Brunswick, Maine.   35

7. CANNA INDICA. From an album of flowers and plants by Winslow Homer's mother. Watercolor. 21 x 13¾. William Wikoff Smith, Bryn Mawr, Pennsylvania.   37

8. WINSLOW HOMER WITH HIS FATHER AND SAM AT PROUT'S NECK. Photograph taken about 1890. Homer Collection, Bowdoin College Museum of Art, Brunswick, Maine.   43

9. THE SHIP'S BOAT. 1883. Watercolor. 16 x 29. New Britain Museum of American Art, New Britain, Connecticut.   60

10. PROUT'S NECK, ROCKY SHORE. 1883. Watercolor. 14 x 21. Worcester Art Museum, Worcester, Massachusetts.   61

11. PROUT'S NECK, BREAKING WAVE. 1887. Watercolor. 15 x 21. The Art Institute of Chicago. Mr. and Mrs. Martin A. Ryerson Collection.   62

12. THE LIFE LINE. 1884. Oil. 29 x 45. Commissioners of Fairmount Park, George W. Elkins Collection. Courtesy of the Philadelphia Museum of Art.   63

13. A HAUL OF HERRING. 1884. Monochrome drawing (charcoal and Chinese white.) 14⅞ x 23¼. Courtesy, Museum of Fine Arts, Boston.   67

14. THE HERRING NET. 1885. Oil. 35 x 48. The Art Institute of Chicago. Mr. and Mrs. Martin R. Ryerson Collection.   67

15. HALIBUT FISHING. 1884. From a photograph signed by Winslow Homer. Mrs. Charles L. Homer, Prout's Neck, Maine.   70

16. THE FOG WARNING. 1885. Oil. 30 x 48. Courtesy, Museum of Fine Arts, Boston.   71

17. STREET SCENE, SANTIAGO DE CUBA. 1885. Watercolor. 11¾ x 17¼. Philadelphia Museum of Art. Given by Dr. and Mrs. George Woodward.   76

18. CONCH DIVERS. 1885. Watercolor. 13½ x 19½. The Minneapolis Institute of Arts.   78

19. THE SPONGE DIVER, BAHAMAS. 1889. Watercolor. 13½ x 19. Courtesy, Museum of Fine Arts, Boston.   79

20. EIGHT BELLS. 1886. Oil. 25 x 30. Addison Gallery of American Art, Phillips Academy, Andover, Massachusetts.   81

21. TROUT BREAKING. 1889. Watercolor. 13⁹⁄₁₆ x 19⅝. Courtesy, Museum of Fine Arts, Boston.   87

22. A SUMMER NIGHT. 1890. Oil. 29¼ x 40. Musée National d'Art Moderne, Paris.   90

23. SUNLIGHT ON THE COAST. 1890. Oil. 30 x 40. The Toledo Museum of Art. Gift of Mr. and Mrs. Edward Drummond Libbey.   92

24. WINTER COAST. 1890. Oil. 36 x 31⅛. John G. Johnson Collection, Philadelphia.   94

25. THE WEST WIND. 1891. Oil. 30 x 43½. Addison Gallery of American Art, Phillips Academy, Andover, Massachusetts.   97

26. CAMP FIRE, ADIRONDACKS. About 1892. Watercolor. 14 x 21. The Art Institute of Chicago. Mr. and Mrs. Martin A. Ryerson Collection.   100

27. ADIRONDACK GUIDE. 1894. Watercolor. 15 x 21¼. Courtesy, Museum of Fine Arts, Boston.   101

28. JOHN GATCHELL. Photograph taken about 1895. Homer Collection, Bowdoin College Museum of Art, Brunswick, Maine.   102

29. CANOEIST, LAKE ST. JOHN, PROVINCE OF QUEBEC. About 1895. Photograph by Winslow Homer. Homer Collection, Bowdoin College Museum of Art, Brunswick, Maine.   104

30. WINSLOW HOMER IN A CANOE. About 1895. Photograph by Charles S. Homer, Jr. Homer Collection, Bowdoin College Museum of Art, Brunswick, Maine.   105

31. THE END OF THE HUNT. 1892. Watercolor. 15¼ x 21½. Bowdoin College Museum of Art, Brunswick, Maine. Gift of the Misses Mary Sophia Walker and Harriet Sarah Walker.   106

32. THE FOX HUNT. 1893. Oil. 38 x 68. Pennsylvania Academy of the Fine Arts, Philadelphia.   109

33. THE COMING AWAY OF THE GALE. 1883. From a photograph, signed by Winslow Homer, of the painting in its original state. Homer Collection, Bowdoin College Museum of Art, Brunswick, Maine.   112

34. THE GALE. 1883 and 1893. Oil. 29½ x 48. Worcester Art Museum, Worcester, Massachusetts.   113

35. Frederick MacMonnies, FOUNTAIN. 1893. World's Columbian Exposition, Chicago. Photograph taken in 1893.   114

36. THE FOUNTAINS AT NIGHT, WORLD'S COLUMBIAN EXPOSITION. 1893. Oil. 16 x 25. Bowdoin College Museum of Art, Brunswick, Maine. Gift of Mrs. Charles Savage Homer, Jr.   115

37. FISHERMAN, ADIRONDACKS. About 1894. Photograph by Winslow Homer. Homer Collection, Bowdoin College Museum of Art, Brunswick, Maine.   118

38. THE NORTH WOODS. 1894. Watercolor. 15 x 21½. The Currier Gallery of Art, Manchester, New Hampshire. Gift of Mr. and Mrs. Frederic Haines Curtiss.   119

39. MOONLIGHT, WOOD'S ISLAND LIGHT. 1894. Oil. 30½ x 40. The Metropolitan Museum of Art, Wolfe Fund, 1906.   120

40. THE ARK AND HOMER'S STUDIO, PROUT'S NECK. Photograph by Philip C. Beam, 1950.   122

41. THE ARTIST'S STUDIO IN AN AFTERNOON FOG. 1894. Oil. 24 x 30. The Memorial Art Gallery of the University of Rochester. R. T. Miller Fund.   123

42. HIGH CLIFF, PROUT'S NECK. Photograph by Philip C. Beam, 1960.   124

43. HIGH CLIFF, COAST OF MAINE. 1894. Oil. 30¼ x 38¼. National Gallery of Art, Washington, D.C. Lent by the National Collection of Fine Arts, Smithsonian Institution.   125

44. Detail: HUDSON RIVER LOGGING. 1897. Watercolor. In the Collection of the Corcoran Gallery of Art, Washington, D.C.   128

45. HUDSON RIVER LOGGING. 1897. Watercolor. 14 x 21. In the Collection of the Corcoran Gallery of Art, Washington, D.C.   128

46. TROUT FISHING, LAKE ST. JOHN, PROVINCE OF QUEBEC. 1895. Watercolor. 13½ x 20½. Courtesy, Museum of Fine Arts, Boston.   129

47. THREE MEN IN A CANOE. 1895. Monochrome watercolor (sepia and Chinese white). 13¾ x 19¾. Courtesy of the Knoedler Galleries, New York City.   129

48. WOLFE'S COVE, PROVINCE OF QUEBEC. 1895. Monochrome

watercolor (sepia and Chinese white). 13⅞ x 19½. Bowdoin College Museum of Art, Brunswick, Maine. Gift of Messrs. Neal W. Allen, John F. Dana, John H. Halford, William W. Lawrence, and Benjamin R. Shute.   131

49. HOMER'S CABIN, TOURILLI CLUB, PROVINCE OF QUEBEC. 1895. Photograph by Winslow Homer. Homer Collection, Bowdoin College Museum of Art, Brunswick, Maine.   132

50. HOMER'S CABIN, TOURILLI CLUB, PROVINCE OF QUEBEC (Second Version). 1895. Monochrome watercolor (sepia and Chinese white). 13⅛ x 19½. Estate of Dr. Simon Stone, Manchester, New Hampshire.   133

51. BEAR BREAKING THROUGH A CANOE. 1895. Watercolor. 13½ x 19¾. The Brooklyn Museum.   134

52. CANNON ROCK, PROUT'S NECK. Photograph by Philip C. Beam, 1950.   136

53. CANNON ROCK. 1895. Oil. 39½ x 39¼. The Metropolitan Museum of Art, Wolfe Fund, 1906.   137

54. AN EQUINOCTIAL STORM, PROUT'S NECK. October 12, 1937. Photograph by Charles L. Homer. Homer Collection, Bowdoin College Museum of Art, Brunswick, Maine.   138

55. NORTHEASTER. 1895. Oil. 34¼ x 50¼. The Metropolitan Museum of Art.   139

56. SUNSET, SACO BAY. 1896. Oil. 25 x 38½. Courtesy of the Sterling and Francine Clark Art Institute, Williamstown, Massachusetts.   142

57. BLOWN AWAY. Probably 1896. Watercolor. 10¹⁄₁₆ x 19. The Brooklyn Museum.   144

58. A SUMMER SQUALL. 1904. Oil. 24 x 30. Courtesy of the Sterling and Francine Clark Art Institute, Williamstown, Massachusetts.   144

59. THE LOOKOUT — "ALL'S WELL." 1896. Oil. 40 x 30. Courtesy, Museum of Fine Arts, Boston.   146

60. THE WRECK. 1896. Oil. 30 x 48. From the Collection of the Carnegie Institute, Pittsburgh.   148

61. Wu Chên, BAMBOO IN THE WIND. Chinese, early fourteenth century, Yüan Dynasty. Courtesy, Museum of Fine Arts, Boston.   160

62. TORNADO, BAHAMAS. 1898. Watercolor. 14½ x 21. The Metropolitan Museum of Art.   161

63. WATERFALL IN THE ADIRONDACKS. About 1894. Watercolor. 14 x 20. Courtesy of the Smithsonian Institution, Freer Gallery of Art, Washington, D.C.   163

64. THE MINK POND. 1891. Watercolor. 13½ x 19⅝. Fogg Art Museum, Harvard University, Cambridge, Massachusetts. Grenville L. Winthrop Bequest.   164

65. CANOE IN THE RAPIDS. 1897. Watercolor. 13½ x 20½. Fogg Art Museum, Harvard University, Cambridge, Massachusetts. Louise E. Bettens Fund.   165

66. OUANANICHE FISHING. 1897. Watercolor. 11 x 19½. Courtesy, Museum of Fine Arts, Boston.   165

67. SLOOP, BERMUDA. 1899. Watercolor. 14 x 21. The Metropolitan Museum of Art.   166

68. RUM CAY. 1898. Watercolor. 14¹⁵⁄₁₆ x 21⅜. Worcester Art Museum, Worcester, Massachusetts.   167

69. TURTLE POUND. 1898. Watercolor. 14¹⁵⁄₁₆ x 21⅜. The Brooklyn Museum. A. T. White Memorial Fund, A. A. Healy Fund.   167

70. THE GULF STREAM. 1889. Watercolor. 11 x 19½. The Art Institute of Chicago. Mr. and Mrs. Martin A. Ryerson Collection.   168

71. THE GULF STREAM. 1899. Oil. 28⅛ x 49⅛. The Metropolitan Museum of Art, Wolfe Fund, 1906.   169

72. WEST POINT, PROUT'S NECK. 1900. Oil. 30 x 48. Courtesy of the Sterling and Francine Clark Art Institute, Williamstown, Massachusetts.   212

73. EASTERN POINT, PROUT'S NECK. Photograph by Philip C. Beam, 1955.   214

74. EASTERN POINT, PROUT'S NECK. 1900. Oil. 30 x 40. Courtesy of the Sterling and Francine Clark Art Institute, Williamstown, Massachusetts.   215

75. THE COMING STORM. 1901. Watercolor. 14 x 20¾. Mrs. Charles R. Henschel, New York City.   218

76. SEARCHLIGHT, HARBOR ENTRANCE, SANTIAGO DE CUBA. 1901. Oil. 30½ x 50½. The Metropolitan Museum of Art. Gift of George A. Hearn, 1906.   219

77. HIGH CLIFF, PROUT'S NECK. Photograph by Robert Macbeth, 1936.   222

78. BREAKING WAVE. 1887. Watercolor. 14 x 20½. Courtesy, Museum of Fine Arts, Boston.   223

79. EARLY MORNING AFTER A STORM AT SEA. 1902. Oil. 30¼ x 50. The Cleveland Museum of Art. Gift from J. H. Wade.   223

80. STOWING SAIL, BAHAMAS. 1903. Watercolor. 13¹⁵⁄₁₆ x 21¹³⁄₁₆. The Art Institute of Chicago. Mr. and Mrs. Martin A. Ryerson Collection.   225

81. WINSLOW HOMER AND GUIDES, HOMOSASSA RIVER, FLORIDA. Photograph taken about 1904. Homer Collection, Bowdoin College Museum of Art, Brunswick, Maine.   226

82. PALM TREES, FLORIDA. Photographed by Winslow Homer about 1904. Homer Collection, Bowdoin College Museum of Art, Brunswick, Maine.   227

83. HOMOSASSA RIVER, 1904. Watercolor. 19¹¹⁄₁₆ x 14. The Brook-
     lyn Museum.   228

84. THE TURKEY BUZZARD. 1904. Watercolor. 13 x 19. Worcester
     Art Museum, Worcester, Massachusetts.   229

85. KISSING THE MOON. 1904. Oil. 30 x 40. Addison Gallery of
     American Art, Phillips Academy, Andover, Massachusetts.   233

86. THE WRECKED SCHOONER. About 1908. Watercolor. 14¾ x
     21⅛. City Art Museum of St. Louis.   235

87. DIAMOND SHOAL. 1905. Watercolor. 13½ x 21½. Collections
     of the International Business Machines Corporation, Armonk,
     New York.   240

88. RIGHT AND LEFT. 1909. Oil. 28¼ x 48⅜. National Gallery
     of Art, Washington, D.C. Gift of the Avalon Foundation.   248

89. CAPE TRINITY, SAGUENAY RIVER. 1904. Oil. 28¾ x 43⅜.
     Guennol Collection, New York City.   250

90. SHOOTING THE RAPIDS AT GRAND DISCHARGE. 1902.
     Watercolor. 13⅞ x 21¾. The Brooklyn Museum.   252

91. SHOOTING THE RAPIDS, SAGUENAY RIVER. 1905. Oil.
     30 x 48. The Metropolitan Museum of Art. Gift of Charles
     Savage Homer, Jr.   253

92. DRIFTWOOD. 1909. Oil. 24 x 28. Dr. and Mrs. Samuel Emlen
     Stokes, Moorestown, New Jersey.   255

Winslow Homer
at Prout's Neck

CHAPTER ONE

The Years of Preparation, 1836–1881

AN INTRODUCTION

IN the annals of art, the story of the youthful prodigy is not uncommon, but the life of Winslow Homer is quite the opposite.
He matured late, working long and hard before he realized his
full potential. Then greatness seemed to come with dramatic sud-
denness. There was a turning point in his life so marked that it
divided his career into two strikingly different chapters, with the
work of his later years standing in powerful contrast to his earlier
work. But behind this turn of events were the years of determined
and exhaustive preparation which, though unspectacular, were
essential to his development. They are the solid foundation of his
final eminence.

In emphasizing the period and place of his greatest achievements, we must not overlook the continuing elements in his life.
Although Homer traveled widely throughout his career, he remained to the end a New England Yankee — practical, self-
contained, sometimes brusque, and always terse. Honest and
fiercely independent, he was plainspoken, but with a dry, salty wit
and a deep interest in people. His travels took him once to Chicago and twice to Europe, but he ranged mainly along the Atlantic seaboard, from Cuba to Canada, and into the Adirondack
Mountains. Born in Massachusetts, he died in Maine.

Yet Homer spoke for all America with a breadth few other artists have achieved. His ultimate reward was a rare attainment, the respect of the most demanding critics and the popular acclaim of his fellow Americans. People could understand him. He was never an abstractionist, a mystic, or a painter of aristocratic elegance. Unlike Albert Ryder, he did not wander in the world of dreams. Unlike Sargent, he avoided the mannered realm of high fashion. He was never a self-conscious stylist, a manipulator of paint and patterns, or an advocate of art for art's sake. Homer painted only a few portraits and even fewer still lifes. An everyday sort of man, both in his life and his painting, he is yet ranked by John Canaday along with Thomas Eakins and John Singleton Copley as one of America's three greatest artists. He differs from them, of course, in many ways, but he shares their fundamental respect for realism and uncompromising honesty. He enjoyed the world around him too much to feel any need to distort it. Not that his approach was mere photographic imitation or surface naturalism. Homer's realism was derived from his thoughtful consideration of what he saw and knew. He was expressing his conception of what was true and basic in the world of nature and of humanity. His art was conceived and created as a service to life and not as a decorative frill. Its worth lies in the way it shows all men a world that is fine and strong and beautiful.

As Homer's insight deepened, his art became at the same time simpler and more profound, especially after his return from Europe in 1882. Gruff, yet not lacking in appeal, Homer could exert great charm. His work was popular during his middle years, and recent exhibitions have excited tremendous admiration. But charm and popularity are not the ultimate proofs of greatness. Homer attained that level only when he added to his lifelong gift for honest clarity a rock-like strength of character, purpose, and execution.

Winslow Homer was born on February 24, 1836, in a house on Friend Street in Boston, near Faneuil Hall and the busy harbor. Salt air, ships, and men of the sea were familiar to him from his earliest childhood. His father, Charles Savage Homer, was a hardware merchant of the district; his mother, Henrietta Maria Benson Homer, a native of Bucksport in down-east Maine. Both came from respectable middle-class families, with a status and outlook which would characterize Homer's own social and economic attitudes as long as he lived.

In 1842, when Winslow was six, Charles Savage Homer moved his wife and three sons to a comfortable house on what is now Massachusetts Avenue in Cambridge, adjacent to Harvard College. The proximity of the college failed to inspire Winslow with a desire for higher education. He was never inclined to book study or literature, and his educational career, which ended in his nineteenth year, was undistinguished. To him school was a tedious hindrance to a carefree outdoor life. On the other hand, he loved to draw. Three of his earliest works are, significantly, a drawing of a boy dreaming in a meadow called *Adolescence* (1846), a watercolor of a *Farmhouse* (1847), and the tiny 1849 oil painting of a haywagon.

Homer loved the small farms and rolling fields around the Cambridge of his day, so different from the streets and docks of Boston. His delight in the countryside permeated the work of his early and middle years; the feeling for the sea was to come later. A boy's normal preference for play instead of work and study characterized Homer's youth and was reflected in many pictures during the coming decades. His early love of fishing, especially, lasted all his life.

Reconciling himself to Winslow's lack of interest in a college education, his father placed him as an apprentice to John H. Bufford, a Boston lithographer, in whose shop he spent about two years learning the craft of commercial illustration. Here he drew portraits of state senators and designed title pages for sheet music, work which he considered drudgery. When he became twenty-one he announced that never again would he work in another man's shop, and he never did. He rented a studio in the *Ballou's Pictorial* building and began his independent career by drawing

[5]

for illustrated weeklies. This would be his chief source of income for the next eighteen years. He drew for *Ballou's* and sent designs to the new *Harper's Weekly* in New York. The promise of the connection with *Harper's* and of New York as an art center led him to move there in the autumn of 1859. In both Boston and New York his earliest subjects were scenes showing the life of the people in the streets and environs of the two cities.

His treatment was youthful and fresh, sometimes broadly humorous, sometimes sedate. He had a remarkable command of perspective, and his pictures of dancers and skaters show an infectious appreciation of swirling motion. Homer, always agile, enjoyed music and loved dancing when he was young, and these pictures reveal much of his own interests. At the end of the '50's he painted one of his first major watercolors, *Skating in Central Park,* now in the City Art Museum of St. Louis, in a medium he was to elevate later to a new level of importance. These subjects were not exceptional at the time. Far from being in any state of isolation, Homer was thoroughly grounded in a school of illustration exemplified by Currier and Ives, and others of his contemporaries.

During his first two years in New York, Homer sought some instruction in art. He attended Professor Thomas Seir Cummings's night classes at the National Academy on Thirteenth Street, and took a few lessons from Frédéric Rondel, a French painter who had formerly lived in Boston. The latter, who may have taught Homer the rudiments of oil painting, such as setting a palette and handling brushes, was afterward listed as his only formal teacher. But the instruction was limited, and Homer was largely self-taught. He had many opportunities now to visit exhibitions and dealers' galleries, but he had asserted vehemently to a friend when he was nineteen that no one who wants to paint should ever look at a picture. This would have been a difficult credo for an artist of Homer's alertness to practice literally or indefinitely. It may have been only a too dogmatic expression of an ideal of independence which he tried to follow all his life. As

[6]

Courbet distrusted the influence of museums, so Homer by nature disliked anything snobbish or pretentious in the arts. Still, his down-to-earth common sense made him favor the visual perceptions of his time as found in the popular art of the illustrated journals, a genre with which he was thoroughly acquainted.

In October 1861, the year so critical in the nation's history, Homer went to the front with McClellan's Army of the Potomac, as artist-correspondent for *Harper's Weekly*. By the war's end he was its leading artist, favored with more full-page spreads, cover designs, and choice positions than anyone else. In response to the demands of *Harper's* readers and a complex war, he ranged all over both the battle and the home fronts. He did not neglect the grimness, the savagery, and the poignancy of the war, which he depicted with an honest and by no means over-romanticized realism. But his shrewd perception led him also to record the inactivity, the waiting, the interminable dullness between engagements, which the soldier knows so well. The horseplay, the entertainments, the everyday activities of camp life, the ways and manners of the Southern Negroes all excited Homer as much as did the battles. He was not primarily a war correspondent, but a painter and sketcher of life and nature who happened to be in a war.

Several fine oils record Homer's impressions of his stay with the troops; one of the most poignant, *A Sketch of a Soldier* (1864), depicts a mere boy, drafted to fill a man's place in the lines, clad in an ill-fitting man's uniform. The 1866 *Prisoners from the Front,* painted from sketches done four years previously, was an outstanding success at the exhibit of the National Academy of Design in New York that year. Encouraged by its reception, Homer (a member since 1865) continued to exhibit for many years, selling his pictures at modest prices, while he gained a solid reputation as a painter.

One of his best war paintings, *A Rainy Day in Camp*, was not completed until 1871. It illustrates Homer's determination to finish any project he started; his insistence on tying up the loose ends of a period before he left it for another — the same tenacity

[7]

which later drove him to finish at Prout's Neck the Tynemouth series he had brought from England.

Homer's war experiences were revealing and even sobering, but it is apparent that they gave him no great profundity of insight. His work of the period was an honest and perceptive record of life as he saw it during the war, but he produced no monumental war art, certainly nothing of the caliber of Goya's *Disasters of War*. Goya was an old man when he created his masterwork; old, embittered, and with a fully developed philosophy. Homer viewed the American Civil War with the eyes of a young man. It added to his experience in drawing and engraving, and it accelerated under pressure the development of his powers of observation, two assets in his later growth. Yet had Homer died then he would be remembered only as a promising but unfulfilled young artist.

With the end of the war Homer, like the whole American nation, turned eagerly to peacetime pursuits. He celebrated the change by taking his first trip abroad. Late in 1866 he sailed for France, where he remained until the fall of the next year. There were several reasons for his going. For one thing, it was the first time he had both the opportunity and means, for *Harper's* agreed to pay part of his expense if he would send them designs for engravings. He had been invited to show his *Prisoners at the Front* at the Paris International Exposition of 1867, and he must have been anxious to see how his work looked in foreign company. Like any young man, he probably wanted to visit the fair, and see Europe's artistic capital and gayest city. Little is known of his stay in Europe from existing letters of his, but we can surmise some of his activities from illustrations he sent back to *Harper's*. One is evidence that he visited the Louvre and saw some attractive girls copying there; another that he watched the dancing at the Casino. He may have done some climbing with a companion, Albert Kelsey, who loved the mountains.

Of more consequence was the opportunity he had to see the contemporary progressive painting being done and shown in Paris, and which would, logically, have interested him more than

[8]

the Academic works in the official exhibitions or even the work of the old masters in the Louvre. Much has been conjectured about this, but there is little documentary evidence. Several years ago Mahonri Young called attention to indications that Homer may have visited the French farm country and come under the influence of Millet. Technical similarities and Homer's love of the countryside make this thesis plausible, though his conceptions of rural life remained pastoral compared to the more sober hardships depicted by the Barbizon master. Homer may also have been attracted to the heavy pigmentation of Courbet, the flat, frontal lighting of Manet, and the sharp patterns and silhouettes of Degas. It seems more than coincidental that in 1867 and immediately afterwards some of his work bears strong resemblance, both aesthetically and technically, to the paintings of these artists. There is a Degas-like quality to Homer's *Musicians* of 1867; the *Nursemaid* with parasol of that year and the sparkling *Long Branch, New Jersey* of 1869 are reminiscent of Manet, Boudin, and other early French Impressionists in theme and treatment.

On the other hand, Homer had painted a very Manet-like *Croquet Scene* the year before he went to Europe. Impressionism was born out of the international atmosphere of the times, and the movement's central problems — color, light, and atmosphere — had always interested Homer. The chief benefits of any contact with the early Impressionists would have been a confirmation of these interests and an opportunity of seeing effective ways of creating luminosity and the feeling of motion. As for the Japanese prints he might have seen in Paris, where they were creating an artistic stir, these had already been brought to the attention of American artists by the publication of the United States Government's report of 1856 on Commodore Perry's expedition to Japan, which included prints of landscapes by Hiroshige, although the French may have demonstrated new ways of putting them to artistic use.

All things considered, anything Homer may have learned from the progressive French artists would appear to have been largely

[9]

technical and decorative, and relatively superficial in immediate effect. The ultimate results of such an influence on his development as a man and an artist pose another and more important question which can best be considered in relation to Homer's work of the next decade.

Homer returned in the fall of 1867 to a gay and relaxed postwar America. Everywhere people were taking to the out-of-doors for vacations, fun, and the sports of sailing, swimming, and fishing. Even ladies were allowed new freedom, and despite layers of skirts and voluminous bathing attire, they turned genteelly but eagerly to croquet, boating, picknicking, mountain climbing, and bathing at resorts and beaches. The rapid spread of railroads following the Civil War quickly opened up New England's mountain, lake, and seaside locations as vacation centers.

Homer, in his early thirties, fell into step quickly and smoothly with this new leisure, and recorded for the pages of *Harper's* many resort scenes, with a noticeable emphasis on pretty girls. But gradually his outlook was taking a more serious turn. Where contemporaries like Eugene B. Bensell were lampooning *How We Went Up the Mountain* in *Godey's Lady's Book,* he was interpreting with a dignified and adult interest. He was outgrowing the popular press style in both perceptiveness and technique.

The same railroads which promoted the rise of resorts also spawned mills and factories along their routes. These industrial subjects, and even the railroads themselves, never had great appeal for Homer. An exceptional melodramatic cover illustration for *Appleton's Journal* of a train crossing a trestle and entitled *Danger Ahead* is far from one of his better engravings. Nor do his few factory scenes have the real feeling of industrial commentaries, but are variations of mere pastoral country mill pictures. He seemed to be ignoring the rising factories, and devoting his attention instead to carefree, apple-cheeked farm boys and genteel, immaculately dressed shepherdesses.

Children at play and the happy, unhurried farmer pervade the whole of Homer's middle period painting and engraving, along with considerable attention to courtship and attractive girls. Couples and groups of young people enjoying the outdoor recreations of the day record his impressions of a gentle and appealing world. Homer, ill-at-ease with girls at thirty-six, treated romance often, but from afar. Especially puzzling for an artist destined to be known for his virile subjects are numerous paintings and drawings of shepherdesses in elaborate and frilly costumes which he rendered in the late '70's.

In 1875 he sent the last of his illustrations to *Harper's Weekly*, abruptly concluding that aspect of his career. His long association with this and similar journals had given him valuable experience as a draughtsman and established his reputation as a popular illustrator. But he probably wanted a change from the thematic restrictions, inherent stiffness, and colorless character of journalistic engraving to a freer and more chromatic medium. Now his production of watercolors increased rapidly, especially after 1872. This increased activity allowed him to exhibit with the American Watercolor Society for the first time in 1874, and gave him improved competence. By the end of the decade he was, technically, a master of the medium, and he exploited it thoroughly. The freedom, freshness, and luminosity of his works of this period make some of them among the deftest and most appealing he ever painted.

Outstanding among them are many studies of boys and girls along the beaches and harbor-front of Gloucester, a favorite painting ground which he visited in 1873 and in 1880. His watercolor *Sailing the Catboat* shows great skill in handling light, color, and water in motion; from it he developed in 1876 the noted oil *Breezing Up*. Together they show the state of his skill in the two media at the time.

These seaside resort watercolors of 1872 to 1880 were technically sparkling, pleasant in content, but not especially deep. Between 1875 and 1879, however, he showed a much more penetrating observation of life in another area. In 1875 he returned to Virginia to study once more the Southern Negroes he had seen during the war. He portrayed them with what was, for that date, an unusual depth of understanding. Several works were remarkably ahead of their time in depicting the Negro with human dignity, and not reflecting the conventional minstrel and Old Black Joe stereotypes. Philosophically as well as artistically, Homer was steadily gaining in stature.

During this middle period of the 1870's, Homer took two other steps which crucially affected his development as a major artist. He began to explore the rugged lives of hunters and woodsmen and their surroundings. More importantly, he turned his attention once more to the sea, and to those who work on it rather than merely play at its edge. These themes were to dominate his later work, but he approached them at this time only occasionally, and almost cautiously. His interest in them was definite, but (and this was typical of Homer) he advanced into both fields step by step, gaining understanding by practice and thought. Even by the end of the decade he was far from his later achievements, and was especially slow in realizing the full possibilities of what was to be his greatest subject, the sea.

He had crossed the ocean, of course, in 1867, but a *Harper's* engraving of that December is concerned more with homeward-bound tourists than the sea on which they are traveling. Several other illustrations during the next few years give faint glimpses of the future, but these sporadic works are little more than dramatic, storytelling, bread-and-butter pictures. One illustration of *The Wreck of the Atlantic* for *Harper's* he copied, almost line for line, from an old Daniel Huntington engraving of Longfellow's *Wreck of the Hesperus,* the only time in his life he felt obliged to depend on another artist's work for an entire picture.

His views of the ocean at this time are tame as compared to later conceptions. It was merely something for nice young people to parade beside, wade and swim in, or sail upon. Even as late as 1880 his Gloucester watercolors continued this theme. The old town's blue-water fishing fleet was as available to him as it was to

Kipling in 1897, but Homer was not yet ready to conceive a pictorial counterpart of *Captains Courageous*.

His progress in deep woods subjects was faster. For one thing, he had always loved outdoor activity, and for another, this was a popular theme as early as 1863 when Currier and Ives had published a whole series of hunting scenes by A. F. Tait. There were sound precedent and an appreciative audience for Homer's pictures of hunting, fishing, logging, and camping out in the mountain forests of the Adirondacks. Engravings and oils of trapping subjects in 1870 were far more advanced than any sea studies he had made up to that time. By 1880 the oil *Camp Fire* shows the ease and naturalness of conception and execution that Homer had attained by participation in the activity he was depicting.

Sea and forest subjects made up only a part of his productions at this time; there were many other themes in his work. Too many, perhaps, for proper concentration. Up to 1875 this variety of subject had been inherent in his profession as an illustrator. One reason he had left the field was to escape having to follow editorial policy and popular demand as much as his own preferences. Yet even afterwards he continued to range widely in his interests and risked spreading himself thinly. If he was to advance in his painting, he would have to devote his energies to fewer subjects and explore them more exhaustively. He was intelligent enough to perceive the problem, but in 1880 he was still uncertain of the answer.

What should be the next step? Not, probably, in the field of technique or style. Such technical lessons as he may have learned abroad had been fully applied, but though he had found subjects enough for a lifetime, he could not exploit them fully. The professional painter was ahead of the man as a thinker. Talent came, but genius lingered. What he needed to grow from the one to the other was no longer in the realm of technique, taste, and refinement, but in that of meaning.

Discerning critics recognized almost at once the originality and promise of his *Camp Fire,* which may have given him some hint of the road to take. For Homer there was now no question of turning back or standing still. He must move on, but a single picture could hardly provide a bridgehead to a whole new career. He had to withdraw for a while from the environment of cities and leisurely seaside resorts and reconsider his life. If the gap between minor prose and powerful epic statements was to be closed, he must depend progressively less on help from the world of art, and more upon the development of resources within himself and his own interpretation of reality. If necessary, he would have to give up all that was fashionable and popular and follow a solitary path far from the influence of others. It was the only road he could take if he was to find himself. When he returned to Europe, he did not go back to Paris.

CHAPTER TWO

An Artist at the Crossroads

TYNEMOUTH, 1881–1882

IN 1881 Winslow Homer was on the verge of an important change. He had reached a point in his development much like that of Rembrandt in 1642, the crucial year of *The Night Watch*. By continuing the conventions that his public had come to accept, he could ensure for himself a steady income and an established position. The alternative would be to attempt to advance his art by experimenting with new forms and conceptions and seeking new challenges on ever higher levels. To continue to paint as he had for the past ten years would have meant popularity and security, but probably an end to growth. To venture into untried fields was to incur the risk of misunderstanding, neglect, and failure. With the new master, as with the old, it was a period of transition and trial that proved decisive. Reviewing this time long afterward, in his essay of 1914, Kenyon Cox saw it as the moment when Homer stood at the crossroads. His summary of the artist's early and middle years is both apt and fair when he says: "In spite of his precocious boyhood and his rapid success as a young man, Homer's talents as an artist ripened slowly. If he had died at fifty he would be remembered as an artist of great promise and as the author of a few pictures in which promise had become performance. It is because he lived to be seventy-four that his career is the great and rounded whole we know."

The early career of any worker in the creative arts is a period of preparation — partly the gaining of technical proficiency, but even more, a slow gathering of experience, judgment, and purpose that ripen with maturity — not only of age, but outlook. In some cases, progress is steady and unspectacular, an inner ripening connected with no particular year or turning point, as it was with Eakins, Homer's profound but undramatic contemporary. Other artists, like Homer, appear to flower to full capacity more abruptly and in connection with some sudden move. When, in these instances, the artist is ready, there comes some event that acts as a powerful and moving stimulus, launching him into greatness. It may be a war, a change of scene, a natural disaster, or a profound emotional experience. The great American Civil War came before Homer was ready — but in 1881 the elements of greatness were combined within him, awaiting only a catalyst that would initiate the reaction. Unconsciously, perhaps, Homer was seeking the critical stimulus for which he was prepared. He found it in the tossing swells of the North Sea at Tynemouth, England, and later at Prout's Neck on the southern coast of Maine. His brief sojourn at the one was the prelude to greatness, his settlement at the other the fulfillment of it.

The years 1881 and 1882 were the turning point in his life, but they are also puzzling. The improvement in his work is as impressive as the motives behind his actions are unclear. We do not know why he went to England in 1881 or what he hoped to find there. What he did find was the inspiration worthy of his talent, and he responded to it with a depth of feeling and a power of execution that carried him, ultimately, to his undisputed place among artists of major stature.

He had visited Europe in 1867 and enjoyed it. He had felt rewarded by his trip to France and had learned some valuable lessons from the then avant-garde Impressionists, but he had shown no desire to return. He never explained his reasons for going, and rarely mentioned anything he had seen there; most of his comments went into his pictures, and like the reticent Rembrandt and

Turner, he felt it unnecessary to add anything in words. But now, in the spring of 1881, all alone, he took passage for England. He was forty-five years old.

In London, Homer soon created a striking memento of his stay, the watercolor study of the *Parliament Buildings*, for many years in the possession of Charles L. Homer and now owned by Joseph H. Hirshhorn. The deep, almost monochromatic tones have the richness of oil; technically the picture seems to sum up all the years of Impressionist practices. But the manner in which the work was done is less significant than what it says. The murky sky through which the sun can scarcely shine, the restless crowds of people reduced to infinitesimal scale on the spanning bridge, the Houses of Parliament darkly brooding over the centuries of history which have permeated this ancient city — here, if ever, is the soul of London, captured and set on paper by the American Winslow Homer. Neither Whistler nor Monet ever painted London better. Yet this was not what he was seeking.

After a brief stay there, he moved on, making his way to England's northeast coast. Here at Tynemouth, facing the North Sea, he settled down to begin what was, probably, the most critical period of his artistic life. When he arrived there in 1881, Tynemouth was a prosperous city of forty-four thousand people, a thriving industrial center, a popular summer resort, and the home of the great North Sea fishing fleet. The sights and sounds of the coastal city, the noise and smoke from the busy factories, the barges literally "carrying coals to Newcastle" — this was what Homer encountered.

Just why he went to Tynemouth we do not know. He was well acquainted with American summer resorts, and may quite naturally have inquired where he could find a similar spot in England, since it was the beginning of the summer season. He had been strongly attracted to Gloucester, and Tynemouth had the same status as a respectable watering place, the same kind of fishing industry, the same interest in small boat sailing (the Tyne rivals the Thames as a yacht-racing center). Perhaps he wanted to do some English versions of *Sailing the Catboat*. In any case to Tyne-mouth he went, and according to Downes's biography of 1911, "In a suburb called Cullercoates he was fortunate enough to find a dwelling which just suited him, a little house surrounded by a high wall, with one gate, to which he had the key, so that he was safe from intrusion."

Here he settled down to paint, and found that something strange had happened to him. That the industrial subjects crowd-ing the river would interest him no more than had similar scenes in Boston or New York was to be expected. But — surprisingly — neither did the colorful life of the summer resort. The pretty girls, the romancing couples, the sunworshippers on the beach — all the carefree, gaily artificial activity that goes on at a seaside vacation spot no longer aroused his interest. Instead, he turned to a more basic and meaningful field. With a mature and purposeful response to surroundings which were not only novel but moving, he painted magnificent studies of clouds, and mist, and fog, the effects of changing light on the sea, the frightening power of the gale, and the great waves that thundered in from the open ocean.

The past few years had refined his technique to a bold, unclut-tered statement of the essential features of his subject, painted with unusual strength and clarity. His sense of composition had developed to an amazing degree, and he had shown consummate skill in employing effective and subtle color. In short, he had mas-tered the tools of his art. In addition, at Gloucester and elsewhere he had demonstrated a significant maturity in his consideration of the physical world, a deeper and more philosophical approach that went beneath the surface of things.

Now, turning from the summer colony to the fishing commu-nity of Tynemouth, he began to relate the powers of nature to humanity. Seemingly for the first time Homer realized the effects of the elements upon the lives of men. Back in America he had depicted a few storms and he had painted people — but even at Gloucester, among those who "go down to the sea in ships," the great and ever-present intimacy between the sea and the people of the sea had never impressed him sufficiently to mark his work. He had not really noticed the fishing village side of Gloucester — perhaps he had been too busy sketching the pretty girls on the beach.

But here on the cold, gray coast of England, facing the North Sea, he discovered a new race of people in the fishing community that was part of Tynemouth. Here were no handy figures to decorate a pleasing scene — these were sober, hard-working people who lived intimately with the sea and its weather and were part of it. The ocean, sometimes beautiful, sometimes terrible in its fury, sometimes bountiful, sometimes cruel, but always to be reckoned with and respected or feared, was as much a part of their lives and thoughts as their neat parlors and warm kitchens and severe wooden chapels. His new understanding of nature brought these people and their ways into Homer's life and his art, and he sketched and painted night and day to capture all the new impressions that came to him. Never had he been more prolific in his work, and never had he stayed so long in one place to paint.

Homer was discovering what Turner had discovered — the forces in the world that make men feel small, and through that humility to think in cosmic terms. Jarred from his comfortable middle-class background, Homer came to appreciate and understand for the first time a modest, unassuming class of hard-working, simple, almost primitive people — and in his admiration and love for them, and his translation of that love into art, he achieved the unmistakable signs of real greatness.

One measure of Homer's stature as a mature and sensitive artist is the manner in which he avoided two obvious approaches to his subject — approaches that would have been easy (and perhaps logical) for him. He might have done a mere documentary series on the life and activities of the fishermen of Tynemouth; or he might have followed the equally shallow but popular trend toward sentimentality, and dwelt with maudlin emotion on the trite and banal aspects of their existence. And this is all the more remarkable in that his background was that of a romantic realist

[19]

and a popular magazine artist, who had concerned himself for years with translating reality into sentimental forms for a mid-Victorian public.

But here we are dealing with a new Homer, who was seeing with an enhanced perceptiveness, weighing and considering with an enriched and thoughtful philosophy, and painting with a new strength and directness of statement. His fishermen were not the tortured, striving figures of a Doré, but the calmly purposeful and somewhat stolid north-of-England workingmen who happened to be in the business of fishing. The women were sturdy, ruddy-cheeked, no-nonsense English girls who were used to hard work, sometimes (but not always) charming — pretty, even — but real.

The women became the predominating theme of the Tynemouth series, and through his studies of them Homer showed much of the lives of the men, who are implicitly in the background but appear comparatively seldom. There is excitement and suspense in a picture of men combatting a raging gale, straining to save one of their number from the clawing sea, but there is something haunting, almost unbearable, in the scenes of waiting, helpless women looking out to sea with calm fortitude and resignation, watching, hoping, wondering. Homer's love for Tynemouth and its people, his sympathy and admiration, and his perfect understanding of their attitudes and situations — all these come to us clearly through his work.

"No growth is spontaneous," says Bolton in his critique of Homer's watercolor development, "least of all an artistic." And although Homer responded to the challenge of Tynemouth in a remarkably short time, he did not achieve greatness overnight. Quite naturally, some of the pictures are more profound in conception than others among the five major themes that he dealt with again and again: girls looking out to sea, women on the beach, men and women in boats, groups watching a storm, and scenes of anxious waiting for the return of the fishing vessels. Not all of the studies are work scenes, of course. Apparently a favorite activity was spending time along the shore. But the girls, strolling down the beach or sitting on the rocks, are different from the youngsters whom Homer had painted at Gloucester; everyone at Tynemouth seems in closer affinity with the sea. Nature, too, was different there. The atmosphere at Tynemouth was heavy, soft, and wet. When the sun broke through the dark, thick clouds to spotlight the sea, it created effects which were spectacular in brilliance and contrast. If Homer had been completely devoid of feeling for the people, he would still have been able to create fascinating studies of this visually rewarding locale. Fortunately he was able to see both aspects of his subject and to combine them in an inspired way.

Homer could hardly have found a place better suited to rendition in watercolor. Under these happy circumstances, which keyed up every faculty, his sense of design matured and developed as he worked. He began to group his models in twos and threes, letting the lines of one repeat those of another in rhythmic harmonies that stand out against the broad reaches of the North Sea. But design was only the means to the expression of a new conception of life. For the Tynemouth fishing families, the beach was the center of that life. When the laden fleet came in, the men, exhausted from the long and strenuous work of harvesting their catch, usually headed straight for home and bed. It was the women who discharged the cargo of fish, took it to market, and did the selling. Then they returned to the boats, cleaned and re-provisioned them, readied the tackle and gear, making all shipshape for the next day's run. Here they met, visited and gossiped, and here they waited and watched for their men to return to harbor at the end of the day. At Gloucester, Homer had seen individuals at rest or play, but at Tynemouth he saw the people as a working community, and he painted and sketched this theme from innumerable points of view.

The violent equinoctial storms which hit the coast of England in the fall of 1881 brought Homer an additional insight into this world and inspired some of the most spectacular of the Tynemouth pictures. His North Sea gale studies date from that time

Fig. 2. WATCHING THE TEMPEST.
1881. Fogg Art Museum.

and mark an important milepost in his development. In an exceptionally dramatic painting, *Watching the Tempest* (Fig. 2), he
shows us a rescue team lined up alongside their lifeboat, ready to
launch it when needed. The woman at the right, anxiously watching around the bow, the second crew watching from beside their
boat, the crowd of people lining the bluff, even the ready jury
mast with sail bent on, tell of the tension and strain felt by these
coastal people during a storm. Technically the dramatic excitement is pointed up by the abrupt clash of light and dark values,
and the playing of neutral grays against the rich but somber reds
and oranges. Looming above the scene is the bulk of the Coast
Guard Station, a major symbol in the lives of these people.

In the station were stored the lifeboats and other rescue gear;
from the observation tower a watch was maintained for vessels in
distress, especially during a heavy blow. From there the fleet was
counted as it returned to harbor, and during foul weather the rail-

ing beside the station would be lined, as in *Watching the Tempest*, with the anxious families and friends of the men who were still out. Homer introduced it into the background of many of his storm pictures; in the series portraying the scenes of waiting, he was quite likely to move in close to it, as if he were joining the people of the town, and identifying himself with human feelings and problems to an extent that he had never done before.

Since time began, women have spent much of their lives awaiting the return of their men from war, from work, and from the sea. At Tynemouth, Homer shared the long watch with them. In what is perhaps the best of this "waiting series," a watercolor which he later converted into an etching called *Perils of the Sea,* the almost heartrending mood of quiet and deep emotion is presented with moving power, its forthrightness avoiding both melodrama and sentimentality because it was something honestly seen and honestly felt.

Many years before, Homer had elected to devote himself to the study of the world of nature and the human inhabitants of that world. But up until 1881 he had seen only a few of nature's moods, and scarcely touched the real emotional depths of his fellow men. Except for what he had observed of the Civil War when he was still young, his world had been pleasant, healthy, and visually delightful. Tynemouth opened his eyes to a much deeper meaning in existence. It is to Homer's credit that he had prepared himself for this chance and when it came he was ready and grasped it. However he came to know the people of Tynemouth, he was not long in recognizing what he found. When he left them he was a more mature man and a more purposeful artist by far than when he had arrived.

Lettered on the hull of a boat in *Fishing Off Scarboro,* a drawing in the Art Institute of Chicago, is her home port, Yarmouth. That center of the herring industry is halfway down the coast of England from Tynemouth, and Scarboro is some sixty miles below the Tyne. This and other evidence seems to indicate that Homer visited other coastal sections, and it is significant that they were similar in character, a fact indicative of a new outlook on life and nature. A drawing of *Boats of the Devonshire Coast* dated 1882 suggests that he may have visited that section of the southwest corner of England, and perhaps sailed home from its chief port, Plymouth.

In any case, by the latter part of 1882 he was ready to go home. He made his way by the most leisurely route, down the eastern coast, probably pausing here and there. Below Scarboro, where the great chalk cliffs jut out into the North Sea some fifty miles east of the ancient city of York, he stayed at least long enough to do a magnificent drawing, *Flamborough Head, England.* As if to show that he had not lost his sense of form in the northern mists, he showed the sculpturesque figure with the same clarity and solidity as the massive wave-eroded cliffs. This and other experiences were rewarding to Homer and brought additional power to his work. Nevertheless, he did not see fit to settle in England. Profitable though the two years there had been, he was a New Englander born and bred, with a country of his own. And so, on down the coast to the south of England and the liner *Catalonia* of the Cunard line that would take him to America. In late November of 1882 he was back in New York Harbor.

CHAPTER THREE

Maturity at Prout's Neck, 1883–1889

IT was late in the year 1882, and once again Homer was back in his old studio in New York. And once again he felt unsettled. He was no longer at home here; after the cold, clean air of Tynemouth and the simple, unhurried existence in England, New York had become sterile for him. It was an old story with Homer — to drop everything when he felt he must, and take up a new residence, a new technique, a new philosophy of life and art when the old no longer fitted in with his constantly developing personality.

We cannot know exactly, of course, how he had felt about joining the staff at Bufford's back in 1855; perhaps it was only a convenient escape from what must have seemed a horrible alternative — that of becoming a haberdasher's clerk in Cambridge. At any rate, by the end of his two-year apprenticeship he was heartily sick of the place and waited not a day after his legal release (on attaining his majority) to leave. We can imagine his excitement during the fitting out of a place of his own — the Boston studio on Winter Street — and yet in two short years, nothing would do for him but New York. Here he had remained since the fall of 1859. True, he had made many excursions to other localities during the twenty-three years — the South, both in wartime and later, to New England, to the Adirondacks, and latest, of course, to England.

[25]

But he had kept a headquarters in New York in the Tenth Street Studios, at 51 West Tenth Street, throughout the '70's, perhaps merely for convenience and the lack of a pressing desire to settle elsewhere, perhaps because he felt he should be located in the cultural center of the country. But now that he had returned from his great adventure in painting, the voyage of exploration into a completely different world of artistic purpose that was to redirect his whole approach to his art, he was once again unhappy, restless, dissatisfied. New York no longer had what he needed — and before the spring was over he was ready to leave it.

He was ready, too, to leave behind him the vacillation from manner to manner which had been like an aimless shopping around among the various forms of Impressionism. This experimentation had sharpened his eye and perfected his craftsmanship, but it had never lured him from the stubborn and determined search for his own way of seeing and painting. Now he had found it, and after 1882 there is nothing in his work to hint of any borrowing from an outside source. Perhaps he knew that remaining in New York would expose him to other men's work too much; perhaps he feared that the confusion of city life would interfere with his translation of feeling into painting. And as for the prestige of living in the artistic center of America, this thought (if indeed it ever occurred to him) would carry little weight with Homer. He was the center of his own artistic world — and to blazes with any other.

J. Alden Weir, one of the artists whom Homer had met in the old New York University Building that housed his own studio, dropped in one day. He found Homer with a pile of drawings and watercolors on the floor. When asked what he was doing, Winslow replied, "I've been offered five hundred dollars for a hundred drawings and paintings, and these are the ones I've picked out. When I get the money for them I'm going to leave New York for good." And he did.

This time he knew precisely where he was going, why he was going, and what he was going to do there. The transition to maturity was accomplished, the work of greatness about to begin. His whole life had been a slow gaining of skill and sureness in technique; at last he had all the tools he needed to express himself. And now, too, he felt with the certainty of conviction that he knew exactly what he wanted to say. He realized perfectly well that during his past years, the developing years, he had enjoyed pleasant seeing for its own sake, rarely looking beneath the surface of things; now he was to probe deeply into the very heart of human feeling — now he was to set out upon the work for which his whole life had been the preparation, and he was impatient to be about it.

At Tynemouth, England, he had discovered the kind of people whose appearance and way of life were just what he wanted to paint; now, back in America, he wanted to live and work among people of similar type and attitudes, and if possible, in a similar setting. An American Tynemouth . . . and he knew exactly where it was. The story of how he happened to know, and of his going there, was told to me by his nephew Charles L. Homer.

In 1874 Winslow's younger brother Arthur was engaged to Alice Patch of Lowell, and visited her on the Isles of Shoals, near Kittery, Maine. They were to be married the next summer, and he looked about for a suitable honeymoon spot. He had heard of the remarkable scenic beauty of Prout's Neck, which, located about twelve miles from Portland, extends almost due south into Saco Bay. Arthur drove there from Kittery, fifty miles over country roads, but apparently was satisfied, for he engaged a suite for the next summer at the Willows, a venerable hotel which was in operation until 1964. Here the young couple spent their honeymoon, and here Winslow visited them and had his first sight of Prout's Neck. This was in 1875. He was not then ready to settle there himself, but he did not forget it. Meanwhile, the association was maintained by other members of the family. Indeed, since that time there has not been a summer without a Homer at Prout's. Arthur and Alice returned in 1876, though with the arrival of their first son, Arthur Patch Homer, the manager of the Willows asked them to find other quarters, and they built a cottage which Arthur called El Rancho to commemorate his many years of business in Galveston, Texas. Here, six years later, was born their second son, Charles Lowell Homer.

In 1883 Winslow and his elder brother Charles decided to settle at Prout's, a part of the township known officially as Scarborough, after the city in England, but always referred to locally as Scarboro. They wanted a place to establish their father and mother and reunite the whole family; a secondary motive was the idea of developing the area as a summer resort. But foremost in Winslow's mind must have been its resemblance to Tynemouth and the possibilities it offered for the continuation of the point of view he had developed there.

It was the eldest son, Charles Savage, Jr., who more or less engineered the plan, for he had assumed the financial leadership of the Homer family. Father Homer as nominal head of the clan actually made the purchase of the Prout's Neck property, though the money came from Charles Jr. Never one to do anything by halves, the old gentleman bought almost the whole Neck. Unlike some of his earlier transactions, this proved to be a wise move.

During the early seventeenth century the promontory was known as Black Point, but the first energetic family to settle there gave the name Prout's to the Neck in honor of their principal forebear, Timothy Prout. During the eighteenth century the Prouts were slowly displaced by the Libby family (originally Lybbey) under the vigorous leadership of Nehemiah Libby. They rechristened it Libby's Neck and applied that term as late as 1879 to a survey of their holdings, but the name never really caught on and Prout's Neck it has remained.

When Captain Thomas Libby died in 1879, the Neck property was left to three of his children, Benaiah, Minerva, and Louise. Although he had hoped to keep it in the family, a way was found to circumvent his arrangements (to the later sorrow of Louise), and the Neck was divided into three large blocks of lots for individual homesteads. Behind this move was a trend common to the

[28]

middle years of the nineteenth century, which saw the growth of summer resorts all over the New England area, and some members of the Libby family had decided as early as the late 1860's to develop the Neck for recreational purposes. Even before Captain Thomas died, a cousin — Captain Silas Libby — had built a small hotel west of the family mansion and Benaiah Libby one to the east. The first was the nucleus of the Cammock House, and the other became the Willows. Meanwhile, another Libby had built the West Point House, Mr. Harry Kaler had established the Southgate Inn, later converted into the present Black Point Inn, and the Foss family had erected the Checkley House (now razed). Thus by 1879 a movement had been established which Captain Thomas's will could not stop.

While these developments were occurring, loud complaints were being made farther up the coast of Maine, particularly at Bar Harbor, that cottagers were excluding others from access to the seashore by building wire fences along their property lines to the water's edge. When the Libby division plan was drawn in 1879 by S. L. Stephenson, a veteran railroad cartographer, a broad marginal way was established around the perimeter of the whole Neck for the common use of all owners. It has been kept free of all buildings by the Prout's Neck Association (formed in 1899), and by longstanding practice the path along the cliffs overlooking the ocean front has always been open to the public. This foresighted provision has been greatly appreciated by residents and visitors alike; Winslow Homer especially benefited by it, for it was along the path on the marginal way that he took innumerable walks while studying the ocean. Furthermore, the creation of a marginal way not only guaranteed the freedom of the cliffs but afforded a wide and open slope almost the whole length of the Neck. Without this unimpeded stretch the view from Homer's studio balcony would not have been nearly so magnificent.

Minerva Libby outlived her brother Benaiah and inherited his third of the Neck, but she died before her sister Louise and left

Fig. 3.   THE OCEAN FRONT AT PROUT'S NECK.
Photograph taken about 1883. Homer Collection, Bowdoin College Museum of Art.

her holdings to her, perhaps in the hope of fulfilling her father's wish that the Neck be kept in the hands of the family. It was in this way that Louise Libby inherited most of Prout's Neck. In the meantime she had married Alonzo Googins, a carpenter; he had built a stable and started the frame of what he hoped would be a large boardinghouse for summer visitors. Lon was a good carpenter but a bad businessman; in low financial condition (owing partly to fondness for alcohol) he sold the stable, house frame, and most of Prout's Neck to the Homers. Winslow's father drove a shrewd bargain and took over the property for a small cash outlay. Perhaps he had twinges of conscience, for he allowed Louise Libby Googins and her daughter to live in the stable loft when she became a widow shortly afterward while he built her a cottage near the Southgate Hotel. In 1883 he finished the building which Lon had begun and christened it the Ark.

A photograph (Fig. 3) taken about 1883 shows only the Ark and stable, the Checkley House and the Southgate, but this open appearance did not last long. Charles Jr. subdivided the land into cottage lots, and (rather to Winslow's regret) summer residents

[30]

Fig. 4. WINSLOW HOMER'S STUDIO AT PROUT'S NECK.
Photograph taken in 1936 by Charles L. Homer. Homer Collection, Bowdoin College Museum of Art.

were attracted in large numbers. Before he died six hotels and sixty cottages had been erected on the Neck. Today only two hotels remain, but there are one hundred and four cottages.

When the family learned that Winslow wanted to settle at Prout's, they were delighted and instructed their builder to include a painting room at the rear of the Ark over what is now the kitchen. Winslow, however, would have none of this. He asked for the stable, hired his own architect, and remodeled it to suit himself into the famous studio home overlooking the cliffs (Figs. 4 and 5).

He loved the family and wanted to be near them — but he also knew that he could not work without a retreat where he could be alone. The Neck was an ideal location to carry on his Tynemouth approach, a project he felt compelled to continue. He had been attracted to the place even in 1875, but now it fitted in so well with his new philosophy that he really fell in love with it, and the

[31]

Fig. 5.   LIVING ROOM OF WINSLOW HOMER'S STUDIO.
Photograph taken in 1936 by Charles L. Homer. Homer Collection, Bowdoin College Museum of Art.

added opportunity of having the family nearby made the arrangement ideal.

Homer has often been labeled a misanthrope, and much has
been made of his "deliberate self-exile" and his artistic independence. Homer's move to Prout's undoubtedly seemed to his New
York friends like the desertion of civilization for a home in the
wilderness, and to leave the "Paris of the New World" for the
Maine coast must have struck his fellow artists as the height of
folly. The reason for his going was, of course, a perfectly natural
and logical one. He had selected the subject matter for his mature
work; it could be found at Prout's Neck, and it could not be found
in New York.

As to his independence, any artist of stature must, sooner or
later, work out his own manner and method of painting, and usually this is a very private and personal thing. Out of observation

and discussion and experiment there emerges what we call a personal style, which is only the particular artist's own way of doing things. The second half of the nineteenth century saw the isolation of many men of genius. In 1883, for example, Manet died after a long, lonely fight, and Gauguin left Bertin's brokerage house to commence an even more bitter struggle. Van Gogh was working alone in Holland, and Cézanne in Provence. It was the year that Renoir made the agreement with Durand-Ruel which lifted him out of poverty and enabled him to spend his last, great years in the South of France. And Degas, although living in Paris, was more and more alone.

In addition to his studio home, Winslow also acquired, from Benjamin Franklin Sanborn, a second sanctuary — a fact I have never seen mentioned in print. It was a one-story shack which he fitted up with a stove and a china closet, on a rise of ground above the beach of Saco Bay still known locally as Ferry Beach or Ferry Rock (after a ferry which plied from there to Old Orchard in Colonial times). The shack was surrounded by a small yard which commanded an excellent view of the ocean, across a flat sweeping terrain quite different from the cliffs of Prout's. For nearly twenty years Homer used it as a storage room for painting materials, and many of his watercolors are of views from the vicinity of the shack. Several times it was broken into during the winter, and he finally sold it to William H. Munroe, who used it to store duck-hunting gear. Munroe had the same trouble with thieves, and eventually tore it down.

On the landward side, Prout's Neck has been eaten away into a triangle that is almost an island. Its woods, beaches, and rocks provide a varied repertory of scenes for the outdoor painter. The tip and the south side look directly out to sea; the cliffs run east and west, and no matter what the direction of the storms, the waves always break from the southeast. The cliffs, part of an ancient syncline, emerge from the water in strata at a forty-five degree angle, making an ideal wall up which the waves can climb. The absence of marine shelves of any consequence and of offshore rocks allows the breakers to roll in with tremendous force.

During the summer months the waves at Prout's are ordinarily light; a sudden violent squall may bring waves of twenty to thirty feet, but even this is rare. A fall three-day northeaster, on the other hand, will create forty and fifty foot waves, and when they break the salt spray will fly like solid shot over the tops of the sixty foot cliffs. If the wind has shifted to the west, as it often does before the waves subside, it blows long streamers called mares' tails from the crests of the great breakers. The summer people rarely see the most violent displays, which usually occur in November and December.

Winslow Homer delighted in these spectacles, studying and painting them from every aspect, as he did the varied formations of the rocks. From Checkley Point to Eastern Point he missed hardly a single spot, and the incredibly varied forms of the rocks seem even more rugged in contrast to the flat and expansive beaches on both east and west. Nearby are farms, sand dunes, marshes, rolling hills and pastures — Homer came to know and love them all.

Prout's was a painter's paradise, and might have attracted a colony of artists had not the Homer family, after buying up almost the whole Neck in 1883, sold lots only to "approved" buyers, usually people of means. Winslow's nephew Charles insisted his uncle never would have stayed there if he had been surrounded by any typical arty group. As at Tynemouth he made friends with the native residents, friendships which meant a great deal to him. Even more rewarding was the chance to live among his own people; especially did he enjoy being with his mother, although this renewed relationship was a brief one, for she died in 1884.

Winslow's family had always encouraged him in his work, but of them all it had been his mother (Fig. 6) who showed the greatest faith and understanding, perhaps because she was herself an amateur artist of considerable ability. Mrs. Charles L. Homer owns a watercolor, *View Near Naples*, which Henrietta painted in 1827 when she was eighteen, and which shows a re-

Fig. 6.   WINSLOW HOMER'S MOTHER.
Homer Collection, Bowdoin College Museum of Art.

markable gift for design. Perhaps her finest work is a collection of fifty-four floral paintings, which she had selected as the best of her studies of over twenty years (Fig. 7). Executed and labeled with the painstaking accuracy of a botanist, the studies also have a freedom and boldness almost prophetic of Georgia O'Keeffe. Her *Sumac* and *Gladiolas* practically cover their 15 by 22 inch sheets, and *Woodbine* shows a fine sensitivity in the delicate treatment of the fragile tendrils. Here, surely, is at least one source of Winslow Homer's artistic heritage.

Winslow Homer recognized his mother's ability and paid it a unique tribute. For many years after her death he kept a group of her paintings — the only paintings by another artist he ever collected. His relationship with her was of the tenderest and most genial sort. From a letter he wrote to his sister-in-law, we can visualize him standing by his mother's bed when she was ill in 1883, enjoying her sense of humor and sharing her intense desire for independence and health.

> *Dear Mattie:*
>
> *I find Mother very much better. In fact to me she seems very well. She laughed at the amusing pictures in The Graphic and stated as to her surroundings that the Queen of England could not be better cared for. That her bed was the best that Father or she had ever had — That the food & attendance she considered unequaled, & she has all the company that she wishes — She wishes it understood that when she gets old her greatest comfort will be to do as she likes — & when she gets sick it will be time enough for her to have a companion.*

A letter to his sister-in-law a year later states, poignantly, that he has been sick with grief over the loss of his mother, who died in that year at the age of seventy-five.

After the death of Homer's mother in April 1884, his father lived on in the Ark during the summers and moved to Boston dur-

Fig. 7. CANNA INDICA.
From an album of flowers and plants by Winslow Homer's
mother. William Wikoff Smith, Bryn Mawr, Pennsylvania.

ing the winters. He survived his wife by many years, living to a hearty old age. During that time he was Winslow's daily companion at Prout's and figures prominently in many of his letters.

From Charles L. Homer and others I heard many a vivid account of the forceful personality that was Charles Savage Homer. Prior to 1886, when Charles L. Homer was first old enough to know his grandfather, the senior member of the clan had been up and down the ladder of fortune many times. At that date he was down and was being supported by Charles Jr., but he lived, as the saying goes, the life of Riley. He had been a forty-niner, but before returning from California had been forced to sell the sumptuous bags which he had had made especially for gold. In fact, he returned to Boston without cab fare, and his wife had to pay the coachman. During the 1850's he traveled abroad. Several letters of 1852 show that he was in London to solicit funds for copper, silver, or gold mines in the United States. His profession was that of a promoter of enterprises of a get-rich-quick nature, none of which ever materialized. He never found the pot-o'-gold, but misadventures did not daunt his confidence; two photographs in the family album show that in the early 1860's he retained his impressive pose and, in keeping with his role of a man of affairs who might conceivably own a gold mine, he wore a winged collar, wide velvet lapels, and a brocaded satin coat that gave him an air of respectability and affluence, though at the time he and his wife were living with their oldest son in Belmont, Massachusetts, and he was destined never to support himself again.

After he moved to Prout's Neck and was established in a home that is still imposing, his normal condition became pompous, garrulous, and flamboyant. Those who knew him well asserted that he was sometimes magnetic, but more often overbearing, and added that when the natives of Prout's referred to him as Old Man Homer it was without connotation of affection. His swaggering would have been appropriate only on the grand opera stage, where his booming voice would have filled an auditorium. He expressed himself in grandiloquent language assisted by a deep baritone and dramatic gestures. Once after he had applied a hot palm to his grandson Charles for a misdemeanor, the mother of the culprit intervened and said that thereafter she would do the honors herself. Afterward, the sire used to refer to Mrs. Arthur B. Homer as "my daughter-in-law the duchess."

In general, he was a martinet who took it upon himself to police the whole Neck. He was especially adamant about fires on the rocks, with some reason, for picnickers might have started a conflagration in the brush during the dry months. One instance of meddlesomeness, however, boomeranged so badly that it chastened him for a short time. Thinking to improve his own property, he hired workmen to build a road bisecting the long stretch of Homer lots and then arbitrarily announced that he was presenting it to the town for upkeep. Whereupon the long-suffering selectmen firmly replied that the care of the road was Mr. Homer's sole responsibility and that he would be liable for any accidents that occurred on it. Later the selectmen realized that the way was beneficial if Mr. Homer's manner was not and relented. Today it is called the Winslow Homer Road.

As Winslow's letters bear out, his father always had a finger in other people's affairs and liked company as much as his son enjoyed privacy. Once, in later years, Charles Jr. wrote anxiously to his brother Arthur: "Father came very near persuading that servant girl to marry him by a false estimate of his wealth but I bust it up by proposing to cut off the cash." The story from Arthur's son Charles is as follows: "Charles Sr. always looked prosperous, and once when he was living at the American House in Boston as a widower, the office secretary at the hotel decided that this distinguished-looking gentleman who paid his bills so promptly might be a good catch. The affair soon prospered by mutual consent to such an extent that Charles Sr. wrote his eldest son saying that he was lonely and had found someone to brighten his final years. Upon receipt of this alarming letter, Charles Jr. hastened to Boston and pointed out to the prospective bride that he had been paying his father's bills for years and would be delighted to have her assume that responsibility. Grandfather at that time was eighty-five."

The master of the Ark was enabled to devote his full attention to these and similar activities by the ubiquitous competence of his housekeeper, Miss Hamilton, in managing the household, so the loss of her services in 1890 was, temporarily at least, a serious inconvenience. While descending the grand stairway she fell and broke her hip, which, because of her age, never healed properly. Hearing of her plight, Mrs. William H. Munroe, recently widowed and seeking employment, called at the house to offer assistance. Mr. Homer met her at the door and demanded imperiously, "Madame, what has sent you?" When she explained that she was both an experienced housekeeper and a trained practical nurse, he replied with obvious relief, "Enter, madame, Providence has sent you!" Thereupon began a stormy relationship that lasted until Mr. Homer died at the close of the decade.

The senior Homer found Mrs. Munroe to be of different mettle from the prim and quiet Miss Hamilton. Born Annie Jane Fearns in Dublin, she soon added her share of Irish personality to the temperamental household and made up for her deceptively small stature by unlimited spunk, as she was required to prove during the third day of her employment. When the proprietor of the Ark shouted at an elderly lady who had inadvertently trodden upon his lawn, "Madame, are you aware that you are trespassing upon my property?" the new housekeeper interceded and apologized for him, so enraging the master that he bellowed at her, "If you ever dare to interfere in my affairs again, I'll punch you in the nose!" Mrs. Munroe faced him and replied, "You do, and you'll get as good as you give." She then explained that if his affront had caused the old lady to have a stroke, he might have become the object of a lawsuit. There was an inescapable logic in this argument which was recognized by the old speculator, always sensitive to points of law. Nor was this the last time that he had reason to be impressed by Mrs. Munroe's common sense, diplomacy, and courage. She was a worthy antagonist, and in the ensuing years the two engaged in a contest of wit and will that caused many a spark to fly.

Charles Savage Homer found life in the Ark sumptuous and exciting as the century drew to a close. Gregarious and hospitable in his heavy way, he filled the house with guests, customarily entertaining the dignitaries who visited the nearby St. James's Episcopal church and enjoying especially the missionaries with their talk of exotic lands. During the summer months the whole clan reassembled: Arthur brought his family to El Rancho, barely a stone's throw from the studio, and Charles Jr. and his wife stayed at the Ark next door to it. Much to the delight of the patriarch, the eldest son also brought with him a retinue of servants from his New York apartment or his home at West Townsend, Massachusetts, over whom Charles Sr. promptly assumed command. The entertainment of guests was lavish and constant, except by Winslow, who more often beat a retreat to some hideaway.

Charles Savage Homer's sons were open-handed in providing for him and saw that he was abundantly supplied with every comfort. In addition to three full-time servants of his own and Charles's staff, he had a standing charge account with the Boston provisioners S. S. Pierce, who regularly shipped him the finest wines and foodstuffs available, the bills being mailed with equal regularity to his eldest son. Also, the Ark was furnished for him with something approaching plutocratic splendor. Like many ambitious failures, Mr. Homer, given the opportunity, avidly surrounded himself with material plenty, following the theory that if a small basket of fruit on the table is good, a large basket is better. Meanwhile, Winslow preferred to live a Spartan life, and these differences in taste instigated several minor but revealing contests. Quite often, when Winslow arrived at the Ark for a meal with the family, he would surreptitiously prune some overloaded mantelpiece or table decoration, after which his father would angrily replace the fruit or objects and belabor Mrs. Munroe for her presumed interference. The preference of the father for ornateness, it must be said in fairness, was merely typical of that day. Winslow's respect for simplicity was years ahead of his time.

Although the elder Homer luxuriated like a country gentleman, he had an unpastoral abhorrence of exercise. Winslow and his brothers had worshipped the out-of-doors from their boyhood days and were devoted to numerous manly sports. They spent every possible spare moment fishing at Prout's, in the Adirondacks, Quebec Province, Florida, and the West Indies; and Winslow, for his part, celebrated the joys of flycasting in scores of watercolors. But Homer père considered these pursuits vulgar and beneath his dignity. He never went fishing or hiking with Winslow and only rarely consented to a token stroll along the cliffs to a point about a hundred yards from the Ark which the family dubbed "Father Homer's rock" (Fig. 8). Thence he would return to the seaward porch of the Ark and watch Winslow through a spyglass until he disappeared in the distance. Notwithstanding, the old gentleman made a great show of Spartanism, and constantly urged on others the therapeutic benefits of cold baths. Winslow saw through this pretense and caricatured it delightfully on the back of a letter to Charles. Utilizing a caption from a newspaper advertisement to label the sheet "Rub Down," he sketched his father calling to his servant, "Lewis, put your finger wet with cold water in the small of my back — That will complete my full bath!" Mr. Homer also contended that some virtue attended shaving with unheated rainwater, which he had caught especially for him in a barrel beneath the drain pipe. Ordinarily this practice was harmless and amusing, but on one occasion it took a comic turn. Mrs. Munroe mentioned that the roof gutters had recently been stained green, but the master ignored her warning, with the result that he appeared at breakfast besmeared with vivid green from ear to ear.

Homer père, humored as he was, came to think that he could do no wrong, until he finally ventured upon one extravagance the family had to veto with a firm hand. Disliking exercise, he never-

Fig. 8.   WINSLOW HOMER WITH HIS FATHER AND
SAM AT PROUT'S NECK.
Homer Collection, Bowdoin College Museum of Art.

theless thought that a gentleman should take a daily airing in
proper style; so, in the face of Winslow's strong objection, he ordered the construction of a stable during the latter's absence on a
painting trip. When the artist returned, his father presented him
with a *fait accompli,* a stable fully furnished with two thorough-

[43]

bred horses and an expensive equipage. This was the last of many straws: Winslow and his brothers held a family council and voted to raze the structure.

There is ample evidence that Charles Savage Homer was always fussing with someone or something. During the summer of 1898, he and the aged S. L. Stephenson, the railroad cartographer who had drawn the Libby division plan for Prout's Neck and had now retired to a house overlooking Kettle Cove, telegraphed daily to the War Department that the Spanish fleet had just been sighted off the coast of Maine; and they continued to send these messages up to the day the fleet was sunk in Santiago Harbor. After the exasperating incident of the stable, Winslow was grateful for this harmless amusement, and lightly reported to Charles Jr., "I go to Prout's on Saturday — hope that Father will go to Boston. By Saturday I shall hear of the whereabouts of the Fleet." To this he appended a humorous drawing which shows an enormous cannon pointing from the bay window of the Stephenson cottage toward the horizon, where the Spanish fleet is preparing to attack Portland Harbor. Mrs. Stephenson, who bore the brunt of the cronies' antics, leans from a dormer window shouting, "I protest!"

When the American victory ended this diversion, the elder Homer, a firm believer in temperance for other people, subscribed to the White Ribbon Society, the prohibition party of that time, and took a vociferous part in its meetings. Meanwhile, it was an open secret within his family circle that he took for a nightcap a water glass half full of the finest Holland gin, absorbed neat. This, he assured the servants, was purely for medicinal purposes.

Winslow must have seen his father alternately as a source of vexation and ludicrous humor, and it is to his credit that the latter view prevails in the majority of his letters. Measuring both himself and his sire in the light of a realistic good humor, he wrote on Christmas Day, 1895, "I shall go home tomorrow. I find that living with Father for three days I grow so much like him that it frightens me." Recognizing this, he conducted himself in an op-

posite manner and made his father's example account for many
of his own best traits. Meeting parental pomposity with patience
and respect, he deferred to his father in numerous ways. Wit-
nesses have testified that the latter had no real comprehension of
anything aesthetic; in fact, he had thoroughly bad taste and only
came to mention his son's work proudly, and with some surprise,
after the arrival of medals and other tangible rewards. Yet Winslow never failed to take his finished paintings to the Ark to receive
his father's nod of approval. And when winter approached he
would set aside his own affairs and escort the older man down to
the American House in Boston, where Mr. Homer spent the colder
months. The son's solicitude is shown in a letter to Mattie dated
December 2, 1886: "Father leaves here tomorrow on a most haz-
ardous journey. He is, in fact, to travel alone for the first time in
many years. No friendly hand at his coat tail to keep him from
the seductive railroad tie. Confidential conversation with the
brakeman — at forty miles an hour — will be in order." Because
Winslow never married, it was expected that he should live near
and care for the older man; and though the legend which has
gathered round the painter stresses his misanthropy, he accepted
his responsibility toward his stimulating but trying parent with a
fierce loyalty and a forbearance that often bordered on the heroic.
In later years, when the father was an aged widower and the
bachelor son well past middle age, their old housekeeper noticed
that the two men depended much upon each other for companionship.

Mr. Homer's winters in Boston produced one result which was
especially beneficial. It was at the American House that he first
met Lewis Wright. A waiter in the dining room, Lewis Wright had
been born a slave in Virginia and possessed magnificent Chester-
fieldian manners and an indestructible good humor. He was one
of the few people outside the family circle who got on really well
with the elder Homer, so when the latter was stricken about 1895
with an intestinal disorder for which he needed extra care, the
Homer brothers induced Lewis to join the staff of the Ark. The

colored man became beloved by everyone on Prout's, and even Charles Sr. forgot his lord-of-the-manor attitude and treated him with a kind of gruff fondness. Lewis, a born diplomat, strengthened this rapport by appearing to take unlimited pleasure in waiting on Father Homer hand and foot; and the phrase-loving patriarch responded by addressing the servant by the Biblical name of Luke and allowing no one else to put him to bed. This event itself was worth seeing, for the master and the servant both enjoyed ceremony and turned the simple chore into a ritual. For one hour every night before bedtime, the old man, enthroned in front of a large mirror, would admire himself while the Negro valet combed and brushed his long flaxen locks and rubbed into his scalp the finest oil available.

Everything the grandsire did he did with gusto. During the 1880's he became very religious and associated himself with a group, of which J. Vaughan Merrick and Thomas B. Merrick, summer residents from Philadelphia, were the prime movers, working for the establishment of an Episcopal church at Prout's. Charles Savage wrote letters to everyone in the vicinity and the Merricks collected the money thus solicited. The building was consecrated in 1887, and Mr. Homer served as vestryman and as treasurer until his death. As if this were not enough, just before he died in 1898 his devotion increased to the point where he let his hair grow in long ringlets down to his shoulders in the belief that they made him resemble some Biblical prophet. The cascade of curls on an octogenarian struck Winslow as very funny, and he chided his parent in a letter of February 24, 1898: "Dear Father, I pray you give up your intemperate habits — *Red Pepper* — & *Long hair.*" To Charles Jr. he sent two sketches of their father: one entitled *Circassian Girl* after the long-haired sideshow girls of the day, and the other called *Prize Old Man.* The latter is the masterpiece of a long series illustrating life with father, for in it are summed up his most prominent characteristics: his astounding health and longevity, his long hair, and his officiousness in bossing Lewis and everyone else. Dressed in a Little Lord Fauntleroy suit and a sailor's hat on whose band is inscribed "Perpetual Youth," he calls to the servant, "Lewis, plant those English split peas in hills."

Father Homer's religion was largely in his hair and was trimmed, like it, to suit circumstances. In saying grace before every meal he would bow his head and begin, "Our Father, we thank Thee for this bounteous —" then, turning his head, he would mutter in the same monotone, "Luke, what have we got for breakfast?" If the menu seemed promising, the blessing would be lengthy and profound; if not, brief and to the point. Few things escaped Winslow's sharp eye, and in the running account of his father's welfare which he relayed to Charles Jr. he reported in a note written in September 1895: "He thanked the Lord — at blessing this morning — Not 'for the luxuries of thy bounty' but for 'the *means* of subsistence,' owing to the difference in the bill of fare."

Doing things with a flourish was second nature to the senior Homer. Consequently, though he was wholly dependent upon his sons during the final two decades of his life, he left a very ambitious will, apportioning to each of his three sons $10,000, and to his nephews and his servants $1,000 each. In addition, he left his grandson Arthur Patch Homer a gold watch and two lots near Eastern Point. Of this goodly estate, all except the last-named items was entirely nonexistent.

The fact that the senior Homer sired a genius is, of course, the reason for any study of the older man, who otherwise would not have left a ripple in history. The relationship between the father and son puzzled many people who knew them well. To Mrs. Munroe's close view they appeared quite unlike. Whereas Winslow was the son most closely associated with the father, he seemed, compared to his large and hearty brothers, to retreat the farthest from the parental example. He shared his father's excellent health but not his ponderous frame and massive head; instead, he was small, lean, and strikingly bald. When occasion demanded, he could dress immaculately, and appeared at Charles Lowell

Homer's wedding impeccably clad; but he preferred hunting boots and flannel shirts. Simplicity was the keynote of his tastes. At the time that his father's mansion was the showplace of a fashionable resort, Winslow lived in a converted stable as austere and poorly heated as a monastic cell (most of the furniture one sees in the studio today was added after the artist's death by his older brother). His character was an amalgam of contradictory elements inherited from two contrasting sources, the tug-of-war within him varying as the characteristics of one and then the other gained ascendancy. Yet it was probably this inner struggle which gave him his vitality. Outwardly self-contained and soft-spoken, he was the recognizable son of a firm, stable, and introspective mother. And in the end he painted as many pictures praising placid mountain lakes as he ever composed of storm-wracked ocean waves. But there was another pole to his wide emotional range. Lodged within him was a primitive drive of great force. It made him hate fetters as intensely as did his freedom-loving father; it caused him to announce when he finished his apprenticeship at Bufford's that he would never again acknowledge any man as master; and it inspired him to travel widely until the end of his life. The same passionate force enabled him to exult in howling autumnal winds, scudding clouds, and thundering surf, and to identify himself with dynamic nature. Outwardly as steady as a rock, he was fascinated by wild and spectacular manifestations of change. Thus, long after the cold and wet had driven everyone else from the cliffs, Winslow would stand transfixed by the untamed power and pounding rhythms of an equinoctial storm. Fishing or dreaming on a sylvan lake, he could be a pastoral poet, but when the nor'easters lashed the rocks, he responded to their epic grandeur. These superb moments he transferred to canvas with such comprehension that the gale seems to shriek through his painting of *The West Wind*. The source of this element of his personality, despite all outer differences between father and son, seems obvious. In the roaring surf

[48]

of the marine paintings, the father, big, blustering Charles Savage Homer, spoke through his son and found his fulfillment.

No one in the family circle around Winslow during the Prout's Neck years was closer to him than his older brother, Charles Savage, Jr., who was described by all who knew him as "a prince" and "a wonderful fellow." Brilliantly endowed, he was a successful chemist and business executive. After graduating from the Lawrence Scientific School at Cambridge, Massachusetts, in 1855 with a brilliant record, he began his career at the Pacific Mills in Lawrence, Massachusetts, at the unheard-of starting salary of $3500. From there he went in the mid-'60's to the Valentine Company in Brooklyn; his contributions to the growth of the firm were outstanding and he profited handsomely. He helped to develop a new varnish for railroad passenger cars and horse-drawn carriages which was so superior that it gave the firm a virtual monopoly. At that time such vehicles were given as many as eighteen coats of varnish, thus making it an extraordinarily lucrative product.

Charles was the tallest and handsomest of the three brothers, if two portraits of him painted by Winslow are fair evidence. He was an outstanding athlete in his youth and a vigorous man of the outdoors until his death in 1917, shortly after his golden wedding anniversary. He shared the distaste of his brothers for illness and confinement to such an extent that it was nearly impossible to keep him in bed during his final illness at the age of eighty-three. On the night before his death, against all orders he got out of bed and wandered around the room until forced to retire. When the end came, he said simply to his wife, "Mattie, I don't feel so well," and expired.

Charles and Mattie were a devoted couple. Mattie was so sentimental about him that she permitted nothing that he had used in the Ark to be moved for many years after his death. There was one habit of his, however, of which she strongly disapproved. Like Winslow, Charles was devoted to tobacco and loved a full pipe of

Gravely, an expensive brand of that day, which he cut himself from a plug. When the odors became a matter of contention, he would retire to a smoking room which his brother Arthur had allowed him to build onto El Rancho, or join Winslow in a long smoke in the studio.

The two men had much in common, sharing the camaraderie of travel and fishing in the Adirondacks and Canada in high good humor over many years, and Charles furthered his brother's career at every turn throughout their lives. Winslow, in turn, was so fond of his brother that he gave him scores of watercolors, especially those which depicted scenes they had known together, while Charles made it possible for Winslow to visit far-off places like the Tourilli Club in Quebec Province and the North Woods Club in the Adirondacks which necessitated expensive trips.

After Winslow's death one of the first things Charles did was to present to the Metropolitan Museum the handsome unfinished oil painting entitled *Shooting the Rapids, Saguenay River*. In the same year, as Winslow's executor, he invited the Metropolitan and Brooklyn Museums to purchase for modest sums many of the unsurpassed watercolors which have since played an important part in Homer's fame, and at the same time presented to the Cooper Union Museum its unexcelled group of Homer drawings. Having offered his brother encouragement, appreciation, and financial aid during his lifetime, he showed equal devotion and intelligence after Winslow Homer's death in placing his work before the public for all time.

Charles was a vigorous man, somewhat larger and more robust than Winslow, and both like and unlike him in several ways. He and the painter shared the Homer sense of humor and delighted in joshing each other, but Charles's more cosmopolitan experience and attitude made him substitute for the painter's forthrightness a perfectly expressionless manner of telling a joke, and he was especially pleased when the more sedate ladies of his wife's circle did not know how to take him. Much more at ease in large gatherings, he was an addition to the conversation of any assemblage and was recognized as a witty after-dinner speaker. Convivial, healthy, and virile, jolly, gracious, and genial, he easily assumed the role of host at his wife's largest parties where Winslow was painfully ill-at-ease. Cyrus Merriam, a summer resident of Prout's Neck, recalled a time when a large party was being held in the Ark to celebrate Charles Jr.'s birthday. Noting Winslow's absence, Cyrus, who had known the artist fondly for many years, made his way to the studio, where he found him sitting by his fireplace in solitary grandeur. Using an old board as a lap table, he was eating a chicken which he had just roasted. He allowed Cyrus to bring him some punch, but much as he loved his brother, nothing could induce him to join the festivities.

During the winters, Charles and his wife lived in a large apartment at 10 West Forty-third Street in New York City, where he devoted himself to business. The spring and fall seasons were passed at West Townsend, Massachusetts, the birthplace of his wife, where they owned a comfortable residence, and summers in the Ark at Prout's, where he had gathered around him the unexcelled collection of Winslow's watercolors later bequeathed to his nephew Charles.

Winslow's favorite lady next to his mother was Martha E. Homer, the wife of Charles and the "Dear Mattie" of so many of his letters. She was the recipient of the large album of flower paintings which had been addressed by Henrietta Benson Homer to "my beloved daughter," and possessed an unusual faculty for inspiring devotion and affection among those who knew her. As a small-town girl Martha E. French had married a rising young businessman and then had blossomed herself. Although physically frail, she lived until 1937, surviving her octogenarian husband by nearly twenty years. Meanwhile, she had added to a lovable personality a considerable number of social gifts; she was not only fond of being an important hostess, but did it well, running her houses like mansions, with plenty of help and money, so that no invitation to a social function at Prout's Neck surpassed hers in prestige. A handsome woman, she possessed a keen mind, was well read, highly cultured, and supported the opera, symphony concerts, and all good works. She lived by a code, did all of the proper things, and in her later years became a leader of New York society. Charles Savage, Jr., took great pride in his wife and her accomplishments. Mrs. Edward G. Vaill, a long-time resident of Prout's, related that one summer a young man was brought down from New York to tune the piano at the Ark. Seeing the mistress of the house, he said to Charles with genuine admiration, "That lady must have been a fine figure of a woman in her day." To this Mr. Homer retorted forcefully, "She is still a fine figure of a woman!" Among those who knew her during the New York seasons was William Witherle Lawrence, a distinguished and distinguished-looking young professor of English literature at Columbia University, a most presentable bachelor and hence a frequent guest at Mrs. Homer's numerous dinner parties. "They were invariably memorable occasions," he recalled "at which conversation flowed, sometimes brilliantly but always smoothly, under the guidance of Mrs. Homer. A natural hostess, she was lively, ultra-feminine, tactful, and intelligent and loved the company of similar people. As an active social leader in New York, she knew a great many successful, cultured, and distinguished members of the worlds of business and the arts. Yet during these years the chief lion of all was a member of her own family, and devoted to her, but conspicuously absent from these gatherings."

In keeping with her station, Mrs. Homer had, during the years prior to the automobile, a stable of blooded horses. These were shipped with the seasons from New York to West Townsend and to Prout's, so that she might be properly conveyed on her social calls. The horses were under the care of a fine English groom named Thomas Roebuck. The period of transition from the horse-drawn vehicle to the automobile, however, found Roebuck too old to master the new machine and forced Mrs. Homer to make new arrangements. She converted a younger groom named Mike Flanagan into a French chauffeur (then stylish) by rechristening him

Alphonse Peabodeau. In addition to drivers of coach and automobile, footmen were needed. So Roebuck trained his son to be a footman for the coach, and "Peabodeau" trained the youth to drive the automobile. When father and son took out the limousine, the father served as footman. The Homer brothers, who loved Mattie in most regards, had an irreverent attitude toward this sort of thing and derived no end of fun from the situation, going out of their way to call Mike Flanagan by his true name.

Older residents of Prout's Neck still remember Mrs. Homer as the most gifted and colorful hostess they have ever had. Her service to art was even more important. Believing as firmly as her husband in Winslow's art, she joined her encouragement to his in every way that she could. That Winslow reciprocated and was extremely fond of her is apparent in his letters. That we have the letters today is, Charles L. Homer asserted, owing to her foresight in keeping them and passing them on to him and his wife. More significant still is the fact that she began to preserve them in the early 1880's, before the principal period of Homer's fame, along with the album of newspaper clippings started by Winslow's mother, to which she added extensively.

Winslow's younger brother Arthur was five years his junior, and for that and other reasons was not as close to the painter as Charles. His business kept him in Galveston, Texas, during the long period after the Civil War and separated from his family. He was known for the affability of his disposition. He had a strong, outspoken way of talking, similar to his father's, and resembled him in his love of company. Neither so elegant as Charles nor so quiet as Winslow, he enjoyed bodily comfort and did not stand on show. Each year he would buy a new felt hat which, regardless of how comfortable it already was, he would wet and force down over a fence post until the crown came up to a peak, achieving what might be called a studied informality. Like all the Homers he had strongly marked idiosyncracies, but was friendly and liked by all for his jolly, robust nature. After Arthur moved to Prout's for the summers, he and Winslow renewed their relationship, and we see in the letters that it ripened into deep affection in the closing years of their lives.

Almost a member of the family was Winslow's dog Sam, a white wirehaired terrier with a black head which the artist had bought as a pup in England. When Winslow had to leave Prout's in the winter his primary concern was for Sam's welfare, and he boarded him at the West Point House like a gentleman. He was as long-lived as any Homer, for he died in 1899 at the incredible canine age of eighteen. The two were inseparable, and it was a question as to whether Winslow owned Sam, or Sam owned Winslow. In Figure 8 he is sitting, as usual, at his master's feet, with Father Homer standing behind them.

So, in 1883, surrounded by his family, his dog, and the warm-hearted local people who were soon to become his friends, Winslow Homer settled down at Prout's Neck in a house and studio of his own, commanding a superb view of the sea. Here he was to achieve his full stature as a major American artist.

Before he could begin this wholly new phase of his artistic career, however, he had some unfinished business to complete. As he had done immediately after the close of the Civil War, he wanted to finish the paintings from his last series. From Tynemouth he had sketches and notes and ideas to develop, and this project occupied much of his time for the remainder of 1883.

Typical of the first studies completed at Prout's was a watercolor begun at Tynemouth called *The Lookout*. For models he enlisted the services of local people, as he was to do so often in the years ahead. According to Mrs. Larrabee, he posed them on the cliff overlooking Saco Bay near the Southgate Hotel or on the beach below — Miss Hattie Carter, Mrs. Ida Harding, Mrs. Maude Libby, Mrs. Sadie Richardson, Mrs. Larrabee — these were some of the women who good-naturedly posed for Winslow Homer, and gained some measure of immortality by doing so.

One of the best of the leftover English paintings is *An After-*

glow, in Boston's Museum of Fine Arts. The massive boats and brilliantly illuminated water are what we have come to expect of Homer, but we can see, too, his eye for simple and appealing human behavior that derived from his long experience as an illustrator. There are other paintings of women watching the sea. The oil *Two Figures by the Sea* is probably only a study, but the free handling of the pigment is well suited to the theme. *Fishwives*, a watercolor dated 1883, conveys perfectly the soaking wetness of a stormy day by the shore, as does a kindred subject in a lighter mood derived from the drawing *Fisher Girl on the Beach*. The finished watercolor *The Incoming Tide* shows the same girl against a background of surf, and is a lighthearted harmony of line and tone. When it was exhibited at the American Watercolor Society in 1883, this lightheartedness led one wit to do a caricature of it under the title "Hoop-la! Dad's Gone!" at which even Homer himself was greatly amused.

Deservedly noted among this group is the powerfully conceived watercolor *Inside the Bar*. But the best of the whole English series is generally considered to be *A Voice from the Cliffs*. Against a towering chalk cliff three fisher girls are set in a rhythmic harmony of attitudes, climaxing the type of grouping Homer had tried before in such sketches as *Three Girls*. The boldly realized figures leap from the hazy background with a startling feeling of mass against depth, but the chief appeal of the painting is in the idyllic mood that Homer has so perfectly created. The composition was finished in his studio in New York in early 1883 and first displayed to the public at the American Watercolor Society exhibition in February of that year.

Homer was frequently dependent upon models, particularly in representing female human figures, and when, after moving to Prout's, he wished to complete other pictures he had conceived at Tynemouth, he needed the services of girls similar to the sturdy, healthy fishermen's daughters he had discovered on the coast of northern England. As a group they had strong arms and regular, almost classic features that were imposing rather than pretty.

Fortunately he was able to find someone of this character near Prout's to continue his English themes. Four women who knew her well identified the principal figure in numerous drawings and watercolors Homer executed at that time as a Scarboro girl named Cora Googins Sanborn. In 1883, when he first engaged her as a model, she was eighteen and considered an outstandingly handsome girl, a consensus borne out by photographs of her. Tall, with especially lovely hands and arms, she was an ideal choice to carry on the Tynemouth type because of her striking resemblance to the central figure in *A Voice from the Cliffs*, and Homer used her as a model for several years.

The mood of this painting was also expressed in an earlier, somewhat similar oil called *Hark! the Lark*, and in an etching of the same subject which he did for popular sale in the middle 1880's, thus treating the same idea in three media, an exception for him. The reason, as Goodrich suggests in his biography of Homer, is that Homer regarded the oil version of this theme as the best picture to come out of his visit to England, and exhibited it at the Royal Academy in London in the summer of 1882. Ultimately, of course, he exhausted the rich Tynemouth vein of inspiration, until by 1884 these subjects, like *Enjoying the Breeze*, became exceptional. It is a fair guess that in some cases he merely added a few final touches to drawings he had only started abroad when he was seeking to add as rapidly as possible to his storehouse of ideas, and then, perhaps unconsciously, dated them 1883 or 1884. An instance of the readiness with which he interchanged Tynemouth and Prout's settings in his own mind at this time and for some years afterward is a watercolor dated 1882 and now called *Breakwater, Tynemouth*, though in an entry for July 5, 1902, in his Day Book a pen sketch of the picture is named *Girls, Pine Point* — a promontory near Prout's. These discrepancies create problems for historians, who must find or wait for clarifying evidence, but fortunately are not crucial to understanding by others. For, to complicate dating further, Homer on occasion apparently diverted himself by retouching earlier drawings and watercolors like *Sailing a Dory* or *Girl and Sheep* and signing these too as 1884, although they had been conceived during the '70's at Gloucester, West Townsend, or Houghton Farm near Cornwall in the Hudson River Valley. He was pulling together the last loose threads of his artistic past.

Homer's moods and methods as observed at first hand during this transitional period when he was adjusting his life from the Tynemouth to the Prout's phases of his career were described to me by Joseph Foss, a resident of Scarboro who knew the artist well and occasionally did chores and favors for him. At some time during 1887 or 1888 Homer wished to finish another English subject. For it he needed models, but as a newcomer did not know where to find them, and asked Foss — who knew everyone — to enlist two girls to pose for him. Joe engaged Sadie Sylvester and Ida Meserve, two sixteen-year-old Scarboro girls. Homer first posed them near Eastern Point, carrying a heavy net. They worked about an hour a day — fifteen-minute poses, then five minutes rest. He was very considerate of his models, asking them frequently if they were tired, paying them after each session, always thanking them courteously. However, he wanted no giggling girls around unattended, and in order to have a proper chaperon obtained the services of Sadie's grandfather, Benjamin Sanborn, to "carry his pencils" — of which there were two.

Mr. Foss recalled that after some dissatisfaction with his first results, Homer decided to drop his original idea and make an etching of a theme he had rendered in watercolor at Tynemouth and called *Mending the Nets*, of two girls mending a net rather than carrying it. He rearranged the girls, made drawings of this new design, and then transferred it to a copper plate, renaming the etching *Mending the Tears* and copyrighting it in 1888. If watercolor and etching seem at first glance identical, it was characteristic of Homer to employ a new sitting for an old theme in order to attain a fresh point of view and give himself a chance to improve his composition. A comparison of his paintings with similar etchings will show that he did this frequently, particularly when he created several versions in the graphic medium. In both instances here, the strong but simple modeling of the two girls, the boldness of their silhouettes against the misty background, and the play of the erect girl's posture against that of the bent-over mender all remind us of the strength of form and design that Homer gained from his sojourn among the people of Tynemouth and rank *Mending the Nets* (or *Tears*) among the best pictures inspired by that locale. It is clear that his visit to the northeast corner of England was an experience which made an indelible impression upon him, coming to the fore not only in the duplication of *Mending the Nets* in etched form but in pictures completed twenty or more years after he returned to America. *Mending the Nets* is significant in another way, for Homer has often been conceived as being as brusque in manner as his painting was powerful but coarse. Here is plainly expressed a chivalrous attitude toward women that is in keeping with the courtesy Joe Foss said he showed toward his young models in real life. Along with his masculine manner he not only knew perfectly how and when to be a gentleman, but he truly had, as a youthful friend said of him, a side that was as "fine as silk."

In 1882, while still at Tynemouth, Homer had sent a few of his English subjects to J. Eastman Chase's gallery in Hamilton Place, Boston. In 1883 he sent a larger group to the exhibition of the American Watercolor Society, in New York, and followed this with another show at Doll and Richards Gallery in Boston. Contemporary newspaper comments indicate the reaction to this new Homer. The Boston *Transcript* (February 9, 1882) called the pictures "sketches in the strongest sense of the word. They are, for the most part, painted with an exceptionally vigorous and free brush; the prime essence, the very spirit, of each scene being surely and easily caught, and details being emphasized strictly in the ratio of their importance." Another critic, captivated by the models, said, "There is a charming feminine grace in these sturdy Christie Johnstones, a grace not only of posture and bearing, but of look and expression." A third praised the sentiment: "What makes these sketches peculiarly valuable in our eyes is a certain unstrained poetic treatment of the various subjects." Of the American Watercolor Society show, the Boston *Daily Advertiser* said, "By almost unanimous consent the first rank is this year assigned to Mr. Winslow Homer." Another paper compliments Homer on his vast improvement after the "trickery and oddity" of the doll-like Shepherdess series of his middle period, noting that two of his paintings were sold on the opening day. Predictably, one critic compared Homer's new work to that of Millet, and lamented the similar "socialistic tendencies."

In 1882, the New York *Times* had been mild in its praise of the Homer sketches shown by Chase in Boston, but the more comprehensive exhibition at the Watercolor Society show led it to say with wholehearted enthusiasm that "travel and change of outlook have benefited his art immensely in one way, that is to say, in technique, and they have also deepened his seriousness." Another colleague described *A Voice from the Cliffs* in superlatives, saying of the artist, "He returned stronger than ever."

Naturally, there were adverse reactions. One anonymous journalist searched vainly (and unhappily) for "stories and morals"; another deplored "a lingering taint of the malaria of Impressionism." A third felt that Homer did not "get into sympathetic relation with the people, and apparently misses the opportunity of showing that they have their joys and sorrows, their loves and bereavements." Of the pictures, he said, "They have every good quality save that of intellectual insight."

Most of the critics and most of the public liked Homer's Tynemouth pictures, and they marked a real turning point in his popularity as a painter. Not that this general acceptance meant much to him — Homer knew what he was after, and it was by no means popular acclaim. Only he could judge the success of his work as measured against the yardstick of his own self-criticism. As Downes wrote in his biography, "The praise or blame of critics

Fig. 9.   THE SHIP'S BOAT.
New Britain Museum of American Art.

never made any difference with Homer, who went serenely on his
way, as unconcerned with such matters as any man that ever
lived."

While he was finishing up his English series, Homer began the
long exploratory walks around Prout's that came to be such a part
of his life there, and little by little came to know and love every
rock and bush, every little outcropping of ledge, and every different aspect of weather and lighting and mood that made his great
Prout's Neck paintings so real. Once, on the long hike to Cape
Elizabeth at the south shore of Portland Harbor, he did an autumn glimpse of the sea with Prout's in the distance. In 1907 he
gave it to Mrs. James Nevins Hyde, who later bequeathed it to her
son Charles. On the then sparsely settled Neck, one can just make
out the Ark and Winslow's studio. But very early among his paintings at Prout's we see him devoting himself to the close studies of
rocks and waves which were to become his great love. In a watercolor, *The Ship's Boat* (Fig. 9), he demonstrates the new attitude
toward the sea which he had developed at Tynemouth. Here is all
the power and threat of mighty seas and cruel rocks, and the imminent danger that is an ever-present part of the lives of those

Fig. 10.   PROUT'S NECK, ROCKY SHORE.
1883. Worcester Art Museum.

who live by the sea, the overshadowing danger that Homer saw at
Tynemouth. But the background is Prout's, and in setting as well
as technique it is prophetic of Homer's coming work, even though
it is backward-looking in its use of watercolor rather than oil for
this type of subject.

During 1883 he ranged all along the cliffs of Prout's, making
such studies as *Surf at Prout's, Light Blue Sea at Prout's,* and
Prout's Neck, Rocky Shore (Fig. 10). The same year, in *Heavy
Surf, Prout's,* he tried his best to capture, through the wetness and
fluidity of watercolor, the massive power of the waves, but the
unfinished painting, later owned by his nephew Charles, testifies
to his dissatisfaction with the experiment. He tried again and
again, in *Incoming Tide, Scarborough, Maine,* painted in 1883,
and *Prout's Neck, Breaking Wave* (Fig. 11), done in 1887, and
finally decided that the problem was insoluble. The mighty ground-
swells, the headlong speed and feathery spray of the breakers, yes
— but the thundering, crashing impact of the tons of solid water
against the great rocks could not be handled by watercolor, at
least not by him. He loved the watercolor medium, with its flexi-

Fig. 11.   PROUT'S NECK, BREAKING WAVE.
1887. The Art Institute of Chicago.

bility and handiness, and had used it for most of his finished
paintings up to this time. But he had never seen anything like the
waves at Prout's. Master of watercolor though he was, the great
breakers defied his best efforts to capture their power, and he
finally turned to oils, almost against his will. Now the difficulty
was overcome, and speedily he painted, in 1884, what has been
called the first of his real masterpieces, *The Life Line* (Fig. 12).

In many of the Tynemouth pictures, and in some of his early
Prout's Neck studies, such as *Prout's Neck, Rocky Shore* (Fig. 10)
and *The Ship's Boat* (Fig. 9), he had shown the eternal battle of
the waves and the rocks, and man's danger when he fights the
sea. But in *The Life Line* these two themes are carried almost to
their ultimate. Barely indicated in the background are the rocks
and cliffs of Prout's; in the upper left is a suggestion of a wind-
whipped sail and a parted line that tell us of the helpless sailing

craft driven onto a lee shore and doomed to break up at any moment. A lifeline has been carried (or shot) from the bluff to the wrecked vessel, and with the aid of a breeches buoy, a coastguardsman is rescuing a woman passenger. The high-flung spray, the choppy sea clawing at the legs of the two figures, the taut hauling line — all these give a frighteningly real sense of man's courage and strength when he is called upon to help his fellows. We see little of the rescuer except his tenacious grasp on the helpless, perhaps unconscious woman, and it is by this almost ruthless suppression of detail in figures and setting that the piece gains its real power. Our eyes and minds would be riveted on Homer's boldly managed forms by the effective, sweeping design alone, even though we could recognize nothing but pattern. A close examination of the canvas reveals part of the reason why Homer had been forced to desert watercolor in rendering subjects like this: much of the violence in the pictures comes from the vigorous brushwork.

Fig. 12.   THE LIFE LINE.
1884. Philadelphia Museum of Art.

At last Homer was satisfied. Through untiring experimentation and self-criticism he had finally found the way to achieve what he wanted to do. He liked the painting so well that he translated it into a series of etchings under the title *Saved*, but of all the media he ever used, etching suited his character the least, and in the numerous alterations that he made we can sense his own dissatisfaction.

At this stage of his career Homer preferred to paint from live models, but in this case he could not get anyone to pose for him in the half-prone position he wanted. Perhaps the Scarboro girls had felt it would be immodest; perhaps the rather proper Homer felt diffident about asking them. He called into service one of several small manikins he had purchased at Tynemouth. Using a wooden bird perch for the breeches buoy, he posed the doll at the desired angle and held it with a garter band which is still tied to the arm of the figure. The clothing is fastened back to look windblown, and the many pinholes show how Homer experimented with various arrangements. But in spite of this artificial model, his painting is a miracle of dramatic power and the female figure incredibly real. Homer sent the final version of the painting to the National Academy Exhibition in the spring of 1884, where it was greatly admired.

In this version our attention is focused on the girl by an adroit touch — Homer has covered the face of the rescuer by the wind-whipped shawl, which somehow makes the whole episode very believable. It is a bit of realism which would have occurred to few painters, but is so completely characteristic of Homer's approach to any subject. According to Downes's biography, Homer had become interested in rescue techniques at Tynemouth, and when he conceived *The Life Line* made a special trip to Atlantic City, in 1883, to study the matter still further.

The model for the coastguardsman was Henry Lee, who was working for Homer as a handyman around the studio. His face is shown in a drawing in the Cooper Union Museum. A poor boy, he had joined the Confederate cause when he was sixteen, and after the war had been brought from New Orleans to Lowell, Massachusetts, by Admiral Porter. Here he knew Winslow's brother Arthur, and later followed him to Prout's with the idea of making a living as odd-job man around the growing summer resort. Although small in stature, he and his sons as well were good workers. Winslow put him to work around the studio, and soon began using him as a model. Henry worked and posed for Homer until the artist's death; later he moved to Portland, where he died in 1925.

Another native of the Neck who worked for Homer was Leonard Libby. When he was thirteen Len, who loved horseback riding, started riding to Oak Hill to collect Homer's mail, and worked for him every summer all through the '8o's (during the winters he attended school in Portland) as valet and general handyman, and off and on thereafter until Homer's death.

Homer made many friends on the Neck — Harris Seavey, the stagecoach driver and mail carrier; Elbridge Oliver, who served for over fifty years as stationmaster; and of course Miss Hamilton, the Homers' housekeeper. Sometime in 1883 she had come as companion to Winslow's mother, and after Mrs. Homer's death stayed on to look after Mr. Homer Sr., and to manage the Ark. A prim New England spinster, she was an ardent churchgoer and very righteous; she irritated Mr. Homer exceedingly, and even clashed with Winslow on occasion, but he was very fond of her.

Even more than human companionship, perhaps, Winslow enjoyed the extraordinary natural beauty of the Neck. As he wrote to his brother Charles on September 1, 1884, "I like my home more than ever as people thin out." From his studio he had a wonderful view of the sea which he enhanced by a lawn and juniper trees trained in Japanese style. He could look eastward toward Scarboro and Higgins beaches and on to Cape Elizabeth; to westward was an unimpeded view of Saco Bay, Old Orchard, and Wood's Island Light; to the south was Stratton's Island and the open ocean. During the '8o's he painted these panoramic views in a series of pictures showing the bay in every kind of weather.

[65]

Small Sloop, Saco Bay and *Schooner on Saco Bay* are very like the Gloucester works, but the two best of the group, *Schooners in the Moonlight* and *Prout's Neck, Looking Toward Old Orchard*, are something quite new in breadth of conception and treatment of the elements. The moonlight painting is similar in feeling to certain Japanese prints by Hiroshige and is hauntingly lovely.

When Homer took up his residence at Prout's Neck in 1883, one of the institutions of the area was the fishing fleet, which could trace its history back to the early part of the seventeenth century. In his *Voyage into New England in 1623*, Christopher Levitt described the six-mile stretch between the Saco and Scarborough rivers and said, "There hath been more fish taken within two leagues of this place this year than in any other land." It is safe to assume that the presence of a village of Maine fishermen may well have been one of the determining factors in Homer's decision to settle there. He had come to know this way of life at Tynemouth, had been inspired by it to do some of his finest work, and further, had grown to understand and admire the people who made their livings from the sea. In any case, he was not long in getting acquainted with the fishermen at the Neck. Unfortunately, most of the old breed are gone now, for when the fish moved on with changing conditions of sea and weather, the deep-sea fishermen went too, or turned to clam digging or lobstering. I was able to find only one of the old-timers, of the type Homer painted in one of his rare portraits, the *Portrait of Captain Smith*. He told me the story behind Homer's second great marine painting, *The Herring Net* (Fig. 14).

Roswell Googins had known Winslow Homer from the time the painter settled on the Neck. He told me that in 1884, the year after Homer arrived, a great school of herring came in by Stratton's Island, opposite Prout's, and attracted a huge fishing fleet. Googins, then a boy of thirteen, rowed Homer out to the fleet and waited until nearly nightfall for him to make sketch after sketch of the men and the boats. These schooners had come out of Portland and from all up and down the coast as well. It was common

Fig. 13. A HAUL OF HERRING.
1884. Courtesy, Museum of Fine Arts, Boston.

Fig. 14. THE HERRING NET.
1885. The Art Institute of Chicago.

knowledge among the fishermen that every fall would see a big school of herring gathering in these waters; when they began to come in, word went from one fishing village to the next, and the fleet swiftly gathered. The men fished from dories with gill nets which caught the herring by the gills as they were lifted to the surface, rather than the more modern pocket nets. It was an old-time method, unsuited to mass hauls, and is little seen today. Homer, said Mr. Googins, showed the scene as it really was.

Soon after the early '80's, for some reason, the herring stopped schooling there and never came back. It may have been continually milder climate that drove them away; it may have been the shifting Gulf Stream current; some say mysterious diseases killed off their feed. Many authorities say the waters were "just fished out" through widespread use of trawls and of seines sometimes a quarter of a mile long. Whatever the real cause, the industry vanished, but fortunately Homer captured it in the nick of time and it will live forever in his pictures.

He sketched innumerable variations of the subject, from the complex *A Haul of Herring* (Fig. 13) and *Schooner at Anchor* to the beautifully simple *Dory* and the quietly dramatic conception called *Study* in the Cooper Union Museum. This last design Homer liked especially, and within a year translated it into his great painting *The Herring Net* (Fig. 14).

To one who knows the many faces of the sea and the sky, the soft orange glow of the fog which has rolled in at sunset is indicative of Homer's accurate observation of nature. The whole piece is conceived in subdued intensities, but the Indian-red float and the scintillating play of light on the silver fish afford an intriguing contrast in both color and brilliance. These, together with the looming, richly deep tones of the central design against the soft delicate background, are worthy of some of the great Dutch masters of two centuries before. It is difficult to agree with Kenyon Cox's statement of 1914 when he says, "Homer's technical handling of oil paint is entirely without charm, and it is abundantly evident that he triumphs not through it but in spite of it."

When the painting was shown in November 1885 the newspaper critics liked it very much indeed. Of the Doll and Richards show, where *The Herring Net* was exhibited, one journalist wrote, "Remembering that Mr. Homer, not so many months ago, declared in disgust (he was incapable of chagrin) that he would show no more pictures in collective exhibitions, because the public is unappreciative, it is very gratifying to see so many of these pictures ticketed 'Sold'!" Another paid him one of the finest tributes accorded him in his lifetime: "We have said much of Mr. Homer's power as a man of thought, because we look to such men as he for the only true development in art which this country can hope to gain."

Homer did not disappoint them. Masterpieces followed in rapid succession, some of them the great paintings that we know and love. In these sensitive and penetrating studies of this little northeast corner of Winslow Homer's America, he captured and preserved forever the vanishing look of the old-time New England fishing industry and the hardy people who carried it on.

His next painting is one of his finest — *The Fog Warning* (Fig. 16). From the late Alexander Bower, a member of the National Academy and former Director of the Portland Art Museum, I learned how this work originated. Mr. Bower never knew Homer, but he lived for many years at Cape Elizabeth just east of Prout's, and was acquainted with several people who knew the painter well. According to those who had watched Homer work out his idea of *The Fog Warning,* he propped up a dory near Alvin Brown's fish house on the beach below the Cammock House, on the west side of the Neck. He spaded up a pile of sand to substitute for a wave, got the dory up onto it at the desired angle, with Henry Lee in position modeling for the fisherman. All afternoon he worked on his eleven by fourteen inch watercolor block, achieving nothing but false starts. Realizing that for this day, at least, the spark was not present, he flipped Henry a five-dollar gold piece and brought the session to an end. It was an inauspicious start, and *The Fog Warning* was to cost him long, hard effort. Some-

Fig. 15. HALIBUT FISHING.
1884. From a photograph signed by Homer. Mrs. Charles L.
Homer, Prout's Neck.

times, with Homer, an inspiration would boil up inside his mind
and the picture would leap from his brush almost of itself; when
it did not he would simply settle down to stubborn hard work,
trial and error, and rigorous self-criticism. Patiently, laboriously,
he would eliminate and distill and consider until at last he
achieved a result which strikes us as the final, uncluttered essence
of his subject. In this painting, as in *The Herring Net*, we can
trace this progress quite accurately.

Mrs. Charles L. Homer owns a photograph which Winslow
signed and hung on his studio wall of an oil study he called *Halibut Fishing* (Fig. 15). In this intermediate study, rather rough in
technique and prosaic in conception, the doryman is hauling on a
line run through the tholepins rather than rowing, but the boat
and the sea are quite patently the parent passages of their later
parallels in *The Fog Warning*. It is a good, honest representa-
tional painting of a fisherman at his accustomed work. The later
version, true, demonstrates far more subtlety in the handling of

the oils, but the chief (and immediately apparent) difference is in its emotional implications. Here is a man used to a small boat in pretty tricky seas, well away from his ship, the fishing schooner on the horizon, tending his lines with care, handling his dory with consummate skill, and yet we know that in his occupation danger, even of death, is always imminent. A snapped oar, a slip of the foot, a moment's inattention to what he is about and he may be swamped or overboard in an instant. To the green-water fishermen, many of whom could not swim, and many of whom were far from young, this could mean a cold and lonely death. One of the great perils of the dory fisherman was to get caught away from his ship by fog or a sudden squall, and in *The Fog Warning* the signs are in the sky of that threatening gray wall that rolls in almost without notice on the New England coast; the doryman has seen it, hauled aboard all lines and tackle, and has manned the "white ash breeze" for the long touch-and-go row back to the schooner. If he has figured the weather signs correctly and used his good sense in time, he will make it. But if he has been careless about keeping his weather eye open, or waited a little too long to head back . . .

Fig. 16. THE FOG WARNING.
1885. Courtesy, Museum of Fine Arts, Boston.

A masterwork like this is not run off in a hurry. Soon after he had sketched *Halibut Fishing* in 1884, Homer painted the dory which was to feature in the more ambitious *The Fog Warning*, and the sea, which was a simplified version of that in the earlier study. But he wanted a sky, and the unfinished work stood against the studio wall, waiting, until the following summer, when an incoming fog at last gave him the right effect — the only effect he would accept.

Homer's reputation as a realist has led to his being accused at times of a slavish dependence on subject matter and props, and a lack of creative imagination in the painting of things and scenes. These two works just discussed represent fishing on the Grand Banks off Newfoundland, the setting of Kipling's *Captains Courageous*, a place where Homer had not been. He could not have witnessed the episode in *The Fog Warning*, but his memories of the North Sea off Tynemouth and his familiarity with Gloucester and Prout's gave him the material he needed, and his fertile imagination enabled him to synthesize these physical elements into a convincingly realistic and very moving composition. This process, of course, is hardly Homer's sole property; every creative artist uses it, even the most loudly self-styled realists; without it they would be producing nothing but photographs in oil.

Both *The Herring Net* and *The Fog Warning* reveal Homer's habit of improving a design as the dramatic conception developed. In the first, he changed the flat and uninteresting sea he had seen near Stratton's Island to a lively and exciting swell that not only gave him a reason for the subtle motion, poise and balance of the men and the boat as they ride the crest of a wave, but endows the whole work with a feeling of action. The eerie, orange-lit fog and the sparkling light give a sense of brilliance, and at the same time a feeling of the infinite vastness of the ocean setting.

When he developed *The Fog Warning* from *Halibut Fishing* he made the dory larger and the schooner smaller, increasing immeasurably the long row ahead of the fisherman, and with it our feeling of tenseness and concern for the outcome. By placing the schooner to the right and turning the fisherman's head toward it, the figure, the halibut's tail, and even the white crest of the breaking wave just above the starboard oar all carry our glance out to the ship and tie together the right and left sides of the design. The horizontal oars, the thwarts, and the flat edge of the fog bank emphasize the broad expanse of the sea, while the harshly diagonal line of the dory is echoed in the streamers of fog in the distance. Lines and tones and masses are played against each other with a disturbing effect of action and strain, and the colors are appropriately cold and somber. Idea and technique join to turn a simple act into a situation of infinitely powerful significance.

There are no more severe or caustic critics of genre pictures than the people whose lives and activities are represented. The comments of a Maine coast fisherman about an inept sea painting, especially one purporting to show him at a common task, would, if printable, make interesting reading. But the laymen liked Homer's paintings of fishermen; Henry Lee, who was not a fisherman but lived close to them, and the sea, was intensely proud of his position in this and other pictures by Homer. "You see the feller in the halibut picture?" he said to Augustus Moulton, author of *Old Prout's Neck*. "That's me." On January 8, 1886, a short time after Homer finished *The Fog Warning,* it was put on display in Doll and Richards Gallery in Boston, and was almost immediately purchased by Mr. Grenville Norcross, a local collector.

Labor Day is traditionally the time when summer visitors (with regret) desert the beaches and the resorts for their winter quarters, and the natives (usually with relief) wave them goodbye. With September, the Neck saw most of the Homers leave; even Father Homer moved briefly into the Falmouth Hotel in Portland before settling down for the winter in the American House in Boston. Winslow, who appreciated and needed the peace of the autumn months for his work, might have stayed even longer than he did, except for a curious development. Shortly after he had settled at Prout's, according to Theodore Bolton, the townspeople of Saco Bay district found in Homer those qualities of sound judgment that made for an excellent juror. Unfortunately for the quality of the Cumberland County legal system, however, Homer detested jury duty. He had reluctantly served in that capacity in New York and in Belmont, and on one occasion had punctuated a letter with the sketch of a harassed juror and the exclamation "No more!" Besides that, it interfered with his work. This unsought honor came as the last straw, and to discourage it he picked up and left before the fall of 1884 ended. The townspeople did not again press him to do jury duty.

He went first to Boston to see his works displayed at Doll and Richards, and while there told a newspaperman that he was going to Bermuda. He gave no reason, and actually went to Florida, then to Nassau for about two months, and finally to Santiago de Cuba at the end of February 1885.

From the very first, the tropics made a tremendous impression on Homer. The brilliant sunshine brought out the richness of the vegetation and the flowers in a blaze of color, and outlined forms and masses and details with a clarity of definition he had never known before. Here was another new world for Winslow to paint, and paint it he did, in a large number of watercolors done in approximately three months during the early part of 1885.

Homer's tropical paintings are of several kinds. Some are landscapes of a local nature; some are architectural studies of various towns; and there is a whole series of paintings of the jungle. In this last group Homer seems to be particularly interested in palm trees, but did not neglect the people. Charles L. Homer owned two of Winslow's local-scene watercolors, *A Town in Bermuda* (probably painted in the Bahamas) and *Governor's Palace, Havana.* This unfinished study shows heavy tropical clouds hanging over the limestone hills, but its chief feature is a fence, intricately wrought in iron. Another panoramic view, this one including a pretty woman, is *The Governor's Wife, Bahama Islands.*

Winslow's brother Charles gave him a small, box-like camera which took a circular photograph; Homer refers to it in the Day Book in the Homer Collection at Bowdoin College, and with it were taken the series of travel photographs from which are drawn Figures 29, 37, 49 and 82. Photography has been of deep interest to painters ever since the announcement of the daguerreotype in 1839 — Samuel F. B. Morse made his first photograph in September of that very year and later opened America's first photographic studio; the men who founded Impressionism met regularly at an early Paris daguerreotypist's gallery; Degas and Pissarro were profoundly affected by the camera's way of seeing. Thomas Eakins, we now know, invented a motion picture camera, and almost certainly Frederic Remington got his ideas of galloping horses from the famous Eadweard Muybridge photographs. Recently Charles Sheeler, like so many other contemporary painters, has used the camera. The chief significance of Homer's photographs is that they show scenes paralleling the subject matter of his paintings. Even a cursory comparison of any of his paintings with the similar photograph is an illuminating comment on the extent of his imagination and departure from actuality in creating those works that we commonly consider the ultimate in realism.

According to Beaumont Newhall, our leading historian of photography, Homer's camera was an Eastman Kodak No. 1, which was introduced in July 1888 at the convention of photographers in Minneapolis. An advanced model for its time, it took one hundred pictures two and a quarter inches in diameter on roll film and was an excellent instrument for a traveling artist. Homer's extensive use of a camera shortly thereafter and throughout the '90's on his own trips shows that he was not only interested in photography but alert to new developments. However, he plainly proved that he knew the difference between a photographic record and an interpretive work of art, and he never confused the capacity of the camera to record details with extraordinary clarity (which misled many weaker painters) with the artist's need to view selectively.

Like most artists from the northern areas of America or Europe, Homer was enthralled, almost intoxicated, by the exotic

Fig. 17.   STREET SCENE, SANTIAGO DE CUBA.
1885. Philadelphia Museum of Art.

beauty of the tropics. The intense electric blue of the sky, the seas
that shaded from ultramarine to turquoise, the blinding white
sand and the rich deep greens of the lush growth surrounding
white and pastel buildings of antique Spanish design — these not
only fascinated him, but presented new problems of seeing and
painting. *A Road in Nassau* is a striking pattern of old white walls
gleaming against emerald foliage and cool distances in a perfectly
peaceful mood. This type of subject was made to order for Homer — it was an exercise in simplification and elimination, and
he repeated it again and again.

The novel architectural forms appealed to him, too, and he recorded them in photographs as well as paintings. He did a whole
series of street-scene watercolors in Santiago, depicting various
aspects of the old town. *Spanish Flag* and *Street Scene, Santiago
de Cuba* (Fig. 17) are typical examples. With a deft hand and
perceptive eye he shows the hilly terrain, the superb arches of the

old buildings, the unusual shades and rich textures of the stuccoed walls, the inviting reaches of the narrow streets, half washed in sun and half in cool shadow. These are the picturesque features that attracted Homer the tourist; but Homer the artist saw as well the blockiness of the houses, the abstracted patterns of their grouping, and the innumerable problems in perspective which would have delighted the soul of a Renaissance Italian master. Like Cézanne, he played with the cube-like forms and tactile appeal of the architecture, but he was a luminist too, and continually juxtaposed the effects of light and those of mass with vivid results.

Here too he saw for the first time the tropical rain forest, that lush jungle growth that is so impressive it almost defies the efforts of writers and artists to do it justice. Like many another before and since his time, Homer tried rather unsuccessfully to paint it, and it was only after many attempts and much hard study that he gradually achieved results which satisfied him. In one early example, *Florida Jungle*, he captures the rich growth of the vegetation, but overdoes it; in another, *In the Jungle, Florida,* he tried to give the subject more meaning by including a forest dweller, but the final effect is confusing. Gradually, laboriously, he achieved the simplification of this complex and psychologically overpowering subject to a degree which kept the feeling of the original, but allowed him to arrange its elements into an acceptable design. A historical conception, *Buccaneers,* shows his advance in its splendid trees, but he was not at his happiest in romantic imagination, and the painting shows it.

More successful was his 1885 *Conch Divers* (Fig. 18). The Negro as a subject had been familiar to him since his Civil War experiences, and the details of the boat were, of course, no problem for him. The infinite possibilities of working with these superbly developed dark-skinned bodies, nude or seminude, against the white boats and the cool marine backgrounds led Homer to paint them for years. In *Conch Divers* he exploits beautifully the play of verticals, horizontals, and diagonals, and the sharp contrast be-

Fig. 18.   CONCH DIVERS.
1885. The Minneapolis Institute of Arts.

tween the dark, round forms and the open sky and flat sea. The three central figures, standing, bending, and crouched over the rail are like three progressive sketches to show the movement of a single model. Homer's ability to use thoroughly mastered techniques in attacking new and less familiar but similar elements of design made this a most satisfying picture; he continued to explore this theme, and in doing so produced some of his best works.

He returned to the subject in 1889 in *The Sponge Diver, Bahamas* (Fig. 19), and again at the end of the century in the famous *Rum Cay* and *Turtle Pound*, but now he had simplified his design to one or two figures and achieved his aesthetic effects by harmonies of attitude and form. The subtle S-curve of the sponge diver's right arm is in delightful harmony with the similar curve of the boat's stern, and the otherwise rather blank right side of the picture is brought into perfect balance by the introduction of the two tiny palms. The interplay of deep reddish browns and rich cool shades gives the work a vitality of color that is as satisfying as its orderly design.

When Homer returned to New England after each of his trips he set about completing his watercolors, most of which he had set down only in the form of sketches and notes. This was his usual practice, according to Charles L. Homer; thus, some of the pieces begun in late 1885 are dated 1886 in their finished form. He showed fifteen tropical studies at Doll and Richards in Boston in 1886, and another group at Reichard and Company in New York in 1887. From now on he was to use the dealers oftener to present his work, and the Academy Gallery and American Watercolor Society shows less. The comments in the contemporary press indicate the delight with which the residents of this northern area examined these revelations of the brilliance of the tropics. Never had his work sold so well or been more enthusiastically received. The artistic discovery of Africa, the Orient, and the tropics was a

Fig. 19.   THE SPONGE DIVER, BAHAMAS.
1889. Courtesy, Museum of Fine Arts, Boston.

major event in the latter part of the nineteenth century, and Homer was an important pioneer. After all, Gauguin never visited Martinique until 1887, and Van Gogh did not find his blinding sunlight at Arles until 1889.

Journeying back and forth between the southern areas and Prout's in keeping with the seasons, Homer continued to paint his brilliant pictures of the tropics in watercolor while pursuing his study of the sea in oil at his studio in Maine. According to Downes's biography, one of the best known of his canvases representing the interplay of human life and the ocean was developed in the following way. In 1883, shortly after he returned from England and before he settled at Prout's Neck, Homer was seeking ways and locales in which he could continue the themes he had discovered at Tynemouth. Visiting an old haunt, Atlantic City, he witnessed a rescue from drowning which gave him the idea for the powerful painting *Undertow.*

Downes is correct in stating that Homer began the work in New York, but he had not completed it when he returned to Prout's in April 1885. Leonard Libby recalled the time during the spring of that year when his sister Isa May Libby, then seventeen, posed for a series of preliminary sketches which was afterward developed as an etching, *Till Death Do Us Part.* From this came the still later painting, *Undertow.* Young Libby's part in the production was to slosh buckets of sea water over his sister. Homer, apparently dissatisfied with the etching, took only a few impressions. He rearranged his design for the painting, and it is more successful, but it met with a mixed reception when shown at the National Academy in the spring of 1887. Although the *Tribune* praised the picture, another press comment remarks on the work's lack of Homer's usual "simplicity and remarkable sincerity," and calls it "discordant, hard and lifeless." It remained on his hands for some time, but was eventually sold in 1889 to Edward D. Adams in New York for $2400 less commission of twenty per cent, a modest price even for the time.

The year 1886 saw the creation of another of Homer's great sea

Fig. 20. EIGHT BELLS.
1886. Addison Gallery of American Art.

pictures, *Eight Bells* (Fig. 20). His nephew Charles told me the story behind it. During the Atlantic crossing on the visit to Tynemouth, Winslow had been fascinated with the process of shooting the sun with a sextant and had painted a small watercolor of the operation. Sometime later he had bought an octant (a similar device) for his studio. His brother Arthur owned a small sailboat, the *Texas,* and Winslow offered to do some decorative panels for the cabin to fill the spaces between the ribs. The model for one of these was Arthur B. himself, complete with sweeping mustache, posed as on the deck of a ship and shooting the sun with Winslow's octant. This vigorous monochromatic study, *Taking an Observation,* apparently gave Winslow an inspiration, for he sud-

[81]

denly turned to his brother and handing him the panel said, "Here, Arthur, you can have this — I've got a better idea." Using as models the long-suffering Henry Lee and a neighbor named John Gatchell, he worked rapidly under the white heat of inspiration, and in a few days finished one of his finest paintings of men at sea, *Eight Bells.*

The perfect harmony of the rich blue tonal scheme, the bold handling of the fatty paint, and the incredibly wide range of chiaroscuro make the picture a visual delight. Never had he painted waves with more assurance, and the heavy clouds that are just breaking up to let the sun through are magnificent. The two figures, so completely natural, are so beautifully arranged that the fact of their arrangement is hardly apparent. For its flawless technique alone, the painting deserved to become famous.

Yet its real strength lies deeper than the paint, in the skillfully suggested human drama. Shooting the sun is a common, everyday occurrence in ship's routine. But here the sea and the sky tell us of the storm that has just ended and of the arduous battle between man and nature that has been won. The two men, still wearing their foul-weather gear, are taking advantage of the break in the weather to take an observation — perhaps the first for days — to determine the ship's position. It is this story behind the story that makes the painting great, and it is the understatement of it that gives us our greatest respect for Homer's genius.

The picture was purchased in 1888 by Thomas B. Clarke for the extremely low price of $400; eleven years later, even with the increase of Homer's reputation, it sold for only $4700. Collectors bought many of his paintings for ridiculously small sums. And C. Klackner of New York, who was franchised on August 1, 1888, as the sole publisher of Homer's etchings, charged Homer half the cost of printing plus a fifty per cent commission on sales. According to a memorandum dated 1892, one series of twenty-one impressions netted Homer only $114.67 — less than $5.50 apiece. This sort of thing he passed off in his letters with sardonic good humor, and he actually was not particularly worried about money. Nor, from all we can gather, about the opinions of either the public or the critics, although both were by this time becoming more and more flattering. He knew very well what he was trying to achieve, and that there could be but one final opinion as to the measure of his success — his own. By the beginning of the 1890's his rigorous self-criticism must have satisfied him in many respects as to his progress, for the years beginning at Tynemouth and continuing at Prout's had seen the creation of works that would rank high among the examples of great American painting.

We have seen that Homer's whole artistic life prior to 1883 was a period of preparation for greatness, a period of learning how to say something in his chosen language — the language of art. At Tynemouth he discovered what it was that he wanted to say, a theme worthy of his whole effort and which he could, fortunately, continue at Prout's Neck. There are many ways of making an artistic statement. We may call them styles, or schools, or manners, or modes of representation, but what they amount to is a choice, on the part of the artist, among the infinite number of things he can do with his medium. Which methods he rejects, which ones he uses and in what combinations he uses them — these make up his particular, individual way of working. What was Homer's way?

Tradition, cultural environment, even schooling can give the artist only an advantageous start; to become a master he must go on from there. Homer, like Rembrandt, had learned by his forty-seventh year about all that his contemporaries and his predecessors could teach him. Beyond that was an unmarked trail that he must explore alone. He rose far above the romantic realists among whom he started, and accomplished so much in his solitary labors at Prout's Neck that his intermediate borrowings from the Impressionists become almost insignificant.

In one sense he was always a realist. His ideas are stated in terms of a nature that seems to be untampered with, in an artistic language readily readable by his fellow Americans. Like so many of the older masters, he emphasized, eliminated, and manipulated the elements of his design within a framework of reasonable objectivity. To this degree, then, we may call him (as he often thought of himself) a realist, even as we appreciate that in his restrained departures from reality he produced something far greater.

With the end of the 1880's, we close a chapter in Homer's life. He had continued at Prout's the line of thought and method which had begun at Tynemouth, and finally achieved his full stature as an artist. Ahead lay the crowning years of his greatness, the golden decade of the '90's, with its rich outpouring of works that were to make him one of the greatest and best loved of American painters.

He and his family had come to be a real part of Prout's. Winslow grew to love the place as he studied and painted it, and this love went into every work along with his colors. His brother Charles, too, felt a deep affection for Prout's, and gave about fifty lots north of the present Winslow Homer Road to the Prout's Neck Association to provide a park for the residents. The Association later acquired by public subscription the adjoining land, which enlarged the area to its present size of about fifteen acres. This rustic park has come to be known as the Sanctuary, and in it is a bronze plaque bearing an inscription composed by Mrs. Charles Nevins Hyde:

In appreciation of the generosity of
CHARLES SAVAGE HOMER
1834–1917
Who gave these woods to the people of Prout's Neck
and the genius of his brother
WINSLOW HOMER
1836–1910
Who with his brush gave Prout's Neck to the world

CHAPTER FOUR

The Nineties

THE PEAK OF A CAREER

T HE art is long, and life is brief" — words spoken not of painting but of the art of healing, by Hippocrates, the father of
medicine. And yet, all down the centuries, how many times must
this same thought have occurred to practitioners of every art or
craft, desperate and solitary seekers of knowledge and skill who
saw their years running out, and still so much to do . . . so much
to learn . . .

Winslow Homer was forty-five before he sensed, at Tynemouth,
the first quickening of future greatness, and he was another ten
years working out an idiom in which to express what he wanted
to say — what he felt he must say.

True, it had been a good ten years. He had discovered Tynemouth, and with it a whole world of fresh images and emotions;
he had found a new home and new friends at Prout's Neck; and,
most satisfying of all, he had overcome most of the problems posed
by his new approach to painting. Step by laborious step he had
progressed from those first powerful statements about the fishing
people of Tynemouth, through the exploratory studies of the
Maine coast, to incomparable achievements like *The Herring Net,*
The Fog Warning, and *Eight Bells.* At the end of the '80's he was
seeing and painting with an ease and effectiveness that comes
only from a clear purpose and a sure mastery of technique. By

1890 two new regions had been studied and mastered: the tropical Atlantic and the north woods.

The closing decade of the century was to be his greatest. Everything in his life had led up to this period, and he produced painting after painting of an incredible variety of subjects and of such high character that sometimes we forget we are looking at pictures at all. We look with Homer out of the window of his mind, and see with his eyes; what he feels, we feel too.

One of Homer's greatest delights — after painting, of course — was fishing. The twenty-five years following the Civil War saw a tremendous growth of hunting and fishing as popular sports. It was a logical activity for Americans, whose ancestors had hunted and fished for food, and the fields and woods were a refreshing change from city and town. Homer was an ardent fisherman and a good one. He wet his line in the waters of the Adirondacks, Quebec, Florida, Bermuda, and the Bahamas — and he carried his sketch block with him.

Between 1889 and 1892 he became thoroughly acquainted with the Adirondacks, where he painted some of his most popular watercolors. He first stayed at the clubhouse of the Adirondack Preserve Association; later his base of operations was the North Woods Club near Minerva in Essex County, New York, of which his brother Charles was a member and which he too joined. The club was an exclusive one, intended to attract not the fashionable socialite, but those devoted sportsmen who loved hunting and fishing and who did not mind rough living and the long ride by buckboard into wild country. Typical of Homer's studies of game fish is *Trout Breaking* (Fig. 21); it is one of a series that grew out of his intimate acquaintance with his subject. The accuracy and life of these studies make them unique in American art.

Early in 1890 Homer paid the first of several visits to Florida and found there, probably in the region of the St. John's River in the northeast corner of the state, one of those lonely backwoods spots he loved so well. Here he settled down for a few weeks to

Fig. 21.   TROUT BREAKING.
1889. Courtesy, Museum of Fine Arts, Boston.

sketch in watercolor (and to fish) as he did everywhere he went. In the Homer Collection at Bowdoin College are several photographs which he took in Florida on this visit or one of his return trips in 1899 and 1904, as well as some for which he posed. In one (Fig. 81) he is seated comfortably in the stern of a boat which a couple of guides are rowing over the mirror-like surface of the river. In a strikingly similar and brilliant watercolor, *Bass Fishing, Florida*, which he signed and dated 1890, Homer intensified the luminosity of the reflections from the water in a way that the camera (at least of that day) could not match. Nor could photography quite convey the sense of light, and of soft, balmy air, so perfectly realized in the little *Rowing Homeward* of the same year.

Like most visitors to the tropics, Homer found the palms of particular interest. And since in Florida they grew more sparsely

than in the Bahamas, he could study them individually, and he
began his superb palm tree series. As with most of his subjects,
the paintings grew bolder and simpler every year. One of his photographs (Fig. 82) shows a typical grove; but in any of his similar
watercolors, what a difference! *The White Rowboat, Florida* depicts the characteristic tufted palms of the region, but with an enhanced effect; *Palm Trees, St. John's River, Florida* reminds us of
the intoxicating beauty of moonlight over tropical water. Both
works, long owned by Charles L. Homer, are striking evidence of
the superiority of artistic seeing and accenting over the more im-
personal eye of the camera.

In May, as usual, Homer returned to Prout's Neck for the summer, and observed a remarkable phenomenon of nature. His father was inordinately fond of rhubarb pie, and like many another
New Englander before and since, kept a cherished patch of pie
plant. It was at the rear of the Ark, near Winslow's studio, and, as
was the practice, it had been covered during the winter with old
boards. But when rhubarb is ready to come up, nothing stops it.
Winslow drew a sketch for his father and accompanied it with a
note:

May 4, 1890

> Dear Father:
>   *Your rhubarb is up two feet although it was not un-*
> *covered. But it came taking with it anything in the*
> *way, three-inch plank, wheelbarrow, old wash tubs, and*
> *whatever was over it, as seen from my window.*
>   W ———

That summer Charles had a larger painting room built on to
his brother's studio. Mrs. Larrabee (Marie Seavey) told me of being invited with her father, Zenas Seavey, to see it. The new room
was rather large and barren, and heated only by a pot-bellied
stove. It was filled with Winslow's pictures, which he showed
them with evident pleasure; on this occasion he chatted continu-

ally, a very unusual thing with him. The exterior of the building looked about as we know it today, quite picturesque, and commanding an excellent view of the ocean. But the shrubbery which Homer had trained and nurtured became a mixed blessing. It almost smothered the windows of the painting room, which were none too large, and made him chronically complain about the lack of working light. When showing his pictures, he would move the portable easel about in an attempt to find a good light, and often gave up in exasperation.

He spent much of the summer of 1890 completing the watercolor sketches begun in Florida, and it was that summer that he did the well-known oil *Cloud Shadows*. One of his models (the Old Salt) was Benjamin Franklin Sanborn; the other was Mrs. Maude Googins Libby, who remembered very well posing for the painting on Ferry Beach just below Winslow's "other studio."

One evening that same summer the family gathered on the rocks with other summer residents to watch the moonlight playing on the great swells that were rolling in. After a little while Winslow disappeared, and when they returned to the Ark he was sitting on his studio porch putting the finishing touches to a charcoal sketch which later became the background of his celebrated *A Summer Night* (Fig. 22).

Downes has stated in his biography that all of Homer's moonlight pictures were painted "wholly in and by the light of the moon and never again retouched." Even if Homer had been able to complete so elaborate a painting in the course of an evening, any practicing artist will agree that it would have been virtually impossible to handle color in such a light. Most painters find even a slight departure from good light an almost insurmountable handicap. We know that Winslow's house had only two poor kerosene lamps (in the living room), and no lights at all in the studio. Even in the daytime the light was so unsatisfactory that whenever the weather allowed, he painted outside. To clear up the technicalities of the question I consulted Mr. Alexander Bower, a professional painter for forty-five years, who told me categorically that

Fig. 22.   A SUMMER NIGHT.
1890. Musée National d'Art Moderne, Paris.

the method would be impossible. Charles L. Homer also asserted that the story of his uncle's painting by moonlight, while it continues to intrigue Homer's admirers, was without foundation, and explained that for nighttime scenes he commonly made a monochromatic charcoal sketch and that he had used that procedure in this instance.

The whole family admired and praised the sketch as unusually beautiful, even for the talented Winslow. His nephew Charles remembered how they urged Winslow to make a painting from it, and how pleased he was at their appreciation. Very shortly he set to work on the noted oil painting, now in the Musée National d'Art Moderne at Paris. The moonlight effect alone was a real challenge, but Homer was bold enough to test his powers by introducing a pair of dancers in the foreground, apparently illuminated by a porch light which cuts across the picture from the right. The painting gains immeasurably from another effective touch, one quite common in Japanese woodcuts, a pinpoint flash of red from Wood's Island Light on the horizon, the only warm tone in the whole design.

Fascinated by the effects of light, Homer had long been intrigued by moonlight; years before in 1874, at Gloucester, he had painted a watercolor called *Moonlight,* and had never ceased his investigation. Mrs. Annie Munroe told me how, this same summer of 1890, Homer asked her to put up a lunch of cider and sandwiches for him, and sat alone for hours on the rock just below the Ark, studying the moonlight. It finally got so damp and chilly that she had to suggest he come inside before he caught cold.

When the time came that summer to put his knowledge of moonlight effects to work, in *A Summer Night,* he knew what he was about. As happened so often with Homer, he saw a subject that appealed to him, made up his mind how he wanted to treat it, gathered the various elements over a period of days or even weeks, and then combined them into a final composition. Homer was no human camera; he did not capture a scene in an instant with brush and pigment, but synthesized subject matter, impressions, technical means, and remembered knowledge into a perfectly harmonious result. And his ability was such that the final design impresses us as being so real, so natural, so unstudied that we find difficulty believing it was built up step by step, piece by piece.

For the two dancing figures in *A Summer Night* Homer posed Maude Googins Libby and Cora Sanborn on an old float at Ferry Beach. For about an hour every day through a whole week he made rapid sketches of the two girls, moving around them, studying them from every aspect. In the finished oil the two girls dancing in front of the moonlit dancing waves lend just the right quality of vitality to contrast with the rock-like silhouetted figures at the right.

Homer stayed late that summer of 1890 to study the effects of

[91]

Fig. 23. SUNLIGHT ON THE COAST.
1890. The Toledo Museum of Art. Gift of Mr. and Mrs. Edward
Drummond Libbey.

the equinoctial storms that hit Prout's each fall. Back in 1885, in
a watercolor, *Breaking Wave on a Shore Line,* he had examined
the problem of light on moving water. By 1890 his skill had
grown, and he did the magnificent *Sunlight on the Coast* (Fig.
23). His nephew Charles showed me one of his own photographs
of the surf at Prout's that records much the same effect of chiaroscuro. It is a striking photograph, but a comparison of the chaotic foam with the strongly ordered diagonal lines in the painting
is a sharp reminder of Winslow Homer's mastery of design.

For twenty-seven years Homer studied the waves at Prout's
from every aspect and under every condition of light and weather.
Sometimes the broken, complex surface he depicts gives only a
general impression; at other times he shows only one or two massive rollers that convey the universal nature of the others which
he barely suggests; occasionally he records the curious phenomenon of the wind-roused chop riding on the mighty ground swells
rolling in from a quite different direction, as in his oil *Backrush.*

A key to the perfect reality of Homer's wave studies is his accurate observation of three essential characteristics of great breakers. One is the combination of churning creamy foam and the solid, mighty, knockdown mass of literally tons of water; a second is the apparent downhill slipping motion in the face of an advancing wave. The third is that offshore waves are like huge cylinders, often fifty feet in diameter, moving forward with a simultaneous rolling and sliding motion. Homer's genius lay in his ability to combine a scientific knowledge of hydrokinetics with a highly refined sense of design. In *Northeaster* (Fig. 55) he illustrates the running downhill phenomenon; in *Early Morning After a Storm at Sea* (Fig. 79) the two qualities of airy foam and solid water; and in *Sunlight on the Coast* that little-known cylindrical wave form which is so difficult to represent in paint. Homer had been experimenting with pictures of surf and rocks ever since his arrival at Prout's in 1883, but this was his first real mastery of the subject.

There followed a number of great marines which are true seascapes with practically no concern for man or his works, except an occasional boat or a lighthouse suggested in the background, and this usually for no other reason than to supply a needed accent in the design. These pure landscapes and marines, of course, add up to only a small fraction of Homer's works. Even with nature playing an increasingly important role in his compositions as he matured, Homer was too concerned with humanity to ignore it. After all, he started as a painter of genre, and his concern for human activity persisted even to the last picture he ever finished.

Perhaps the truest explanation of the absence of people in these marines is that he did them in the fall, when most of the summer visitors had left, and when the fishing boats were not around. A summer resort out of season, like a school building in holiday time, seems almost unnaturally deserted — and in *Winter, Prout's Neck* (originally titled *Winter by the Seashore*), Homer captured perfectly this unreal desolation. Even the house has a strangeness about it; after the superb architectural details of the

Fig. 24. WINTER COAST.
1890. John G. Johnson Collection, Philadelphia.

Santiago series, it has a disturbing quality of being not quite square, of being almost distorted. I walked the cliffs for several hours with Homer's nephew Charles, but we never could find a viewpoint that gave us the same effect. The painting is unquestionably by Homer, and the 1890 date about right — the painting appears in a photograph of Homer's painting room taken that year. Nothing but the Homer establishment comes close to being the building in question, and we could only conclude that it is indeed the Ark, but highly altered, perhaps to give the very effect of unreality that we get from the picture.

There is still greater desolation and wintry chill in *Winter Coast* (Fig. 24), also done in 1890. The rock-covered slope which creates so effective a diagonal cross-cutting is within view of Homer's studio. A feeling of bone-penetrating cold pervades the picture, and yet it has an austere beauty about it, quite like the Maine coast itself. In the tradition of Pieter Brueghel or Kuniyoshi, Homer made the figure of the hunter smaller in proportion to the surroundings than it was in reality, an effective device. His knowledge of Prout's in winter was gained at first hand, for he stayed on there until well into December, as a letter written on December 10 to his older brother attests. In it he says that he is cutting ice from his pond on Eastern Point, which is "seven inches thick and clear as glass," and concludes with an indication of the way the winter scene exhilarated him: "Thursday morning — the most beautiful day in the winter."

During this time, as he indicated by a sketch in his letter to Charles, he completed one of his best illustrative paintings of life at sea, *The Signal of Distress*, showing the launching of a lifeboat in answer to a call for help. This work and *Sunlight on the Coast*, *A Summer Night*, and *Winter, Prout's Neck* were shown in New York in 1891; the press notices were highly complimentary. The critic of the *Evening Post* compared Homer's use of impasto in the winter scenes to Courbet's handling of pigment, and asserted that Homer showed greater ability in expressing movement. The critic for the Boston *Transcript* was especially charmed by *A Summer*

Night — "a new painting that deserves to be called great, a masterpiece of moonlight, and a truly inspired poem of the sea, as novel, so far as art is concerned, as if no one before Mr. Homer possessed the eyes to see or the soul to feel this nocturnal splendor and majesty." So gratifying was the response to the exhibition of Homer's four paintings that Klackner reproduced *The Signal of Distress* for popular sale by the then new process of photogravure. This relieved Homer from the necessity of preparing an etching, rather to his relief, for etching was not his favorite medium.

Homer was much on the move in 1891 — at Prout's in May, in New York in June to see Charles and Mattie off to Europe, and most of the summer and early fall in the Adirondacks. But he did paint one canvas that summer which is unusual in that it speaks for the oceanside at Prout's during the warmer months and the tourist or vacation season. He called it *Watching the Breakers.* He had always found the cliffs near his studio very useful and introduced them into numerous paintings. He had used them in 1884 in the background of *The Life Line* (Fig. 12), and in 1891 virtually the same formations appeared in *Watching the Breakers.* The latter is reminiscent of some of his Tynemouth studies of girls watching the ocean; two girls (perhaps summer visitors) are looking at the aftermath of a squall. The wind has gone down, but the great breakers are still rolling in under an angry sky. The tones of the picture are low in intensity, but the great range of chiaroscuro gives it dramatic quality, and there is a most effective accent of color in the clothing of one of the girls. The handling of the pigment and the rendition of the foamy waves is extremely free.

Homer returned from the Adirondacks in time for the fall storms, and this year did what is perhaps his finest painting of the autumn gale in all its savage fury, *The West Wind* (Fig. 25). The great waves in the picture are almost level with the cliffs — only when they achieve a height of sixty feet can they be seen from the angle of observation the painting shows. The lashing wind is whipping flying mares' tails from the crests of the towering

[96]

Fig. 25. THE WEST WIND.
1891. Addison Gallery of American Art.

breakers, and at precisely the most effective spot is the figure of a
woman, struggling along the marginal way that runs by the foot
of High Cliff. The work is an excitingly vivid image of the subject;
it is, as well, an incomparable example of occult balance of forces
along a sweeping diagonal line.

Charles L. Homer told me that sometime before painting *The
West Wind*, Winslow had been dining with John La Farge in New
York; the two were devoted friends but had many conflicting
ideas about art, especially in the field of color. La Farge criticized
Winslow for using too much brown and said his paintings were
too dull-toned. Unlike Homer, he was an avowed admirer of European techniques, especially the rich color of the Venetians. Winslow wagered him a hundred dollars that he could paint a picture
in browns which would be accepted and admired by critics and
the public as well. After Reichard, the dealer who exhibited *The
West Wind*, had reported to Homer the obvious popularity of the
work, Winslow wrote to La Farge: *"The West Wind* is brown. It's

damned good. Send me your check for $100." It is good. Most people call it one of Homer's greatest. Thomas B. Clarke bought it for his collection, and it is now in the Addison Gallery of American Art.

Winslow's brother Charles had taken his wife to Europe that summer; they returned in October, and Winslow wrote them from the club house of the Adirondacks Preserve Association.

Oct 15th 1891

Dear Charlie

I have not heard anything from home since I left Scarboro —

I am working very hard & will without doubt finish the two oil paintings that I commenced Oct 2nd & great work they are. Your eye being fresh from European pictures, great care is required to make you proud of your brother.

The original idea of these paintings are in Watercolor & will not be put on the market, but will be presented to you with the one that I made expressly for you

Yrs

WINSLOW

All Well
Love to Mattie

Europe was not unknown to members of the Homer family. Perhaps the trips of the others have misled historians as to Homer's trips abroad. Theodore Bolton wrote in his *Estimate* in 1932: "This is stated by Mr. Mahonri Young on very good evidence: Homer went to Europe on several occasions other than the well-known trips of 1867 and 1881. He made a number of short trips, probably to glance at pictures, and hasten home again." If this were true it would change our whole theory of Homer's Prout's Neck period, in which his work, unlike that of the '60's and '70's, shows few traces of outside technical influences, either

American or European. More than at any previous time in his career he seems now to be painting purely in his own intensely personal manner, explained (we have always supposed) by the long periods of working by himself away from museums and exhibitions.

To settle this question I asked Charles L. Homer, Leonard Libby, Mrs. Munroe, Mrs. Vaill, and Mrs. Larrabee about any possible trips to Europe. They had, taken together, known Winslow intimately from 1883 to 1910, and all of them (including his nephew) said positively that the artist had never once crossed the Atlantic during that period. This would leave only the years from 1867 to 1881, and during this time Goodrich has traced Homer's whereabouts in his biography of 1944 so exactly that only the briefest of trips could have been fitted into the few gaps that exist. Furthermore, it seems significant that Homer, who was very prone to keep his family posted on his whereabouts and traveling schedule in his letters, never mentions a trip to Europe in any of his communications from the time he settled at Prout's until his death. Actually there is not the slightest evidence that there were any European visits after 1882, except for the Bolton-Young statement. If, however, it could be established that Homer did go abroad between 1867 and 1881, or after 1882, it would shed new light on the puzzling matter of his relationship to European art during his later years.

The watercolor which Winslow refers to in his letter of October 15 as having been painted for Charles is *Guide Carrying a Deer*. He gave it to his brother at Christmastime, 1891, as we can see by the inscription written along the top. One of the oils he mentioned is *Huntsman and Dogs*, now in the Philadelphia Museum of Art. It is a variation of *Guide Carrying a Deer*. Adirondack subjects appear in his work more and more during the 1890's. As was usual with him, he made sketches on the spot, but the majority of both oils and watercolors were finished at Prout's.

The same four friends of Homer's whom I questioned about the possible trips to Europe identified the boy in *Huntsman and Dogs*

Fig. 26. CAMP FIRE, ADIRONDACKS.
About 1892. The Art Institute of Chicago.

as John Gatchell's son Wiley. Mrs. Larrabee added that Winslow
had bought the hounds especially for this picture, but wanted no
rival for Sam, and gave them to her uncle Harris Seavey. Wiley
was fourteen at the time; he and his brothers posed for many of
the pictures in the Adirondacks series, and their father appears
over and over as the lanky, grizzled guide. We can find him in
Woodman and Fallen Tree, in *Camp Fire, Adirondacks* (Fig. 26),
and *Adirondack Guide.* For this last picture Homer ordered a
hand-built birchbark canoe from a company in Old Town, Maine,
to be delivered to him at Prout's. Here, during the summer, he
posed Gatchell in it; this may account for the guide's being so
lightly dressed in the winter scene.

Mrs. Larrabee, who told me about the Old Town Indian canoe,
also identified the craft in *The Blue Boat* as a popular type among
Prout's Neck summer people. In this study John Gatchell and one
of his older sons are the models. Wiley Gatchell posed for the re-

Fig. 27.   ADIRONDACK GUIDE.
1894. Courtesy, Museum of Fine Arts, Boston.

turning hunter in *Adirondacks,* now at the Fogg Art Museum in
Cambridge. This is a wonderful painting of heavy forest growth,
with a giant tree providing a massive counter to the general verti-
cal design, all in cool, low-intensity tones very like those of cool,
shady woods. I am quite certain that this was painted at Prout's,
probably in the thick growth of the Sanctuary. According to Winslow's nephew Charles, the setting of these and many of the Adirondack studies was the Sanctuary and a large pond called Great
Massacre Pond in a nearby wooded section at the base of the
Neck.

Few of his works were finished on the spot where they were
begun. Some were, certainly, when time allowed and the theme
worked out smoothly; at other times he made rough sketches and
notes, completing the piece elsewhere. So consummate was his
skill that neither the speed with which he painted an on-the-spot
picture nor the weeks — sometimes months — of delay between

Fig. 28.   JOHN GATCHELL.
Photograph taken about 1895. Homer Collection, Bowdoin College Museum of Art.

the idea and the final painting seem to have affected the high quality of the result.

He was foresighted enough to find suitably similar models in the various localities where he worked. His female models at Prout's Neck made quite acceptable Tynemouth girls, and in the Adirondacks he found in Rufus Wallace, Orson "Mountain" Phelps, and Harvey Holt, a well-known guide who lived in Keene Valley, three models who bore a remarkable resemblance to John Gatchell and personified the "type" of older bearded guide, while

another resident of the area, Mike "Farmer" Flynn, was inter-
changeable with Wiley Gatchell when a younger type of man was
needed. By this arrangement Homer covered all contingencies.
Holt is plainly the model for *Adirondack Guide* (Fig. 27), though
the picture was probably finished at Prout's, for it is signed and
dated 1894, and Holt had died the year before.

John Gatchell (Fig. 28), whom Homer immortalized in *Eight
Bells* and used in so many Adirondack pictures, came to be his
most famous model. A local Scarboro boy, he had married red-
headed Carrie Ellis, who bore him seven sons. Their house was
tiny and, according to Mrs. Charlotte Googins Stevens, required
so little housework that Mrs. Gatchell sat most of the day making
lace. John seldom found enough odd jobs to make much of a living. Mrs. Vaill described him as "stubborn and obstreperous, and
not very well liked." She told me about one example of his stubborn streak. He was about to put a stick of wood into the rusty old
stove and Carrie observed it was too long and cautioned him
against it. That was enough for John; in it went — and right out
through the back. After he became incurably addicted to the bottle, Carrie left him; nobody was very surprised.

Homer felt sorry for the old man and the seven boys, gave him
what work he could around the Ark and studio, and used him
frequently as a model. John was grateful, and managed to keep
reasonably sober during the '90's, at least when he was working
for Homer. But April 1901 saw the beginning of the telling entries
in Winslow's Day Book (sometimes for several days in a row),
"No Gatchell!" Finally the old man went to pieces because of his
drinking and became too wayward and unreliable to employ as a
model or handyman.

None of Homer's models were identified by name in the titles;
he was less interested in them as portrait subjects than as natural
parts of a design, along with the trees, rocks, and boats. Many of
his figures, it is true, are readily recognized people, and some, like
Lee, Gatchell, and Holt, might well stand alone as superbly
painted portrait studies, but this, to Homer, was incidental. For

Fig. 29.   CANOEIST, LAKE ST. JOHN, PROVINCE
OF QUEBEC.
Photograph by Winslow Homer about 1895. Homer Collection,
Bowdoin College Museum of Art.

him they served to show the relationship between man and nature. Sometimes they were fighting an unfriendly environment, at
other times they were enjoying a peaceful and delightful spot
away from the hurly-burly of civilization, but in all cases it was
man in relation to his setting, rather than as an individual, which
was stressed.

Homer loved nature's every mood, gentle or savage, and his
fondness for the outdoors is always apparent in his work. A photograph (Fig. 29) is one of his records of rippling reflections on
calm water, and in a drawing of 1897, *Adirondack Scene*, at the
Cooper Union Museum we can see how he has simplified the visual image into a subtle yet effective design. In *Boy Fishing*, owned
by Dr. Anthony T. Ladd, the placid waters are yielding up a trout

[104]

Fig. 30.   WINSLOW HOMER IN A CANOE.
Photograph by Charles S. Homer, Jr., about 1895. Homer Collection, Bowdoin College Museum of Art.

to a young fisherman, probably Wiley Gatchell. The master
painter of roaring gales and mighty seas could also devote himself
no less capably to the serenity and gentleness of a warm summer
afternoon.

Above all things, Homer loved the freedom he enjoyed, and
which so many of us lack, to travel and spend time out of doors.
Thoreau had preached the rewarding nature of this kind of life,
but it is a far older dream. The Chinese had said the same thing
in their books, poems, and paintings nearly a thousand years before, after they had been driven from the north of China in the
Sung period. Homer's *Boy Fishing* and Ma Yüan's *A Solitary Angler* have more in common than the visible subject.

A photograph of Winslow in a canoe on a glass-calm lake (Fig.
30) is very like his watercolor *Young Ducks*. The strong horizon-

Fig. 31.   THE END OF THE HUNT.
1892. Bowdoin College Museum of Art.

tals of this painting emphasize the restful feeling of the water; the heavy clouds hanging over the dense woods and mirror-like lake are very characteristic of the Adirondacks.

Sometime after the end of December 1891, Homer finally left Prout's for the winter, returning to Scarboro in April 1892. In June he wrote to his brother Charles, poking some fun at the latter's boat, the *Mattie*. He indicated that he would be through work for a while by July and proposed a trip to Canada.

That summer and early fall saw a lot of work on the Adirondack watercolors, especially hunters in boats. In *The Boatman* Wiley Gatchell is rowing a flat-bottomed scow across a lake, and in *The Guide* we see John Gatchell in the same craft. The two appear together in *After the Hunt* and again in the similar *The End of the Hunt* (Fig. 31). All of these watercolors show Homer's remarkable ability to paint with fluid washes, so appropriate to the cool, damp forest shadows. More and more he was coming to use these in very low intensity tones, accented only by a touch of red in a hat or a sleeve. In *The End of the Hunt* he whitened the reflection around the boat by scraping with a knife through the wet wash to the paper. He was a master at exploiting the water-color paper itself; once he understood this technique he rarely afterward used body color for his lights.

Perhaps the culmination of the series is the famous *Hound and Hunter*. Homer had done a simple watercolor sketch of Wiley Gatchell lying in a canoe, his weight sinking the stern as he holds a cornered deer by the antlers, while the hound swims in for the kill. From this he developed the finished work in oils. It is a perfect study of dense undergrowth over the water's edge, but even more striking as an understanding of weight relationships shown by the boy, the tipped canoe, and the supporting water.

Near the North Woods Club was a sizable hill which had been burned over by forest fire. Homer used it in the background of many of his Adirondack pictures, and alone in a watercolor, *Burnt Mountain*. The rugged guides and the equally rugged fallen tree are admirably done, and the picture is a popular one. He used a strong diagonal design, even signing his name on a slant. The careful attention to detail gives a feeling of age and wildness and shows the same intimate knowledge of nature that we find in his *Old Settlers, Adirondacks*. During the same period he was painting other works with less detail and more dependence on pattern, and a generally more romantic feeling. *North Woods Club, Adirondacks* and *Guide Hiding a Canoe* are typical. He was less general in his thinking than the Oriental painters, whose simplified panoramas and empty spaces speak with such eloquence; at the same time he was not as explicitly romantic as Constable. Hardly another painter ever achieved such perfect balance between detail and pattern.

In November 1892, Thomas B. Clarke, one of Homer's steadiest patrons, bought the canvases *Visit from the Old Mistress* and *Coast in Winter*. The latter, less stormy than *The West Wind* and not so bleak as *Winter Coast*, is worthy of comparison to Hokusai's *The Great Wave*. Without technical derivation from the Japanese artist, Homer shares with him the supreme mastery of marine painting, leading the Western school as Hokusai does the Oriental.

The art critic of the Philadelphia *Telegraph* in October 1892 wrote a column on the Clarke Collection. He said of Homer that he had been "a great painter at one period of his history" (meaning the Civil War), but that "with the production of *Eight Bells* [which was shown at the National Academy in 1886] Mr. Homer seems to have given up all idea of pleasing the public." He called *The Life Line* and *Undertow* mere experiments, and denied that Homer had since then exhibited anything of importance. He said that "having apparently gone off too far on his own line to care about we others who are still lingering in the land of the Philistines, unable or unwilling to follow his lead," was a result of Homer's solitary life, and finished, "Seclusion may do well for a priest — it is fatal to a painter." Another (unidentified) journalist, speaking of *Huntsman and Dogs*, wrote the same year, "He has come dangerously near the commonplace." The writer could see in it nothing but a brutal hunter. This sniping at Homer persisted through the years.

Yet the Boston *Transcript* reported in the same year that of twelve watercolor sketches at Doll and Richards, seven were immediately sold to well-known Boston connoisseurs. It also told of an "eminent artist" who always called at the gallery to see if they had anything new of Homer's, and quoted his opinion that "$250 for a sketch by Homer is a ridiculously low price, and that $1,000 would be nearer the right figure." The artist was probably John La Farge.

Homer wrote to his sister-in-law Mrs. Arthur B. Homer on December 29, 1892, to thank her for a Christmas present and to say that he was leaving Prout's soon, but this winter he returned earlier than usual; an idea was simmering in his mind. He was back toward the beginning of March, and immediately asked Ros-

Fig. 32. THE FOX HUNT.
1893. Pennsylvania Academy of the Fine Arts.

well Googins, a good hunter, to get him a dead fox and some dead
crows. Ros supplied the crows, but another hunter got a fox first
and delivered it to Homer.

Winslow arranged the crows as if in flight on a snowdrift outside the studio window and let them freeze stiff. Googins told me
how he and the artist with sticks and string posed the fox in a
running attitude. With fox and birds frozen in position, and the
background rocks clearly in view, Homer set to work on *The Fox
Hunt* (Fig. 32). Unfortunately he had started a little late in the
season, and Mrs. Charlotte Stevens described his irritation because "the weather keeps thawing, and the crows get limp." After
he had made some progress he asked the opinion of Elbridge Oliver, the Scarboro stationmaster, about the crows in his painting.
Oliver was not one to flatter Homer or anybody else, and his criticism was terse and honest: "Hell, Win, them ain't crows." Homer
was as honest a painter as Oliver was a critic; without a word he
picked up a brush and painted them out.

He returned with Oliver to Scarboro station with some corn,
and for the next three days they lured in crows, while Win made

[109]

innumerable sketches on telegram blanks. Back to the studio, this time to paint the crows as they appear today, but he did not consider them finished until he had called in Oliver again and got his approval. When Mrs. Munroe and Winslow's father came in May to open the Ark, Homer showed them the completed painting, and she remembered that the artist cleared off the mantel and displayed the picture to obtain their impression of it.

When the critic of the Boston *Transcript* saw it in the Doll and Richards Gallery, where it was first exhibited in March 1893, he called it the most important example of Homer's work since *A Summer Night,* exhibited the previous year. He said: "There is something very impressive and solemn about this stern and frigid landscape, and it is a fit scene for the impending tragedy that threatens the fox. The painting of the drifted snow in the foreground is exceedingly interesting in the delicate graduations in the values on the undulating surface, in the delicacy of its color, which is apparently very simple yet is full of variety. The sky also is one that probably no other painter except Homer would have the courage to oppose to such a foreground, or, rather, that few other painters would be able to put in its right place."

Another critic wrote of the same painting: "There are two American painters whose work I never look upon without experiencing a sense of pride that I belong to the same country as they do. These men are George Inness and Winslow Homer."

The Fox Hunt is stark and cruel drama, related with admirable understatement. The tragic possibilities are suggested and the rest left to our minds. The design of the work is a harmony of attitudes arranged along diagonal lines, and reinforces the story to a marked degree. Homer painted the snow in a heavy impasto to convey a sense of substance, as Courbet loved to do.

Stylistically, the painting is an important one and demonstrates several features of Homer's mature work. In conception it shows an outstanding similarity to Japanese art, in the clear-cut pattern created by the sharp outlines and strong value contrasts, in its asymmetrical balance, and in the consciously neat use of the signature as a part of the design. In his excellent introductory essay on the art of Homer for the 1958 Homer exhibition at the National Gallery, the Metropolitan Museum and the Museum of Fine Arts, Boston, Albert Ten Eyck Gardner points out the extensive influences of Japanese art on the work of Homer, Manet, Degas, and others. He stresses the fact that they did not copy specific Japanese prints; instead, they assimilated the essential principles of the Oriental design makers into their own Western and personal styles. Sharp outlines and contrasting values (as in Currier and Ives's *Central Park in Winter*) were inherent in American art and had long been part of Homer's technique. Japanese painting confirmed his interest in design; it showed him new examples of precision, lucidity, and orderliness combined with narrative content. It gave him badly needed precedent and support for his belief in himself, for America was chiefly concerned at that time with almost photographic illustrative painting. *The Fox Hunt* shows how well he learned his lesson without sacrificing his personal manner of expression.

During the summer of 1893 the World's Columbian Exposition was held in Chicago. Blessed by the efforts of Charles Follen McKim, William R. Mead, Stanford White, Charles B. Atwood, Daniel H. Burnham, Louis Sullivan, and an impressive galaxy of artists including Augustus Saint-Gaudens and Frederick MacMonnies, the "White City" culminated a quarter-century of unparalleled material progress. The Philadelphia Centennial had trumpeted America's mechanical achievement; the Grand Concourse at Chicago hailed an era of culture and beauty. Louis Sullivan sneered that the pseudo-classical plaster palaces would retard American architecture for a half-century or more, but the admiring sightseers paid no attention to him. No fair before or since has so impressed a most impressionable people.

Homer sent fifteen paintings to Chicago, and was awarded a gold medal for *The Gale* (Fig. 34). He was fifty-seven years old,

Fig. 33. THE COMING AWAY OF THE GALE.
1883. From a photograph, signed by Homer, of the painting in its
original state. Homer Collection, Bowdoin College Museum of Art.

and this was his first publicly conferred honor, even though many
considered him one of America's leading artists. Thomas B.
Clarke purchased the painting for a ridiculously low $750.

Homer had used the same theme before. The idea was born at
Tynemouth in such watercolor studies as *Fishwives* and *Fisher
Girl,* and in the oil sketch *Watching a Storm on the English Coast.*

In his biography of Homer, Goodrich describes *The Gale* as
having been painted over another and similar painting, *The Coming Away of the Gale,* which Homer had exhibited in 1883 and
which some critics stated had been lost. Charles L. Homer lent me
a photograph of this "lost painting" (Fig. 33), which confirms
Goodrich's deduction and the evidence of X-ray shadowgraphs.
Winslow had kept the figure and made it the central dominating
interest. The old Tynemouth watchtower and the boat had been
painted over into typically Prout's Neck ledges, and Homer had
even taken a bite out of the flat foreground ledge to give it more
the appearance of a Maine formation.

Fig. 34.   THE GALE.
1883, repainted 1893. Worcester Art Museum.

The critics (perhaps justly) had been caustic in their treatment of the original version; the new simplified design is far more
effective, more powerful, and better balanced. The difference between the two designs is the clearest possible evidence of Homer's
advanced skill in the distillation of a trite subject into a simple,
completely lucid statement.

It was a quality, unfortunately, not to be found in many of the
other artists who exhibited at Chicago. Similarities to Homer's art
are apparent in several of the paintings shown; but the banal or
sentimental treatment is painful to behold in such contemporary
American pictures as Walter Langley's melodramatic *Disaster*
and Julius L. Stewart's maudlin *Yachting*. Yet even these are
easier to take than the productions of the European academic ec-
lectics, who were laboring under the domination of the French
Beaux Arts tradition. They wasted incredible technical skill on
wholly insipid subjects like Royer's *Cupid and Psyche*, *The Ant* by
Dubuffe, and *Calling the Worshippers* by Alma-Tadema. These

Fig. 35. Frederick MacMonnies, FOUNTAIN.
1893. World's Columbian Exposition, Chicago.

dreadful productions were typical of the majority shown at the
exposition, and it is worthwhile to resurrect them from a well-
deserved oblivion only to demonstrate how remarkably ahead of
his time Homer was. The recognition accorded his *Gale* by the
jury was, in fact, far from typical of the artistic outlook of his day
and did not denote any sudden and universal appreciation of his
worth. On the contrary, in the official guide to the fine arts exhib-
its at the exposition, which was published by the George Barrie
Company of Philadelphia under the editorship of Charles M. Kurtz
to direct visitors to the best paintings on display, three hundred
and thirty-six pictures are illustrated — most of them unbearably
saccharine by present-day standards — yet Homer's name is nowhere mentioned in the book.

This was the greatest spectacle of the Gilded Age, this sparkling, pretentious, bawdy, raucous, wonderful World's Fair of 1893
— where things of wonder and beauty elbowed the most appall-

[114]

Fig. 36.   THE FOUNTAINS AT NIGHT, WORLD'S
COLUMBIAN EXPOSITION.
1893. Bowdoin College Museum of Art.

ing monstrosities. Perhaps the most conspicuous monument to bad taste was the enormous fountain by Frederick MacMonnies which dominated the lagoon of the Grand Concourse. Homer selected the least objectionable aspect of it (Fig. 35) for his only on-the-spot painting of the fair, *The Fountains at Night — World's Columbian Exposition* (Fig 36). When he returned to Prout's he gave it to the wife of his brother Charles, and she bequeathed it to Bowdoin College. According to her, Winslow painted it at night by the electric lights which illuminated the fair; this is plausible, for the oil is painted in nearly neutral grays, black, and white. Had hue been more important it would have been quite a different matter, as we have seen in the discussion of *A Summer Night*, but Homer could evoke such brilliance from chiaroscuro that he frequently used only a sparing touch of color, and in this case, almost none.

Homer certainly caught the excitement of the fair in his image

[115]

of the gondola and his representation of the artificial illumination. Electric lights were a distinct novelty in 1893; they fascinated the crowds, who called the exposition a fairyland; Homer
had put his finger upon the exact aspect of the fair that was its
most striking feature.

Once the precedent had been set by his gold medal award from
the fair, honors were accorded him in rapid succession during the
rest of his life. The fair had also brought him a new audience, the
Middle Westerners, who saw his fifteen paintings and liked them
immensely. Later in the year O'Brien and Son of Chicago offered
to represent him in the Middle West, and Homer replied from
Scarboro on October 23, 1893, that he would be glad to accept the
offer when the time seemed opportune. They did become his
agents for that section of the country, and the relationship was a
long and pleasant one. There was one curious note in Homer's
letter, however. He concluded, "At present and for some time past
I see no reason why I should paint any pictures." It is not clear
what he meant; there was no apparent reason for him to be de-
spondent about his work or lack of general appreciation. It may
have been that he was irritated by some one critic's barb, although this was not like him. Or he may have meant that he felt,
at the moment, no pressing financial reason for working and selling. Again, he could have been indicating that at that particular
time there was no red-hot idea for a painting in his mind.

In any case, he was working and observing as usual in December 1893, and with his accustomed interest in visual phenomena.
He was intrigued by the way in which on some winter days the
mist rises from the surface of water, and painted a picture (*Below Zero*) of two fur-clad hunters observing the same effect. He
evidently spent that whole winter at Prout's, but without his dog
— he said in a letter to his brother Charles, "I have put Sam out
to board as his winter habits are not agreeable."

He must have had a good winter, for he loved Prout's no matter
what the weather, and especially without the summer crowds.

The summer and autumn of 1894 saw him working with renewed intensity, making it one of his most fruitful years. He produced four of his most famous canvases and several others nearly as good. One of them was the final development of a theme originally conceived at Tynemouth in 1881. There he had seen the sturdy fisher girls climbing the point with heavy nets over their shoulders, and had tried the theme in a watercolor, *On the Cliff*. In 1883 he had revived the idea at Prout's using local models, but had become absorbed in the ledge formations in *Women on the Rocks*. Now, in 1894, in *The Fisher Girl* he concentrated on one massive figure, hiding all extraneous details in a coastal mist. His model was sturdy, blond Ida Meserve from Pine Point, who had posed about six years before for his etching *Mending the Tears*. He hired her for the whole month of May, paying her for every day whether or not the weather allowed working. In the background are the cliffs, looking toward Cannon Rock, and in the lower right some rose hips on straggly stems, to supply the little red accents Homer loved.

Ida Meserve Harding gave me a graphic description of the artist at work. According to her he was all business while painting, very serious, and hardly speaking, although after the session he would talk at great length and tell innumerable stories. Once he had fixed his ideas, he would paint directly on the canvas with little preparation. Extremely considerate, he worked with her only about an hour a day, in order to avoid tiring her, although he would continue for hours without her; as he approached the completion of the picture he painted very rapidly and intensely.

Homer first called the picture *Girl in a Fog*, but when it was sold for $750 in 1904 to Mr. Burton Mansfield, the artist retitled it *The Fisher Girl*. It is now at Amherst College. The late Professor Thomas Means of Bowdoin College (Mr. Mansfield's nephew) informed me that Homer once told his uncle the picture was "a most careful study direct from nature of the best single figure that I remember having painted." Actualiy Ida stopped posing about the end of May while Homer was still making preparatory sketches, as she was to be married to Charles Harding in August. She returned and posed for further sketches in November, and the painting was completed that fall.

During the enforced delay Homer went to the Adirondacks, now his favorite spot for early summer. Here he conceived the design for the watercolor *The North Woods* (Fig. 38). From it the Prang Company (for whom he had drawn his lithographs, *Campaign Sketches*, in 1863) made several chromolithographs by a new process. This method reproduced the low intensity tones of

Fig. 37. FISHERMAN, ADIRONDACKS.
About 1894. Photograph by Winslow Homer. Homer Collection,
Bowdoin College Museum of Art.

Fig. 38.   THE NORTH WOODS.
1894. The Currier Gallery of Art.

the original with marvelous fidelity; unfortunately the plates were
so delicate that only a very limited number of impressions could
be made. The medium was promising, but allowed no greater
popular sale of Homer's work than had the etching process or
Klackner's photogravure. According to Winslow's brother Charles,
the painting was based on Winslow's having seen in the woods
a fisherman using a fly rod (Fig. 37).

Later in the summer of 1894, Homer did a whole series of
studies at Prout's showing the ocean in its calmer moods. After
seeing these perceptive, systematic studies I cannot agree with the
comment of John W. Beatty, who wrote in an introductory note
for Downes's biography: "Indeed, when I knew him he was comparatively indifferent to the ordinary and peaceful aspects of the
ocean, referring to the sea as a 'mill pond,' as it possessed little
interest for him in that mood."

Fig. 39.   MOONLIGHT, WOOD'S ISLAND LIGHT.
1894. The Metropolitan Museum of Art, Wolfe Fund, 1906.

Actually Homer painted scores of pictures of calm seas. *Break-ing Storm, Maine Coast; Prout's Neck, Evening; Breakers Near Rocks, Prout's Neck,* and the magnificent *Sunshine and Shadow, Prout's Neck* are all concerned with varying degrees of serenity. One of the most exhilarating and impressive of all his marines is the lovely oil *Moonlight, Wood's Island Light* (Fig. 39). It shows almost the same view as *A Summer Night* (Fig. 22), but the figures and other distracting elements have been eliminated; even the waves are the gently pulsing ones so characteristic of the summer sea at night. The picture is a supremely beautiful culmination of Homer's long study and appreciation of moon-light.

[120]

He was no less interested in sunlight. Mrs. Vaill said he would paint all day long at his shack near Ferry Beach, and as he came home would walk backward most of the way in order to observe the sunset. If he encountered her or her mother, Mrs. Kaler, he would apologize for not stopping to talk — he didn't want to miss the slightest change in the sky.

He often made thumbnail sketches of these elusive phenomena in a pocket notebook; occasionally he would carry a piece of cardboard, illustration board, or even a thin sheet of wood on which he could make quick oil studies of some passing instance of natural beauty. A brilliant example is *Sunset over Saco Bay*. Here are no subdued values — the sunset rays burst through the dark cloud masses in riotous color, painted in full, fatty strokes like a plein air by Manet. One scarcely misses the lacking detail, in the completeness of the "impression."

As Whistler was discovering at the same time along the dirty Thames, Homer found that fog can transform the ugly details of a commonplace view into a design of beauty. He did an oil of the Ark and studio looming up over the cliffs, silhouetted against the sun and shrouded in mist. Like a Baroque artist, he gathered the ledges and cliffs into one mass, leading the eye toward the buildings. It is a greatly rearranged view, as we can see from a photograph (Fig. 40), and immeasurably more effective. He wrote on the back of the stretcher *Winslow Homer's Studio in an Afternoon Fog*. The painting (Fig. 41), like *The West Wind*, is a brilliant oil study in browns.

Looking in the opposite direction, from the same vantage point he painted the view toward the east in *Coast of Maine* (1893), a study of the wild terrain and wind-twisted junipers, done in heavy pigments. From this oil he did a watercolor in 1894, *The Watch, Eastern Shore*. Together with *The North Woods* it was reproduced by the Prang Company as a chromolithograph in a very few impressions, now quite rare, though one may be seen in the Metropolitan Museum. According to Homer's nephew Charles,

Fig. 40.   THE ARK AND HOMER'S STUDIO,
PROUT'S NECK.
Photograph by Philip C. Beam, 1950.

the old man in the watercolor was lifted by his uncle from a newspaper advertisement for Dr. Munyon's famous "Paw-Paw Remedy."

The Gilbert Rocks at Kettle Cove (near Eastern Point) are easily recognized in *Weather-Beaten* (originally *Storm-Beaten*), a superb marine oil owned by Mr. and Mrs. Charles S. Payson. Homer altered the rocks into repeated diagonals for the sake of design, but they are still clearly the Gilbert Rocks, and the rhythmically rolling waves look as they do today. The painting sold originally for less than two thousand dollars, but in 1896 was awarded the gold medal of honor at the Pennsylvania Academy of the Fine Arts in Philadelphia.

About halfway along the face of the Neck is High Cliff (Fig. 42). In *High Cliff, Coast of Maine* (Fig. 43) Homer shows the ancient conflict between the clawing sea and the unyielding

Fig. 41.   THE ARTIST'S STUDIO IN AN
AFTERNOON FOG
1894. The Rochester Memorial Art Gallery of the University of
Rochester.

rocks. The ledges are slightly changed in the design, but they are
nevertheless essentially faithful to the original formations. As in
Winter Coast, he reduced the scale of the figures on top of the
cliff, not only to make the rock formations seem larger but to
show the inconsequence of man in contrast to a powerful and
rampant nature. Homer never lost his interest in humanity, but
he was here studying it from a different standpoint. Earlier he
had featured people and their reactions to the natural environment which was the background in his paintings; now it was his
purpose to emphasize the environmental factors and merely suggest the human element.

[123]

Fig. 42.   HIGH CLIFF, PROUT'S NECK.
Photograph by Philip C. Beam, 1960.

Most of the great landscape painters have seen and studied nature from two viewpoints, distant and close, maintaining a balance between synthesis and objectivity. And so it was with Homer. At the same period of his sweeping panoramic views of the
sea at Prout's, he was also painting close-up studies of the great
trees in the Adirondacks, like *Big Pines* and *Old Settlers, Adirondacks*. Sometimes they are detailed studies of massive trunks,
sometimes patterns of silhouetted forms. In *Hunting Dog Among
Dead Trees*, the dog gives scale to the giant fallen tree; in *Old
Friends* and *Woodman and Fallen Tree* the measure is given by
human figures. By his use of appropriately rough washes and low
intensity tones Homer conveys the cool, wild feeling of the forest,
and his rugged woodsmen are perfectly in keeping with their settings.

As 1894 drew to its close, Homer could look back on it as an unusually satisfying year. In *High Cliff* (Fig. 43) and *Weather-Beaten* he had reached a new peak of achievement; when the latter was exhibited that year in Boston, the critic of the *Herald* was enthusiastic in his comments. In March of the same year, the Norcrosses (Miss Laura and Mr. Grenville H.) presented *The Fog Warning* (Fig. 16) to the Boston Museum of Fine Arts. It was the first honor of the kind; later the museum was to acquire, by gift and purchase, a superlative collection of his works. Most of his best-known paintings would eventually hang in the leading museums of the country and belong to the public.

Just before his birthday, in February 1895, Homer wrote to his brother Charles rejoicing in his freedom. He was especially jubi-

Fig. 43.   HIGH CLIFF, COAST OF MAINE.
1894. National Gallery of Art, Washington, D.C. Lent by the National Collection of Fine Arts, Smithsonian Institution.

lant at having escaped jury duty, and calculated that on the basis of the usual month's term, he had gained a full year in the last twelve. He was "willing," he said, "to pay the community in work more agreeable to me. *And of more value to them.*" He was getting wonderful enjoyment out of life, nature, and his work, and in the same letter is an especially revealing paragraph: "The life that I have chosen gives me my full hours of enjoyment for the balance of my life. The Sun will not rise, or set, without my notice, and thanks."

Life and the visual world — always something new to paint, or something old to paint in a new way, a new statement about nature or humanity — Homer's world and Homer's philosophy to be set down in pictures for other men to see. Everything had to be examined, studied, painted. When even the beloved familiar ground of Prout's grew a little stale, Homer would suddenly, without warning, be off somewhere else for a fresh world to observe, to dissect, to record in sketches and notes; then back to Maine and his studio, where he could relax and finish the work that he had conceived elsewhere. And always he returned to find something right there on the Neck that he had not painted before — at least, not from this new approach.

He had settled on four main locales for his work: Prout's Neck, the Adirondacks, the tropics, and Canada. In 1893 he and his brother Charles took the first of their trips to the Province of Quebec, and Winslow liked the area so well that he returned in 1895. On their initial trip the Homer brothers stayed at the Tourilli Club on the shore of Lake Tourilli, near St. Raymond in the Province of Quebec. The club site consisted of a group of cabins owned or leased by the members, and although located only about thirty miles northwest of the city of Quebec, it was in densely wooded and isolated country, sparse in tourists and excellent for fishing. Charles and Winslow joined this exclusive group of sportsmen and became extremely fond of the club and the lake. Their second haunt was Roberval on the southern shore of Lake St. John, a large lake about one hundred and twenty miles north of Quebec. Reaching this site meant an arduous trip up the Saguenay River from the mouth of the St. Lawrence over rapids, shallows, and portages in the upper reaches above Chicoutimi. Here among the gigantic cliff walls of the Saguenay, Homer found a primitive grandeur unlike the sylvan lakes of the Adirondacks that added a new dimension to his representation of nature. He recorded the trips to Canada with his camera, and his photographs give a fair idea of some of the scenes which he painted. Although he did no painting on his introductory trip with Charles in 1893, which both may have intended to be only a fishing excursion, he produced soon afterward, beginning in 1895, a large number of outstanding watercolors in sepia and full tone, using the region around Lake Tourilli, the nearby gorge-like valley of the Sainte Anne River, the spectacular Saguenay Valley, and Lake St. John as settings. Although the pictures were little appreciated when first exhibited in Boston late in 1895, they are now considered to be among the strongest he ever painted in the watercolor medium and show him at the height of his mastery of that vehicle. Especially striking or novel are those rendered in sepia monochrome accented with Chinese white in and around Quebec and in the vicinity of Lake Tourilli, and those conceived along the Saguenay and at Lake St. John are truly inspired.

The wildness of backwoods Canada not only failed to daunt Homer but delighted him, even during the rigors of a Canadian winter. An insight into his mental and physical toughness at the age of sixty can be gained from a letter he wrote to his brother Charles from Roberval on February 23 (probably 1896): "The place suits me as if it was made for me by a kind of providence — But I pity any other man who would expect to be satisfied by the accommodations he would find at the Island House at Roberval, P.Q. I stay until March 27th."

On the Saguenay and at the lake he was faced with the same painting problem posed by the deep Adirondack woods and the

Fig. 44.   Detail: HUDSON RIVER LOGGING.
1897. In the Collection of the Corcoran Gallery of Art.

Fig. 45.   HUDSON RIVER LOGGING.
1897. In the Collection of the Corcoran Gallery of Art.

Fig. 46. TROUT FISHING, LAKE ST. JOHN, PROVINCE
OF QUEBEC.
1895. Courtesy, Museum of Fine Arts, Boston.

Fig. 47. THREE MEN IN A CANOE.
1895. Knoedler Galleries, New York City.

tropical jungle — communicating the character of the woods through synthesis and suppression of details, avoiding a clutter in which one "could not see the forest for the trees."

In *Canada Skyline* the detail is skillfully suppressed to enhance the sense of the wildness of the deep woods as a whole. Figure 44, a detail from his *Hudson River Logging* painted in the lumbering region near the headwaters of the Hudson in the Adirondacks, shows a high degree of artistic abstraction in the treatment of the two tall evergreens, the undergrowth, the far riverbank, and the clouds. Yet in the entire painting (Fig. 45), these abstractions blend into a harmonious and satisfying whole that gives an acceptably "real" impression of the scene as it must have looked to Homer. In Canada and the Adirondacks he learned to use an abstract harmony of characteristic shapes to convey the essential quality of the forest, and at the same time to maintain a vital and personal expression. The combination of angular, pointed forms and curvilinear shapes became one of Homer's favorite means of design, amounting almost to a signature. His hard-won technical skill in such devices distinguishes his realism from the literal, the illustrative, and the photographic.

In the brilliant sepia *Two Men in a Canoe,* Winslow attacked another problem: to push the forest into the distance and concentrate on the placid water. The same effect is seen in *Trout Fishing, Lake St. John, Province of Quebec* (Fig. 46). Here he suppressed details to the extreme, and through the most fluid washes imaginable achieved a striking and poetic result. The glass-calm of the lake, the startlingly bold white line of the boat's wake, and the magnificent sweeping curve of the rod and line are positively Oriental in conception. But to me the gem of the whole series is *Three Men in a Canoe* (Fig. 47). During a lifetime of incessant experimentation, Homer had touched upon and rivaled the attainments of many artists and many schools of painting. Here, in this work, he caught the same sense of man's smallness in the out-of-doors that is so characteristic of Sung landscape paintings, and with a greater objectivity conveyed much the same mood and at-

Fig. 48.   WOLFE'S COVE, PROVINCE OF QUEBEC.
1895. Bowdoin College Museum of Art.

mosphere. In short, he achieves the same end as the Chinese painters of nearly ten centuries before him, but in a manner wholly Occidental, completely his, and perfectly appropriate to his own time.

Only a few miles west of Quebec, on the north bank of the St. Lawrence near the Plains of Abraham, is Wolfe's Cove. Although it is today a bustling marine depot, when Homer saw it in 1895 it looked like a jumping-off place, a frontier outpost where one could obtain supplies and little more. Its very bleakness appealed to him, and he depicted the scene in a manner both brilliant and somber in *Wolfe's Cove, Province of Quebec* (Fig. 48). He used a sepia monochrome appropriate to the desolate feeling of the place, and the absence of color allowed him to work out an interesting emphasis on light and dark contrasts. Detail is minimized; in the foreground the simple wash becomes a beach with Homer's few strokes suggesting flotsam and water marks. A broken wash tells us all that we need to know about the rocky bluff behind, with its barely suggested sod and trees at the crest. The buildings even merge at their foundations with a daring economy of means, and a few flicks of the brush suffice to suggest the single figure beside the rail fence.

Always, Homer found people worth studying wherever he went; on this trip he became interested in the Indians he saw in Canada, and he painted them in *Indian Camp, Montagnis Indians, Pointe Bleue, Quebec* and in *Indian Camp, Roberval, P.Q.*

Fig. 49.   HOMER'S CABIN, TOURILLI CLUB, PROVINCE
OF QUEBEC.
1895. Photograph by Winslow Homer. Homer Collection, Bowdoin College Museum of Art.

Fig. 50. HOMER'S CABIN, TOURILLI CLUB, PROVINCE
OF QUEBEC (Second Version).
1895. Estate of Dr. Simon Stone, Manchester, New Hampshire.

Either Winslow or Charles took a photograph of their quarters
at the Tourilli Club (Fig. 49), and in Figure 50, one of two boldly
rendered sepias (both entitled *Homer's Cabin, Tourilli Club*), we
can see how the artist reduced the scene to its essentials,
strengthening the visual impression. The photograph also shows
the Homers' canoe in the cabin clearing, which provided Winslow
with a delightful subject, *Bear Breaking Through a Canoe* (Fig.
51), in which he recorded an actual occurrence.

Although Homer was an ardent fisherman, he rarely hunted.
He loved animals and was a sympathetic painter of them. As with
everything else, he was a patient and shrewd observer, and studied their forms, moving or at rest, their habits, and the "personalities" of different species, as is so apparent in *Hound and
Hunter* and *North Woods Club*. The comic character of the lumbering bear, the pathetic grace of *The Fallen Deer*, the soft coat
and charming posture of *Deer Drinking,* all show Homer's inter-

[133]

Fig. 51. BEAR BREAKING THROUGH A CANOE.
1895. The Brooklyn Museum.

est as a naturalist as well as a painter. He can quite properly be
ranked with Barye and Delacroix, two other masters of animal
painting of the nineteenth century. Here is yet another facet of
Homer's insatiable interest in all of nature — man, animals, the
landscape, the weather. All of these things he painted with seemingly equal facility and skill. Like Turner, who also showed an
unusual versatility, Homer painted in his maturity nothing except
what interested him and moved him deeply.

Mrs. Munroe told me a story of one of the Homer brothers' return trips from Canada, which Charles had recounted to her. Late
one September, at India Wharf Station in Portland, they got off
the train from Quebec. Hungry and thirsty, they asked a cabby to
drive them to a saloon. The "Maine Law" prohibiting the sale of
intoxicating beverages had been on the books since 1851 but was
only occasionally enforced. Apparently this was one of the occasions, for the bartender informed them with a wink that all he
had was some "strong coffee." It was strong, and served in a cup,

but this "coffee" had more affinity with Jamaica than Brazil. After several cups apiece any thought of supper was forgotten, and they ordered the driver to take them sightseeing. In the small hours of the morning the cabby, also in a state of induced happiness, wound up the tour of Portland and drove them the twelve miles to Prout's. The two brothers, about sixty at the time, apparently suffered no ill effects from this sprightly wind-up of their vacation.

Their father, as has been mentioned, was a White Ribboner not averse to a drink under certain circumstances. Downes in his biography quotes William J. Bixbee, who knew the Homers in 1896:

> The relations between father and son were altogether ideal, and as the former grew a little more childish in his last few years, Winslow's untiring devotion was more than ever beautiful. He was all that a son should be. The old man's pride in his son's success was touching. He could hardly understand it, but it gave him infinite pleasure. He was a strong temperance man, and he did not approve of Winslow's habit of taking what the New England folk call an "eleven o'clocker." When he was at Prout's Neck, Winslow tried to induce his father to take a little something for his stomach's sake. At eleven o'clock he would bring him a cocktail, and the two regularly went through with the following dialogue:
> "Now Father, don't you think you'd better take this? It will do you good."
> "Is there any alcoholic liquor in that, Winslow?"
> "Yes, Father."
> "Well, I won't touch it, then."
> "Father, if you don't take it, I'll drink it myself."
> "Well, Winslow, rather than have you destroy the tissues of your stomach by drinking this alcoholic beverage, I'll drink it."

It was about this time, in the mid-1890's, that the Homer household gained its new member Lewis Wright. The first colored servant at Prout's Neck, he was originally looked upon as a curios-

Fig. 52. CANNON ROCK, PROUT'S NECK.
Photograph by Philip C. Beam, 1950.

ity by the natives, but among the servant population he soon
earned the title "Mr. Wright" because of his dignity, good disposition, and impeccable manners. He would elegantly sweep the
ground with his hat when he bowed, and whenever someone
wished him "Good morning" he would reply "Nicely, thank you"
with a broad smile. As he put it, he was "the most politest man on
the Neck." He soon became quite a personage and was liked and

Fig. 53.   CANNON ROCK.
1895. The Metropolitan Museum of Art, Wolfe Fund, 1906.

respected by everyone. He was able to send his son to Tuskegee
Institute; but to his great grief, the boy was accidentally killed the
year he was to have been graduated.

Winslow had always found Negroes charming people to be
with, and he grew very fond of Lewis, as did the other members of
the Homer family. The elder Homer loved to exert his authority
when he could, and his heavy-handed ordering about of his new

Fig. 54. AN EQUINOCTIAL STORM, PROUT'S NECK.
October 12, 1937. Photograph by Charles L. Homer. Homer Collection, Bowdoin College Museum of Art.

bodyservant must have been trying to Lewis, but the two were
actually very fond of each other. During meals Lewis would be
right at Mr. Homer's elbow; if in a gruff mood the old gentleman
would say "Stand back, stand back!" but Winslow would wink at
Lewis, who would reply with a big grin. During the previous ten
years Winslow had taken great care of his father, but little by
little Lewis took much of the burden on himself and freed the
painter for his work. The two enjoyed constant jokes together; as
Lewis grew older Winslow used to accuse him of using shoe
blacking on his graying hair. A photograph in the Homer Collection taken outside of the studio shows the two men smiling at
each other with unfeigned affection.

After Winslow's death in 1910 and that of his brother Charles
seven years later, Martha Homer kept the studio open on Saturday
afternoons during the tourist season of July and August to accom-
modate the visitors who were already coming in sufficient num-

bers to turn it into something of a shrine. On these occasions Lewis was always at the door to bow in the guests, and he took great satisfaction in the homage paid to the memory of his departed friend. During the summer of 1925, a very old man, he could no longer carry on, and the Homer family was deeply saddened when they received a telegram in West Townsend from his wife informing them that their old friend and servant was dead.

During the summer and fall of 1895, Homer painted three of his most famous and popular wave and rock pictures, *Maine Coast, Cannon Rock* (Fig. 53) and *Northeaster* (Fig. 55). *Cannon Rock* shows a well-known rock formation of the Prout's Neck cliffs, which looks very much like a cannon and even has sound effects — at low tide the waves, breaking under an adjacent ledge, produce a loud booming noise. The painting is a clear example of Homer's rearrangement of elements for the sake of design. The rock is in sight of his balcony window, but I for one missed seeing it until Charles L. Homer pointed it out. Winslow,

Fig. 55.   NORTHEASTER.
1895. The Metropolitan Museum of Art.

in his painting, isolated it from the panorama of ocean, changing its height and angle to give its silhouette more prominence and interest. From nowhere on the cliff can it be seen exactly as it appears in the painting. Mr. Robert Macbeth and I both tried to photograph it as Homer showed it, but even the closest possible photograph (Fig. 52) is quite different.

In *Cannon Rock*, Homer had picked just the right tide, just the exact condition of the sky and of the sea — but he had seen a wave tumbling in toward the little inlet beside the rock. For a number of weeks, with the picture on the easel, complete but for the wave, he waited and paced the cliffs and watched . . . and finally he saw it again, that just-right wave, and this time he studied it more carefully, then returned to the studio and swiftly painted it in. The picture was really done now, and he never touched it again.

Not since Turner had there been anything in seascape painting comparable in pure energy to *Northeaster*. Waves like this do beat on the cliffs of Prout's Neck, but they are rare, even in the worst equinoctial storms. Winslow's nephew Charles photographed innumerable waves at Prout's, but in his whole collection there was only one photograph (Fig. 54) that even approached Winslow's wave in *Northeaster*. The rock formation in the painting is no particular spot we could locate, and the matter is unimportant; our whole attention is directed to the surging, creaming sea. Back in 1883 Homer had made an unusually fine study of this type in *Prout's Neck, Rocky Shore* (Fig. 10) and four years later several others (see Figures 11 and 78). But, bold and alive as those waves are, they seem pallid set against the massive, deadly might of the mountainous seas in *Northeaster*. Even the admittedly unusual breaker in Charles L. Homer's dramatic photograph is less effective. For anything comparable we must turn to something like the *Tidal Wave* of the master Japanese sea painter Hokusai.

The winter of 1895 was spent at Prout's Neck, punctuated with periodic trips to Boston, where Winslow stayed with his father at the American House. They had Christmas together, and that day

Homer wrote to his sister-in-law thanking her for her present. She had sent him one of those fascinating mechanical pencils which write in brown, red, blue, and black, and the sentences in the letter to her are written in a variety of colors.

Dec 25 1895

Dear Mattie

 I wish to thank you for this beautiful pencil — One that can never get out of a pocket — being so heavy with solid and valuable silver, I find now that I needed it very much —

 Father & self have had a very pleasant Christmas — I shall go home tomorrow   I find that living with Father for three days, I grow to be so much like him that I am frightened. We get as much alike as two peas — in age & manners — He is very well — only he will starve himself — I shall go to Boston once in two weeks this next month to give him a dinner —

Yours very truly

WINSLOW HOMER

Other letters to Charles and to Arthur during the winter and spring show his keen interest in the building going on at the Neck; in one he includes a diagram showing the lines of some of the lots and their identifying numbers, saying, "I own half of 492 with fifty feet on M'way [marginal way] giving me a front & back of 70 feet the finest lot on the Neck." In a letter to Charles dated March 21, 1896, he included another drawing, and indicated that he was taking a hand himself in the development of the area. In this letter he says, "I am in receipt of your invitation to visit N.Y. It is too soon — I have things to do here that interest me more — I have just returned from burning brush over on the eastern Point. I will take N.Y. after I get through with this place, that will be about the time Father arrives here."

During the summer of 1896 Homer painted the quietly brilliant

Fig. 56.   SUNSET, SACO BAY.
1896. Sterling and Francine Clark Art Institute.

Sunset, Saco Bay (Fig. 56) at Checkley Point on the southwest corner of the Neck, overlooking Saco Bay. Here the sloping ledges make a natural platform, on which Homer posed Maude Googins Libby and Cora Sanborn, the same models he had painted dancing in *A Summer Night*. Once again Benjamin Franklin Sanborn did duty as pencil-bearer and chaperon as he had previously when Homer etched *Mending the Tears*. Shown at the Pennsylvania Academy of the Fine Arts that year, the painting was awarded the Converse Gold Medal; later it was purchased for $1000 by the Lotos Club of New York, through a fund devoted to the encouragement of American art.

A few feet off the cliffs, and within plain sight of Homer's studio balcony, is a good-sized rock continually washed by the sea. Homer knew it well, for he caught tautog just inshore of it many times, and even today it is a favorite casting spot for fishermen. He had also considered it as a possible subject for a painting, but visually, under normal conditions, it is only mildly interesting.

What he needed was something to make it more dramatic, and during the summer of 1896 he found just what he was after. Mrs. Munroe told me what happened.

Captain Thomas Boynton, who owned a small sailboat, had taken some young children out on the bay. Without warning a sudden squall struck violently, accompanied by torrential rain and a gusty wind that blew the chairs off the porch of the Checkley House, next door to the Ark. Mrs. Munroe went upstairs to close the windows, and when she came down, moments later, Winslow had put on his heavy raincoat and gone down to the shore. Captain Boynton, who knew the hazards of a lee shore, had put out away from the dangerous cliffs of the Neck to ride out the storm in safer, open water. The mothers of his passengers thought he was being driven off by the storm and would be wrecked on Stratton's Island, but Winslow assured them he was taking the only feasible action, and that if he could maneuver between the island and the shore he would keep out of trouble. Under the captain's firm control, the little boat rode out the storm safely, and when it had passed, as swiftly as it had come, he set his young passengers ashore, damp but unharmed.

The unusual and spectacular squall made a deep impression on all those who were there, especially Winslow and his family, who had joined him on the shore. As they were walking back to the Ark, Charles said, "He'll have that on canvas soon." He was quite right; his brother retired to his studio and was furiously busy for several days. About two weeks later he came into the Ark carrying the nearly completed painting now entitled *A Summer Squall* (Fig. 58).

It was a synthesis of several elements. Homer had watched the storm from Checkley Point, but he had borrowed the tautog rock, actually some hundred yards to the east. Knowing that the drama of the danger-threatened children would mean little to anyone who had not been there at the time, he painted a different boat with spritsail flying free, its mainsheet blown out of the helmsman's hand. Actually, it is a type commonly seen on the English

Fig. 57.   BLOWN AWAY.
Probably 1896. The Brooklyn Museum.

Fig. 58.   A SUMMER SQUALL.
1904. Sterling and Francine Clark Art Institute.

coast but only rarely in America, and is reminiscent of the fishing boats in his Tynemouth series.

The Brooklyn Museum owns a handsome little watercolor called *Blown Away* (Fig. 57), certainly the source of Homer's boat in *A Summer Squall*. In the watercolor as well as the oil, without departing from pictorial devices peculiar to the Western art idiom, Homer has caught the headlong race of a storm-driven boat with much the same feeling (and with equal success) as Sesson's Japanese masterpiece *Sailing Vessel in a Storm*.

The handling of the oil in *A Summer Squall* is extraordinarily vigorous and dashing, and the color harmony of bluish-green tones is superb, but these were qualities not easily achieved. According to Homer's nephew Charles, the artist could not immediately complete the painting to his satisfaction and kept it for several years in a closet in the studio. Finally, in 1904, he added the last touches, and signed and dated it that year.

Another important work of the summer of '96 resulted from much study and preparation. With a theme in mind, Homer rummaged the junk shops of Boston until he found a large ship's bell he liked; with it he returned to Prout's. There he posed John Gatchell in a sou'wester and painted *The Lookout — "All's Well"* (Fig. 59). Downes in his biography says that in preparing for this work Homer studied the rigging in his earlier sketches, but was unable to find what he wanted and made a trip to Boston to look at ships in the harbor there. Downes also states that Homer painted this picture entirely by moonlight, a theory which I cannot accept, for reasons already mentioned in the discussion of *A Summer Night*.

However it was done, the painting is an enthralling design, one of those "Japanese fragment" compositions that Homer, like Degas, handled so well. As in an ukiyoe print, the frame cuts the figure, and the bell serves as a symbol of the whole ship. Just over the side, the dimly seen crest of a single wave suggests the whole expanse of the ocean. Organized tonally in a harmony of blues,

Fig. 59.   THE LOOKOUT — "ALL'S WELL."
1896. Courtesy, Museum of Fine Arts, Boston.

the spatial design is a tantalizing asymmetrical balance of lines and shapes.

As in so many of Homer's sea pictures, this work carries a deep and sympathetic social comment on the humble yet romantic nature of the sailor's life and work. As Professor Frank J. Mather, Jr., points out in *The American Spirit in Art*, Melville and Dana had treated the theme in literature, and it was further developed by Kipling and Conrad, but in painting it was a new and thoroughly American note. "It seems strange," says Mather, "that the fisherman who for some three centuries has been plying his trade from the American coast should wait so long for his artistic recognition."

On March 14, 1897, replying to a letter from Thomas B. Clarke, Homer told him of *The Lookout*, mentioning that Doll and Richards had shown it to a representative of the Cunard Line who "greatly admired it." Mr. Clarke, when he saw the painting, also greatly admired it — he bought it for his collection, which numbered thirty-one Winslow Homers, making him the artist's greatest single patron.

If we arrange all of Homer's works not by technique or by date but by theme, it falls into groups that are quite unlike in subject matter but remarkably similar in structure. Like a library of collected works, each group is a volume devoted to one subject, in which we see Homer sketching, experimenting, repeating, and finally distilling the idea into one magnificent (and usually simple) climactic statement of his theme. *The Lookout* is such a culmination. From the rather slight prefatory studies at Gloucester, Homer's "Men Against the Sea" volume describes the Tynemouth fishermen, then the grim chapter of *The Fog Warning*, next the quiet but powerful *Eight Bells*, and finally the simple, almost mystically significant statement of *The Lookout* — "All's Well."

Homer's translation of his own personal experience and reactions into his art was achieved by a method peculiar to him. Picasso works intensely upon a single problem for a year or two; Homer might spend a decade or even longer. Once a theme had

Fig. 60. THE WRECK.
1896. Museum of Art, Carnegie Institute.

occurred to him, it might be stored in his mind, then would move to the forefront of his consciousness periodically over several years, to be considered and worked on, then pushed back again for a while. Finally there would emerge a masterwork that brought the theme to a conclusion, and that usually he could not surpass. This was his method, and it produced in 1896 one of the most important works in his whole oeuvre, *The Wreck* (Fig. 60).

He had first become interested in rescue work at Tynemouth, fifteen years before, as is illustrated by *Watching the Tempest* (Fig. 2) and *The Wreck of the Iron Crown*. Factor by factor he analyzed the operation — working now at boats, then at waves, then at the straining forms of people. He studied the honest, workaday boats, so different from the graceful dories and sailboats of Gloucester. Next he combined boats with people in a stormy setting — uncertainly at first, then with a surer hand. One good instance he captured in the moody watercolor *Scotch Mist* and repeated in *Storm on the English Coast*. In a series of drawings such as *Fishermen Beaching a Boat* and *Study* he came

[148]

nearer his final theme by close observation of how the men handle their boats as they put them in or out of the water. Fascinated by the subject of rescue from death by drowning in the ocean, he continued to examine it from different points of view over the years in *The Ship's Boat* (Fig. 9), *The Life Line* (Fig. 12), *Undertow* and *The Signal of Distress*. Detail by detail he was gathering the component parts, the building blocks which he would someday combine.

And then, one day in 1896, he saw a wreck along the shoreline of Charles Jordan's farm near Higgins Beach, whose sand dunes are quite unlike the terrain of Prout's Neck. He had no materials with him except a pen and an envelope, but in a few strokes he sketched a crew manning a lifeboat and enclosed it in a letter to his brother Charles. And more important, he conceived the idea and the design for what was to be his concluding statement, his summing up of the rescue theme. Back to the Neck, his studio, and John Gatchell — and to weeks of patient, careful hard work. As the composition progressed he would check his ideas against the evidence of nature, waiting weeks if necessary to confirm his opinion. All during the summer of '96 he worked on *The Wreck*, until on October 5 he could write to Thomas B. Clarke: "After all these years I have at last used the subject of that sketch that I promised you."

In painting this superb work Homer took the neutral tones of the sand as a guide to his tonal organization, relying for dramatic effect on a wide range of values, setting lights against darks in abrupt juxtaposition. In this way he ended with another of those masterful studies in browns like *The West Wind* of 1891. The somber tones, dramatic chiaroscuro, and fluid brushstrokes seem particularly appropriate to the idea of the rescue. Perhaps the most astonishing thing about the picture is the manner in which Homer has said almost everything about the wreck — its drama, tragedy, terror — all without showing the wreck at all. The boat being rolled swiftly to its launching point, the tense group of watchers silhouetted at the crest of the dune, the shore end of the breeches-buoy line, the commanding figure of the coastguards-man in charge of operations, standing like a dark statue in the foreground, making us a part of the rescue party — and what lies over the dunes? We have to imagine that.

Homer sent the work to the first International Exhibition at the Carnegie Institute, and was unhesitatingly awarded the chronological gold medal and a prize of $5000, one of the highest honors accorded any American artist of that time. On December 5, when the jury's decision was made public, Homer's father wrote to Charles Jr.

December 5, 1896

> *My dear Son*
> *Solitude befits an old man who can from the events of his life, gather here and there acts that prove his life to have been serviceable to others as well as profitable to himself.*
> *Winslow first prize!! you ought to have seen the news in the Boston Globe I sent you. — Bless the Boy*
>
> *Affectly*
>
> FATHER

Although *The Wreck* became the property of the Carnegie Institute, the $5000 first prize was a greater sum than Homer was receiving for his best paintings at the time. He remained modestly at Scarboro during the awarding of the prizes, but soon had to answer the letters of congratulation that poured in. To his patron and good friend Thomas B. Clarke:

Scarboro, Me. Dec. 9, 1896

> *My dear Mr. Clarke, —*
> *I thank you for your very kind note of congratulation on my success. It is certainly a most tremendous & un-*

*precedented honor and distinction that I have received
from Pittsburgh. Let us hope that it is not too late in my
case to be of value to American art in something that
I may yet possibly do, from this encouragement.*

Yours very truly

WINSLOW HOMER

There were, of course, still those who held to older styles in
painting and shook their journalistic heads at Homer's successes.
We read in the Pittsburgh *Dispatch* (December 6, 1896):

The first prize picture, Winslow Homer's "Wreck," is a
striking example of the best American school, vigorous in
conception and careful in detail and finish. But had Lavery's
"Lady in Brown" been eligible for the prize, it would have had
strong claims for the prize as combining the best quality of
Whistler's atmosphere with the detail of Carolus Duran's
portraiture.

Since Sir John Lavery was not American, he received only a "first
medal." Others went to Raffaelli's *Notre Dame* and Cecilia Beaux's
Ernesta, while the second-prize money was awarded to Gari Melcher's *Shipbuilder*, which was described as a good example of
American painting in the French style.

And across the Atlantic, Homer's status as an artist was hardly
what his contemporary work deserved. This same year (1896)
Richard Muther, one of the foremost European critics of the time,
published (in London and New York) a translation of his *History
of Modern Painting* in three volumes which in many ways still
merits attention. Lamenting that American art was a mere "ré-
sumé of European art," he comments:

One is not brought into the "Wild West" by these American
masters. Hordes of Indians, grazing buffaloes, burning prai-
ries and virgin forest, gold-diggers, fur-traders, and Roman-
ticism of the "Leather Stocking" order may be sought in their

works in vain. The many-sided Winslow Homer, the painter of Uncle Tom's Cabin, is striking as the only one of them who represents in his subjects what we should understand as peculiarly American. He took an interest in the colored population, and had the secret of kindling an interest for them in Europe also. His Negro studies, his representations of the land and the people, his pictures of the American soil with the race of men whose home it is, are often rather naïve in painting, but they are honest and sincere, baptized in American water. He was a vigorous realist who went straight to the mark and painted his open-air scenes in sunlight fluently from nature. Thus he was the first energetic representative of open-air painting in America.

Many of these comments, especially the last sentence, are perceptive, but they were twenty years behind the times. *A Sunday Morning in Virginia,* Muther's only Homer illustration and undoubtedly the Uncle Tom's Cabin he alludes to, had been painted in 1876. And Homer's status was not helped by putting him in a class with two nonentities, Alfred Kappes and Robert Blum. But when we consider that the index of the *History* (which included thousands of now-forgotten hacks) did not mention Toulouse-Lautrec, Gauguin, Van Gogh, Pissarro, or Cézanne, perhaps Homer did well to appear at all.

Homer spent the Christmas season at the Hotel Rudolf in Atlantic City, where he took a five-mile hike every day on the boardwalk, wrote letters, and relaxed. By mid-January of '97 he was back at Scarboro. His brother Charles had offered to send him a dog to replace his beloved Sam, who had died. The artist replied on January 14, 1897, "On *no* account send me a dog — the only companion I want is a Bobolink (bird) & the next time I go to Boston I shall get one." He had come to like bobolinks in Florida, and had done a watercolor entitled *Florida Bobolinks.*

From Scarboro he wrote other letters to his father and to Charles. To his father he wrote: "When I got home about 1 o'clock I opened my fish & cooked two shad roes & cut up a cucumber in cold water — then, with a quart of South Side Scarboro cider —

I knew that I was again in my own house. I send you herewith that is by Ameri Ex a gallon of 'said' cider."

And to Charlie: "These are tough days   Very cold deep snow   I am glad that I returned here as soon as I did as I was in time to answer a request for pictures for the Society of Ameri Artists — & as I found in Boston that they liked that 'Lookout' the 'Man with the Bell' I have sent them that & Saco Bay. Other things, big things, are booming. I have made $100 cash. $120 of it will go for frames & that is my seasons profit —" His letters indicate that there were several periods when he made little or no money from painting. He survived and met his traveling expenses mainly through the sale of his share of the house lots on Prout's Neck and with the aid of his prosperous and open-handed older brother.

With the Homers settled down on the Neck for the summer of '97, Winslow did one of his important works, the well-known oil *A Light on the Sea*. The model was Ida Meserve Harding, who was placed to the left, in one of Homer's favorite occult balances. The painting was shown at the Carnegie Institute in November 1897, and in February 1898 at one of the exhibitions at the Union League Club in New York. Critics thought the model vulgar-looking and stiffly posed, but the Corcoran Gallery nevertheless bought it for $2500 for its permanent collection in 1907.

A curious item from 1897 is a Shepherdess drawing, clearly signed and dated that summer. This apparent return to a theme Homer had worked on nearly twenty years before is explained by a careful study of the drawing and confirmed by a conversation with Mrs. Munroe. The figure in the picture looks suspiciously like a boy in anatomy and attitude, while the crook appears to be an afterthought. Mrs. Munroe had refused an offer to model occasionally for Homer before she went to work for the family, as the remuneration was insufficient for her needs as a widow. But she remembered that after she started working at the Ark in 1890, she did pose once so that he could finish a drawing that was nearly completed. All she did was to hold a shepherd's crook in the right position for about half an hour while Homer put the finishing touches on a sketch that had been in his portfolio for years. It is a safe guess that this was the drawing, and also that the original model was Sergeant Joseph Keenan of the Belmont, Massachusetts, police, who posed as a boy in shepherdess costume for the girl-shy Homer when the artist was doing his shepherdess series in the Belmont area during the late '70's. Why did Homer want to complete the drawing? Perhaps it was nostalgia, perhaps he just couldn't stand to see a job unfinished. We do know that he always treasured these old *Shepherdess* drawings and used to show them to visitors at Prout's.

Homer rarely attended exhibitions that included his own work, but for the November 1897 show at the Carnegie Institute where *A Light on the Sea* was hung, he agreed to act as one of a jury of ten artists. A fellow judge, Edmund C. Tarbell, who was an old friend of Homer's from the New York days, told Alexander Bower about the judging. To relieve the strain on the jury, Mr. John Beatty, art director of the Institute, had thoughtfully set out a table of drinks, and soon after the jury convened at ten in the morning, Homer said to Tarbell, "Ed, I usually have an eleven o'clocker about this time," whereupon the group adjourned to the improvised bar. Shortly before noon Homer consulted his watch and said, "Ed, I usually have a drink before lunch, and it's almost lunchtime." The ritual was observed again. The afternoon session was punctuated by "three o'clockers," "four o'clockers," etc. This was the sort of jury duty that Homer could enjoy.

To illustrate winter life at Scarboro for Charles and Mattie, Winslow sent them a page of delightful sketches which he entitled *Bachelor Homes — Prout's Neck, Winter of 1897–1898*. Across the top is High Cliff, decorated with a porcupine; Homer's own studio house with Homer himself painting out-of-doors; and the Checkley House guarded by its caretaker James Sanborn, son of Benjamin Sanborn. At the bottom is John Gatchell chopping wood outside his shack. The middle row shows Alvin Brown's fish house (where he had propped up the dory for *The Fog Warning*), his abandoned portable studio, now occupied by lobsters, and the "Hotel de Wiggin," with barefooted John Wiggin himself.

[154]

John was born on the area of the Neck where the golf course is now located. He was the stationmaster at Oak Hill, about four miles west of Prout's, when he fell in love with the cook at James Thornton's, married her, and gave her all his savings (several hundred dollars) to go to New York and buy furniture. If she did, the furniture never got back to Prout's, nor did the bride. John went to New York to find her and to set up a small business. Both projects failed, and he returned to Prout's discouraged about business and understandably bitter about women. He settled as a squatter on his brother Joseph's land and found solace in drink. When he "felt a toot coming on" he would take off his shoes and run a red flag up on the flagpole. He ran a tiny store, where he sold groceries and soft drinks and made barely enough to live on. His brother paid his taxes, and every week he sent a basket of clams to a friend in Boston, Sam Davis, who sent him in return a basket of provisions.

The children loved "Captain John," who gave them incomparable home-fried doughnuts, and any missing child was more than likely to be found at his place. He once hired a visiting organ-grinder, complete with monkey, to play all afternoon from the top of his shed for the children's amusement. He christened his store the Hotel de Wiggin, and, just for fun, in 1896 issued an elaborate prospectus done up in high-flown language by a friendly printer, yellowing specimens of which are still treasured by people of the Neck. He and Homer were great friends in spite of the radical differences in their personalities.

The sketch of the abandoned "portable studio" leads to the necessity of clearing up a misunderstanding. The chapter entitled "The Portable Painting House" in Downes's biography of Homer describes it in detail:

> For the purpose of painting the sea in cold or stormy weather, Homer had a little portable painting house built, and this was set on runners, so that it could be moved to any point where he desired to work. This little building was about eight by ten feet in ground dimensions, with a door on one side and a large plateglass window on the other side. In a

northeaster, when it would be impossible to manage a canvas of any considerable size out-of-doors, and when exposure would be disagreeable and uncomfortable, he would have the painting house moved down on the rocks of Eastern Point, and, installing himself in this snug shelter, with his materials, he could place himself in the position that commanded his subject, and work as long as the light and other conditions were favorable.

Downes's story caught on well and contributed immensely to the legend of Homer's originality, if not downright oddity. Robert Ripley even used it in one of his Believe-It-or-Not cartoons, although his Nassau palms look a little peculiar for Prout's Neck. Even though the story had thus been officially adopted into American folklore, I had certain doubts, because moving a portable studio over the cliffs and rocks of Prout's seemed a physical impossibility, and questioned half a dozen people who had known Homer well and watched him at work. All seemed completely mystified, and all denied any knowledge of such a structure. Win, as they referred to him, had made studies in oil out-of-doors on sheets of illustration board, quick and simple things; he did have the old shack at Ferry Beach, and it was there and in his regular studio or a fenced-in garden enclosure adjacent to it that he did all his painting on canvas. They all agreed that no heavy wood structure on runners could have been manipulated over Prout's rocks and ledges, even with a pair of horses; furthermore, the consensus was that "Win wouldn't never have bothered with such a clumsy rig." Which had been exactly my own opinion.

Then Winslow's nephew Charles explained the whole thing. During the late '90's, when the artist was considering Eastern Point as a subject, his well-meaning and sometimes over-helpful brother Charles had the portable studio built for him. Winslow, trying not to offend his brother, had the thing hauled across Charles Jordan's farm and the adjoining surf beach to Eastern Point and tried to use it there; he even had it mounted on a small scow and launched in shallow water as the only feasible way to move it. Unfortunately, spray on the outside of the window and steam on the inside made it almost totally opaque, and he was unable to overcome the persistent problem of "visibility zero." After a short and hectic experience he finally gave up. As we can see in Homer's sketch, some errant lobsters took over the "studio," but one season of winter storms broke it up, and that was the end of it, except in the legends, which refuse to die. Actually Homer painted only two pictures near Eastern Point, one watercolor and the famous oil of 1900.

The summer of 1898 brought the death of Winslow's father at the age of eighty-nine; he was buried beside his wife in Mount Auburn cemetery in Cambridge, Massachusetts. The family agreed that Charles and Mattie should take over the Ark, and they did, redecorating it and adding an outside chimney as well as a Richardson Romanesque tower to provide space for a billiard room and a tea room, and in this form it remains today. The Homers had loved the old gentleman very much, in spite of his undoubted eccentricities. Winslow in particular had been very close to his father, tolerant of his habits and devoted to his welfare. Life with Mr. Homer was often trying, but rarely dull.

Homer received a new and signal honor in March 1898: the Union League Club devoted its annual exhibition to a Homer–George Inness show. Thomas B. Clarke, chairman of the club's art committee, lent twenty-five Homers from his own collection, the finest privately held group in the country. The show, which included the cream of Homer's output, was the artistic sensation of the year, and even the diehard criticism of the anti-Homerists began to fade.

Since the start of the development of Prout's as a summer resort, Winslow and his brother Arthur had been arguing over property lines along adjacent lots they owned, especially as land values on the Neck increased. In September 1898 they finally decided by tossing a coin which of them should have the front lots and which the back on Eastern Point. Winslow lost the toss and got the back lots, but he also received the front half of a triangular piece of land outside the marginal way, and later made this the subject of one of his most famous paintings, *Eastern Point, Prout's Neck* (Fig. 74).

Homer was in good health at this time, working hard and enjoying life as much as ever. He was well liked at Prout's and had many close friends there. Frank Coolbroth, an amateur naturalist, went for frequent walks with Homer and was often asked to comment on new paintings. Like Homer he knew Florida, for he went there every winter on business. On their walks he would carve knotty canes, often from apple branches, and frequently gave them to Winslow. There are dozens of them around the studio to this day. Another close friend was Charles Walker, the Scarboro station agent, who had succeeded to that position after Elbridge Oliver carelessly let the building burn down. Walker ordered Homer's supplies from Boston and New York, and since he was an enthusiastic amateur photographer like Homer himself, frequently took pictures for the artist; his orders were to make two or three prints and then destroy the negatives. Another friend was Bartlett Pillsbury of nearby Pine Point, a long-time butcher for the Scarboro area. He supplied Homer with meat, and with commonsense criticism of his work. He even named one of his sons Winslow. When he retired, his successor, Harvey Urquhart, continued to supply Homer, and became one of his good friends. These people, as distinct from the late-comer summer residents, were the true permanent citizens of Scarboro township and many could trace their family names — Libby, Oliver, Brown, Walker, Seavey, Larrabee, Meserve, Wiggin, Foss, Coolbroth, Pillsbury — back through a proud line of ancestors who had settled in the area in the seventeenth or early eighteenth century, defended Scarboro against attacks during the bitter French and Indian War, and served with Washington at Valley Forge.

In 1899 the Carnegie Institute honored Homer with an exhibition of twenty-seven of his watercolors of life and scenes in the Province of Quebec. But the high point of that year was the sale of the Thomas B. Clarke collection. Clarke, like a nineteenth-century

Lorenzo de Medici, did more to encourage the art of his own time and country than any other wealthy American of his day. Of Homer's work alone he had purchased thirty-one paintings, and had helped such other artists as George Inness. The prices at the sale, though high for that day, seem ridiculously low today — the highest was the $4700 paid for *The Lookout — "All's Well"* by the Boston Museum of Fine Arts. But even more important than the money was the interest of the museum in Homer's work; together with the Carnegie Institute it performed an invaluable service in furthering Homer's reputation, even before his death.

Altogether, Clarke and the widely publicized auction of his collection benefited Homer greatly. As Homer's principal Maecenas, he purchased the artist's paintings to the point where he needed a special room in his house for them, wrote him encouraging letters, persuaded his friends to buy Homer's work, and through his position in the New York art world saw to it that Homer's work was displayed in the club exhibitions which were an important means of recognition at that time among well-to-do and cultivated patrons. As Goodrich observes in his biography, Clarke was, outside of Homer's immediate family, the strongest influence in his professional life during the peak of his career. The sale of the Clarke collection stimulated almost at once the sale of Homer's paintings, increased the prices paid for them, and enhanced his reputation among the general public, which, then as now, often measures artistic worth by monetary value. It also improved the economic position of contemporary American art at large, which up to that time had invariably brought lower prices than comparable work from the hand of any European artists.

During the last two years of the century Homer moved about as actively as ever, but concentrated especially on the tropics. In 1899 he did only one outstanding oil, but his watercolor brush worked overtime. The two years saw him rounding out several different series of subjects he had been working on since he first saw the Bahamas in 1885.

One series was concerned with designs that included architec-

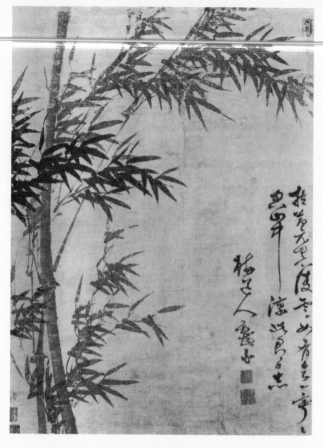

Fig. 61. Wu Chên, BAMBOO IN THE WIND.
Chinese, early fourteenth century, Yüan Dynasty. Courtesy,
Museum of Fine Arts, Boston.

ture, vegetation, and the ocean background, as if he had turned his back to the picturesque perspectives of hilly Santiago to face the sea. The whole group is characterized by broad washes and orderly designs. *The Shore at Nassau* shows the expansive panorama of an incredibly blue ocean; *Flower Garden* and *Bungalow, Bermuda* stress the forms and colors of the vegetation. *Salt Kettle* is of reflections in a placid cove, while *Wall, Nassau* plays with the textures of the wall and the scarlet flowers on it. A variation of the same theme in *Nassau, N.P., Bahamas* is a study in the geometric patterns that attracted Homer's eye.

He also continued his series of studies of the tropical palm, sometimes showing the stately trees under storm conditions,

Fig. 62.   TORNADO, BAHAMAS.
1898. The Metropolitan Museum of Art.

when they sway so expressively with a kind of inner life. When the fourteenth-century Chinese painter Wu Chên achieved much the same effect in his *Bamboo in the Wind* (Fig. 61) he had centuries of tradition as a start; Homer, on the other hand, began his study of palm trees completely on his own, in 1885. In *Mountains and Palms, Cuba,* the small scale of the palms was related to the huge limestone mountains; in *Royal Palms, Cuba,* he moved in and studied the trunks and branches in detail. The careful observation which went into all these studies becomes apparent in such finished works as *Palm Tree, Nassau,* in the Metropolitan Museum. No matter what part of the world he was in, Homer loved to add the excitement and aliveness of high winds to his studies of nature, and he was not long in trying his hand at the spectacular storms of the tropics.

Up north he had used the pounding of the surf against the rocks to epitomize the fury of the storm; here he used as his symbol the sullen, brooding, heavy sky. Picture after picture shows the building clouds, the lowering light, the feeling of tension in the air. In *Windstorm, Bahamas* and *Palm Trees, Nassau,* back in 1885, he had shown the trees bent like taut bows under the violent pressure of the gale. Now, in 1898, he combined his thoroughly mastered elements into a piece charged with mood but rigorously ordered — *Tornado, Bahamas* (Fig. 62). The storm, more accurately called a hurricane, is indicated with great power by the striking value contrasts and the somber low intensity tones; the palms, expressive as they are, are generalized to suggest the nature of all palms without representing any particular ones. It is a wonderfully satisfying and moving example of a maximum effect achieved with a minimum of means, again like the effect in Wu Chên's *Bamboo in the Wind.* It is difficult to avoid the belief that Homer derived more than perhaps even he realized from the art of the East.

We know that Homer had examined Oriental paintings, and even done some pastiche studies in Japanese style; furthermore his friend John La Farge had been to Japan and the South Sea Islands with Henry Adams in 1886 and brought back a portfolio of brilliantly colored watercolors, several of which are in the Bowdoin College Museum of Art, which Homer may well have seen. According to Charles L. Homer, La Farge was the only colleague with whom his uncle enjoyed discussing theories of art, and he may have given Homer many ideas that he had picked up in the Orient. Whether he did or not, Homer certainly shows the same restraint, simplicity of design, and appreciation for the universal attributes of nature that we think of as characteristic of Oriental art.

Homer could no more ignore humanity here than he could anywhere else, and in *After the Tornado, Bahamas* he shows the tragic aftermath of a tropical storm. Under the date of July 5, 1902, in his Day Book, a small sketch of this picture is called *After the Tornado, Texas,* a subject probably suggested by one of his visits to the winter home of his brother Arthur in Galveston. Moving north and south with the seasons, he portrayed now na-

Fig. 63.   WATERFALL IN THE ADIRONDACKS.
About 1894. Courtesy of the Smithsonian Institution, Freer Gallery of Art, Washington, D.C.

ture, now man, and then the two in their many relationships, from the completely harmonious to the grimly tragic. He kept up his visits to the Adirondacks, developing his fishing themes, always working from the complex to the simple, always with more and more technical skill. *Fisherman's Holiday* and *Adirondack Lake* stress general atmosphere and the dexterity of his washes at the expense of emphasis; *End of the Day* and *Fishing in the Adirondacks* bring us closer to the sportsman, with a gain in emphasis, and Homer's impressionistic treatment of light and atmosphere parallel Monet's.

End of the Day is sheer visual poetry, but it carried Homer to the brink beyond which reality dissolves and, always unwilling to carry anything to an extreme, he drew back a step or two. Thus in *Waterfall in the Adirondacks* (Fig. 63) he struck a balance between atmosphere and light, expression of the movement and en-

Fig. 64.   THE MINK POND.
1891. Fogg Art Museum.

ergy of the water, and the design which frames the fisherman in a
neat parallelogram. Homer's great fondness for fishing comes
through in these studies, and his love of nature beckons to us with
the persuasiveness of a siren. In an extraordinary picture of a
lovely microcosm, *The Mink Pond* (Fig. 64), Homer stole upon a
tiny corner of the outdoors and set it down with a charming intimacy and gentle sensitivity that is rarely found outside Chinese,
Japanese, or Persian painting.

Yet he could also appeal to our love of the dashing, active life of
the "back country." *Canoe in the Rapids* (Fig. 65) is exhilarating
with its sense of danger, and the swirling waters seem to move
even in the picture. *Ouananiche Fishing* (Fig. 66), painted at
Lake St. John, creates a feeling of excitement and tension by contrasting diagonals. *Hudson River Logging* (Fig. 45), with its bristling trees, shallow choppy rapids and the massive log hung up on
a rock in the river, gives all the feeling of the rugged, laborious

[164]

Fig. 65.   CANOE IN THE RAPIDS.
1897. Fogg Art Museum.

Fig. 66.   OUANANICHE FISHING.
1897. Courtesy, Museum of Fine Arts, Boston.

logging industry. The real secret of Homer's phenomenal success in dealing with subjects so utterly unlike in both content and feeling lies in his sure instinct for the treatment proper to the theme at hand. Only a supreme command of technique and an almost superhuman sensitivity to many moods enabled him to create hundreds of pictures in an essentially personal style which is at the same time consistent and endlessly varied.

His tropical themes show as great a variety of moods as his northern ones. In *The Shore at Nassau* and *House and Trees in Nassau* he captures the charm of the relaxed and balmy days in this peaceful island haven. In *Bermuda*, in the Metropolitan Museum, the two massive antique cannon hint at buccaneers and buried treasure; *Shore and Surf* is just a good, honest Homer investigation of an offshore reef and the character of the choppy waves that wash it. He returned to an old love of his, a graceful boat at anchor, in *Sloop, Bermuda* (Fig. 67), in which the composition is unified with rhythmically patterned curves and a color scheme amazingly rich in both an abstract and a descriptive way.

Fig. 67. SLOOP, BERMUDA.
1899. The Metropolitan Museum of Art.

Fig. 68.   RUM CAY.
1898. Worcester Art Museum.

Fig. 69.   TURTLE POUND.
1898. The Brooklyn Museum.

Fig. 70.   THE GULF STREAM.
1889. The Art Institute of Chicago.

He studies the beautifully proportioned bronze forms of the native Negroes in *Rum Cay* (Fig. 68) and *Turtle Pound* (Fig. 69),
concentrating on one or two figures which he sets boldly against
light blue or emerald, reminiscent of *The Sponge Diver* (Fig. 19)
of 1889. All his life Homer regarded watercolor and drawing as
ideal media for unpretentious subjects, and oil as the logical medium for bigger ideas. Yet, curiously, it was in his drawings and
watercolors that he achieved some of his fullest realization of
three-dimensional form (as in *Flamborough Head*), while he
tended more and more to flatten his oil forms.

Homer often said that he would probably "live longer and
please more people" with his watercolors than with his oils, yet he
frequently turned to the heavier medium of oil for his summing-
up pictures, the grand works that seem to synthesize the accumulated experience of years of investigation. So in 1899 he prepared
to paint on canvas a tropical perils-of-the-sea theme which had
been simmering in his mind for fifteen years. Back in 1885 he
had been intrigued, if not attracted, by the repulsive-looking
sharks, and he confided to a fellow passenger on the boat to Nassau that he would like to paint one. This chance acquaintance

sent word, after Homer had been in Nassau a few days, that he
had a shark for him. Meanwhile the artist had found no difficulty
in getting sharks; in fact, he was oversupplied. So he said, pleas-
antly enough, to the messenger, "Tell your friend to go to Hell! I
have a dozen sharks!" He worked his way for fourteen years
through a long series of drawings and watercolor studies. That
first year he painted two Negroes who had just caught a shark,
and called it *Shark Fishing*. In 1885 (or possibly 1886) his *Study*,
in the Cooper Union Museum, showed a derelict schooner with
some stalks of sugarcane aboard; a slightly different boat called
Derelict and Sharks (1885) has the savage fish around the bat-
tered hulk. In 1889 he combined some of these elements into a
watercolor, *The Gulf Stream* (Fig. 70), depicting a Negro on a
dismasted sloop, sustained by sugarcane and threatened by
sharks. This was the theme of his more highly developed canvas
of 1899, also called *The Gulf Stream* (Fig. 71), in which a hurricane provides the *raison d'être* for the subject. Homer worked for
months until he felt the painting was ready to exhibit at Knoedler's late in 1900. He showed it again in the National Academy

Fig. 71.   THE GULF STREAM.
1899. The Metropolitan Museum of Art, Wolfe Fund, 1906.

Exhibition of 1906, and the violent cleavage of opinion it aroused is apparent in press clippings of the day.

The critic for the New York City *Bulletin* reported that the painting had been "purchased by the Metropolitan Museum at the suggestion of the Jury, as being the strongest work in the exhibition," but plainly preferred Paul Dougherty's *Land and Sea*. The New York *Herald* stated: "Those who saw *The Gulf Stream* say that it is an unusually strong canvas, even for a Winslow Homer. It should, so artistic opinion runs, eventually bear the same relation to marine subjects by this American artist that Turner's famous *Slave Ship* does to that artist's works. . . . The selection and purchase of *The Gulf Stream*, artists believe, is an indication that the Metropolitan Museum realizes its duty toward contemporary American art, or to be exact, toward what is best in contemporary American art." The New York *American* called it "the picture of the show." The *Times* praised it, but deprecated *A Light on the Sea* and finally said of Homer, "No living painter quite reaches him." The *Evening Post* called it "that rare thing in these days, a great dramatic picture, partly because the horror is suggested without a trace of sentimentality and partly because every object in the picture receives a sort of over-all emphasis that shows no favor to the dramatic passages. As a result the story never outweighs the artistic interest."

There were, however, other opinions. The New York *World* said, "Because the Metropolitan Museum has purchased Winslow Homer's canvas, *The Gulf Stream* was naturally the center of attraction, but it was by no means the best painting on view." The *Sun* pretended to commend the committee for showing mediocre work that would appeal to the masses, and as an example cited *The Gulf Stream*. They too rated it inferior to *Land and Sea* by Paul Dougherty, and said it was "too crowded with naturalistic melodrama," "huddled in composition," "less fantastic than cruel," and rated "the quality of the paint as neither pleasant nor translucent." Riter Fitzgerald of the Philadelphia *Item* called it a "unique burlesque," renamed it "Smiling Sharks," and claimed that the *American Art News* was being sarcastic when it wrote a favorable review of the painting. Downes, ever Homer's defender, upon reading Fitzgerald's remark that the picture had been "laughed at" when shown in Philadelphia, replied in the Boston *Transcript* that "They laugh best who laugh last." But the most revealing aspect of the contemporary newspaper critical reviews is the perspective in which most of them placed Homer when, as we now see him, he was at the peak of his artistry, by heaping praise upon scores of nonentities and feeble paintings which have long ago been forgotten and by considering him perhaps better than these examples but not remarkably superior. In the eyes of the majority he was part of a large group of worthy artists but not head and shoulders above it.

Kenyon Cox, Homer's perennial critic, wrote (for the *Nation*), that he would have been glad of a finer painting at the apex of the show, and the justification of the committee lay in the absence of works of outstanding merit and individuality. For the New York *World* he did a piece speaking of the picture's "evident crudities." In a monograph on Homer eight years later he made the astonishing assertion that Homer in his later days was partially color-blind, and quoted the touch of scarlet on the boat's stern as evidence that the painter "did not see as we do, and that his eye was growing insensitive to red." He mentions other instances of this scarlet spot, as well he might, for it was one of Homer's favorite little touches and a most effective one. Cox, of course, always preached harmony to the point of weariness, although judging by his own work he was himself a poor and discordant colorist. His criticism is strangely like the statements about the "myopia" of El Greco, Van Gogh, and Cézanne! Cox is fairly answered by Arthur Pope in *The Painter's Terms* when he says that "aesthetic experience is a question of reaction to emotionally, as opposed to intellectually appreciable order"; and that "two things are ordinarily necessary for this emotional experience: first, definite order or organization, and secondly, some element of contrast, of novelty, of surprise, of disorder, in fact, but which serves as a means to emphasize the elements of order, and without which the order would seem monotonous, and uninteresting." Today Homer is, in the opinion of most people, a master colorist, especially in his watercolors, where he stressed color more than in his oils. More and more he is coming to be appreciated as one of the most intelligent, expressive, and effective colorists in modern art.

Homer had never been especially irritated by adverse comment, certainly not to the point where his technique was influenced. He knew what he was attempting, and had he not been satisfied the pictures in question would not have left his studio. He wrote to a dealer who had passed on to him some of the comments about the "horror" of the subject:

> *The criticisms of The Gulf Stream by old women and others are noted. You may inform these people that the Negro did not starve to death. He was not eaten by the sharks. The waterspout did not hit him. And he was rescued by a passing ship which is not shown in the picture.*
>
> *Yours truly,*
> Winslow Homer

To us the barbed criticisms directed against such painters as Manet, Cézanne, and Homer seem almost inane, but it is only fair to consider these comments in the light of the times in which they were made. During the '80's and '90's, Homer was ahead of most painters of his day and several jumps ahead of the critics. In that period, art criticism was nontechnical. The reviewer for the Indianapolis *News,* for instance, devoted the top of his column to praise for the works by Sergeant Kendall, J. G. Brown, Albert Herter, and Mrs. Ella Condie Lamb, and was concerned in his passing remarks about *The Gulf Stream* mainly with the practical questions of why the deck of the derelict was not wet with sea water and how the Negro kept himself from sliding down the steep slope of the deck without any cleats against which to brace his feet. Pictures were described, not analyzed, and the descriptions were usually written in a romantic and flowery literary style. Most critics wanted paintings to tell a story, and the more story the better. Such technical discussion as there was generally had to do with how close the picture came to photographic accuracy. If the critic possessed any real technical knowledge or painting experience he would often become involved in an interminable academic discussion of luminosity.

By Victorian standards, Homer's content was deemed vulgar; it lacked the polite elegance of the day. Adherents of the accepted slick academic finish in oil painting regarded Homer's vigorous brushwork as crude, and completely missed its expressive qualities and appropriateness to his themes. His form was admired for its resemblance to, rather than its subtle departures from, photographic naturalism, and so the essence of his artistry was wholly overlooked. Yet, with only two or three exceptions, even those who criticized Homer most harshly still considered him the strongest American artist of the period.

CHAPTER FIVE

The Man and the Artist

AMONG the penalties of fame are the unfounded "facts" invariably related about anyone in the public eye. The more fanciful the invention, the more readily it is believed, and legends once accepted are difficult to dispel. Perhaps this is why they are called popular misconceptions. Artists, composers, and writers are especially liable to this sort of untruth or half truth. To the ordinary person, anyone working in a creative field must be a little odd on the face of it. About such people you can believe anything! Misconceptions start, as one contemporary writer says, "God knows how, and end God knows where." In many cases they originate in the misguided efforts of a newspaper reporter who feels he must produce something sensational.

The extraordinary thing about a creative artist is what he creates, and, to a lesser degree, how he goes about it. But the reporter, rarely qualified in art criticism, and his reading public, untrained (and even uninterested) in art generally, want something more. When the journalist makes the most of any odd fact or personal trait he can discover — sometimes, regrettably, he invents one — the public is delighted. The glamorous exaggeration is repeated until it becomes "common knowledge," and is finally picked up by a serious and well-meaning journalist who accepts it as fact, includes it in his report, and thus makes it official. "Everybody knows" that Van Gogh was a lunatic who sliced off his own ear, Rembrandt a bankrupt, Poe a drunkard, and Casanova a casanova — even though they cannot describe one of the major works of any of these artists or give any sound information as to his influence on his own time and ours.

And so with Winslow Homer. "Everybody knows" that he was a recluse, a misanthrope and a woman-hater, ill-mannered, abrupt, insulting, stubbornly self-sufficient — in short, a bad-tempered monster, who ignored other artists and refused to look at pictures, working out his own way of painting completely on his own, in hermit-like seclusion.

This is hardly the Winslow Homer we have been discussing, nor is it the Homer that I pictured after talking with members of his family, his acquaintances in the art world, and people who had known him intimately at Prout's Neck. True, Homer had always been independent and self-sufficient; and the very fact of his leaving New York for the Maine coast must have seemed to many of his fellow artists like self-exile. But this is not really enough to justify the distorted version of his personality which seems to be so widespread. How did this exaggerated picture originate? The earliest printed version I have found appeared in the November 1893 *Corcoran Art Journal*, apparently from the pen of an embittered girl who had been disappointed in an attempt to make an unannounced call on Homer at Prout's Neck while he was working.

AN EXCEPTIONAL CASE

On the sea-shore away from the dust and heat of a large city, an art student was recovering from the effects of a year's study in a life class.

Having heard that a famous marine painter had a studio several miles away, she proposed to see him. There were two ways of reaching his abode, one by train and stage, the other by rowing. However, the "art student pocketbook" settled the question, and taking her father for ballast the young woman started seaward.

The row was a hard and dangerous one, the waves rising

at the most unexpected times and places, rather upset one's calculations, but the prospect of seeing the great painter strengthened the student's arms and she pulled vigorously at the oars.

When they landed they made the unfortunate mistake of taking the wrong path, which led them to a most unprepossessing back fence with no available entrance. The thought of walking back to the main road was not pleasing, so they crawled in through an opening in the fence and walked through a potato patch, a liberty that might have offended the artistic eye of the owner, had he seen it.

Then began a search for the front door, which wearied even the indefatigable art student. They were almost deciding to enter by one of the studio lights [windows], when they discovered the object of their search guarded by a dog, who lifted his voice and did excellent service as a door bell. Almost instantly there appeared the artist, fairly bristling with wrath at being disturbed. His eyes flashed with anger, his hair stood on end (naturally) while his shoulders were raised to their greatest height, giving him the appearance of a cat with his back up.

The student and her father seemed rooted to the ground as firmly as the hardy bushes which grew about the water's edge, while the great artist informed them that his was a private dwelling; that he had nothing to show them; that they were intruding. Disheartened and discouraged, they started for their boat; not daring this time to tread the insect-guarded potato patch, they climbed and stumbled blindly along the rocky paths. They had left "greatness" behind them, but it was with a sense of relief rather than regret.

— DAISY B. KING

Now this was in 1893, shortly after Homer had been awarded the gold medal for *The Gale* at the Chicago Exposition, where his fifteen exhibited paintings had made him a nationally known and discussed artist among people who had never heard of him before. Readers of the *Corcoran Art Journal* had become familiar with his name, and here was a juicy little anecdote, one of those have-you-heard-the-latest-about things that people love to repeat.

And repeat it they did, in conversation over tea, and in art galleries and museums, and even in newspapers — especially in newspapers. No journalist could report on Homer without mentioning the fact that he was a hermit, a recluse, bad-mannered. Serious biographers like Downes and Goodrich have tried to correct this impression, but the general public hates to have a legend contradicted by cold facts, and the false conception of Homer's personality lives on.

I have spent many hours talking with members of the Homer family about Winslow, and many more with people of Prout's Neck and Portland, Maine, who knew him — some of them intimately and over a period of nearly thirty years. His family remembers him with great affection as well as pride, for the Homers were always close to each other, and he was no exception. At Prout's, as at any summer resort, there are two populations — the year-round residents and the summer people. Between the latter and Homer was a gulf which he rarely attempted to bridge. It speaks well for Homer's character that in a remarkably short time after he settled at Prout's he was accepted by the native residents as almost one of them rather than as "summer folks." His simple way of living, his complete lack of pretense or affectation, and his undeniable love of hard work fitted in well with their own traditions. And perhaps his willingness to swap New York for Prout's Neck endeared him to these Maine coast people. As an artist, of course, he was "different," but they admired him and respected his work — partly as honest work, and partly because it was so concerned with their own land and sea and even themselves. Homer's affection for Prout's came through in his painting and his attitude, and to them anyone who loved their place was one of them. When I spoke with people who had known him there, it was apparent that they thought of him as a fine man, a good friend, hardworking and exclusive but by no means boorish or a hermit.

The younger generation of summer people at Prout's during Homer's lifetime never came to know him; he was frequently in

Canada or the Adirondacks during "the season," and when at Prout's was usually too busy working to become part of the social activity on the Neck. As one of them put it to me, he gained the reputation among them of being "an old grouch who locked himself up with a barrel of rum and painted all summer." It is regrettable but perhaps understandable that they held this opinion; just as it is natural that the older natives, who were, like most country people, shrewd judges of character, came to like and respect Homer for what he really was. From a sort of composite of their descriptions and stories, together with the comments and information given me by Homer's nephew Charles and others of the family, Winslow Homer seems to have been quite a person.

He was not a large man — he stood only five feet seven — but his manner and carriage were such that he seemed, somehow, imposing. Light-framed, wiry and thin, he weighed about a hundred and thirty-five pounds. In 1900, when his brothers had developed impressive paunches, he was trimmer than his pet terrier, and almost as active and quick. He had small hands, which were nevertheless strong, graceful, and very expressive. His face was thoughtful, frequently serious though not frowning; his clear hazel eyes were bright, often sparkling with fun, and when he spoke with anyone he looked straight at him. He had a well-shaped head and face, with a prominent Roman nose and a neatly trimmed, luxuriant mustache. His brow was full, his chin firm, and all in all his face, if not particularly handsome, was strong, intelligent, even distinguished. His shoulders were sloping rather than square, but never stooped or rounded. Always unusually fit, his erect bearing, quick step, and alert manner gave a general impression of brightness and energy.

It is said that men reveal themselves by the dogs they keep. Homer, during his life at Prout's, had a terrier which was his constant companion. A common sight to his friends at the Neck was that of Homer and his dog Sam, skipping over the rocks in all kinds of weather. The man was as agile as a mountain goat, as

quick and graceful in his bodily movements as a dancer or boxer
— perhaps a clue to his love of movement in his art.

Until his late thirties he had a heavy shock of reddish-brown
hair, but after that the top of his head went completely bald,
much to his distress. He developed almost a phobia about drafts;
outdoors he always wore some kind of head covering, a hat, cap,
or the tam-o'-shanter he had bought in England. Indoors he wore
a black skullcap or the red Zouave fez he had kept from his Civil
War days. The only photograph of Homer at work shows him
painting on *The Gulf Stream,* his famous oil, in the dead of winter, clothed in a flannel shirt and heavy coat. For this important
documentary picture he went so far as to pose bareheaded. But
even when he attended parties, sometimes formal ones, at the
Ark, he wore a silk skullcap. He used his baldness to justify the
refusal of invitations to teas on the Neck. Often these came
through Mrs. Munroe, and he once said to her, "Annie, all they do
is put me in a draft and serve me coffee jelly, both of which I
hate."

By nature he was careful, even vain about his appearance, and
this was undoubtedly part of the reason why he kept his head
covered. Like many bald men, he was obsessed with the care of
what little hair he had left. Zenas Seavey was the only man on
Prout's Neck who could trim Homer's hair satisfactorily; the artist
even gave him one of his watercolors at a time when they were
bringing several hundred dollars apiece. When Zenas was away,
his brother Benjamin Franklin Seavey would send his own son
Winslow (named for the artist) to do the tonsorial honors. But he
was not the master barber his uncle was, and often Homer would
go to Boston just for a haircut, since Portland had no barber who
could please him.

Homer's attention to his appearance extended to his dress; he
was quite the antithesis of the "dirty bohemian," or early American beatnik, who even then typified a painter for so many people.
Nor did he affect the velveteen jacket, slippers, flowing tie, and

velvet beret of the Parisian artists of the Quarter, made famous by Murger and Puccini. Rather he maintained the appearance of an English country gentleman, and had a fondness for checks and heavily patterned tweeds. His nephew Charles told me that for many years Winslow patronized Brooks Brothers. The firm's old records were burned in 1915, but a Brooks Brothers label pasted on the edge of a drawing in the Cooper Union Museum dated December 9, 1899, seems to confirm the story. Mrs. Charlotte Googins Stevens told me that her sister, Helen Googins, worked during the '90's for Cohling, Portland's best tailor, and that Homer had a standing order for a new pair of trousers every month. On one occasion when she was on her way to Prout's, Mr. Cohling asked her to deliver the "trousers-of-the-month," adding that Homer insisted on having them by the first, or he would refuse them.

One of Homer's few extravagances, his wardrobe, assumed staggering proportions, and included enormous numbers of shirts, socks, underwear, and miscellaneous haberdashery. Leonard Libby recalled that it was one of his duties to keep the suits brushed and pressed, and his mother did Homer's laundry, under very explicit directions. Len would arrange the returned items each in its designated drawer, and in exact order, under Homer's watchful eye. As with everything else in his life, Homer's taste in clothing was impeccable. His criteria were quality, comfort, and harmony. With a strong check or plaid, he always wore a quiet tie, and chose his shoes, hat, even his stick to go with the ensemble. Among his nephew's most vivid memories are those of his Uncle Winslow heading for the water's edge, fishing tackle in hand, and immaculately dressed, always with a clean collar and bow tie above a white shirt. His sneakers might be soaking wet as he stood fishing off the rocks, but the trouser legs would be carefully rolled up out of the way.

Homer, conservative in so many things, was less so in his dress than either of his brothers. It may have been a taste inherited (or adopted) from his flamboyant father. Even more to the point is Winslow's lifelong admiration of youth, and youthful vitality. The pattern and cut of his own clothes, he hoped, made him look younger than he was. He was proud of his lean figure, the year-round tan from his outdoor life, and his inordinate energy and health.

To those who knew him, his vitality seemed inexhaustible. Without being nervous, he never seemed to run down. Always busy, always active, he was never restless or irritable. With company that interested him he could relax and talk for hours, but this was only when he wanted to. He never seemed to require rest because of exhaustion. Even in his last years he scoffed at daytime naps and poked fun at people who needed them. Proud of his own health and energy, he admired those of like make-up, particularly men who worked in the open, and was rather unsympathetic toward less vigorous people. An exception was Charles's wife Mattie, who was of a delicate constitution and, as the saying is, "enjoyed poor health" all her life. Winslow's great love for his older brother was extended to Mattie, to whom his letters were frequently addressed.

Actually, aside from his frequent complaints about cold or heat, he was scarcely sick in his whole life. He continually abused his health, but apparently got away with it until his final illness. His letters repeatedly contain the underscored statement, "I am very Well." About the only complaint from which he suffered was an occasional touch of indigestion from overeating, and this he considered a huge joke, that one so hardy could possibly be subject to the ills that attack common mortals. In the summer he would eat whole bunches of radishes from his garden and then jokingly complain of "radishes on the heart." His attitude was that ordinary health precautions did not apply to him. He went out for hours in the foulest weather to watch the sea and the sky, and sometimes in stormy weather would not be seen in the Ark for days. Father Homer loved to sit in the comfort of his glassed-in porch and watch the gales from his rocking chair. With his telescope he would sometimes spot a lonely figure far away on the cliffs and exclaim, "Why, there's Win!"

Of course, he was a born out-of-doors man, and loved fresh air. He preferred to work in the open, and his fenced-in private yard was his favorite studio. Long after the cold weather had driven the summer visitors from the Neck, he was still at Scarboro, often well into the winter, even in his advanced age.

Up until the very end of his life Homer's mind was keen and quick, his memory unimpaired, his hand steady as a rock, his energy amazing. He took a diabolical satisfaction in fooling those who thought he was on his last legs, right up until his final sickness. A large fireplace in his living room and a pot-bellied stove in the painting room provided the only heat, and during the bleak season he hired first John Gatchell and later Henry Lee to stop by every morning to see if he was still alive. This was no mere eccentricity — during the off-season he could have died in his studio and no one would have known about it, perhaps for weeks.

When he was working he took no interest in food except as fuel to keep him going. He worked until hunger forced him to pause; then he would eat whatever was on hand, cooking it himself, paying little attention to what it was. In cold weather he would hang a turkey, duck, or chicken outside; when he was hungry he would slice off a leg or a "chunk" and roast it over the coals in the open fireplace. During his off-duty periods, however, he was a real gourmet. His letters are full of references to food, and he was not only a master cook but skilled at carving, which he was always invited to do when he ate at the Ark. Mrs. Vaill remembered vividly how he would order choice beef for an Ark party, and have her hang it to age in the icehouse for at least three weeks. The day of the dinner he would sharpen the carving knife on his own grindstone and whet it to a razor edge.

He was especially fond of wildfowl, and had a standing order with Roswell Googins to keep him supplied. These he would hang until "high," and cook them in the English manner, quite rare, so "the blood followed the knife." Often he would send portions to his friends. He made frequent gifts of fish or fruit (especially to Mrs. Kaler) and would usually wrap them in paper; if none was at hand he would cut off a piece of his tablecloth for the purpose. This is not quite as drastic as it sounds, for Homer's table covering was a laborsaving invention of his own. His long dining table was pushed up against one side of the room, and hung on the wall above it was an enormous bolt of red cloth a little wider than the table. Winslow would pull out enough to cover the surface, and with a pair of shears cut it off at the roller end. "Saves laundry," he once told a pair of guests. "When this length gets too dirty, I throw it away and roll out another!"

He enjoyed cooking when he had the time; his equipment was a swinging crane in the fireplace and a set of kettles, which he scoured in the old-time manner with wood ashes. Leonard Libby told me that Homer would scrub potatoes until they were nearly skinless, bury them in the ashes, and then set him to watch and turn them until they were just right.

When Homer was fond of any food he liked it very much. He introduced oranges and grapefruit to Prout's after one of his southern trips, and consumed them in huge quantities. One of his few pictures that even approach the still-life type is a watercolor, *Oranges on a Branch.* He was also devoted to the onion. At the end of any summer season there were always stray cats about the Neck, and Winslow once took compassion on several, and attempted to feed them onions from his large supply. When the cats refused them, he was hurt by their ingratitude and quite disturbed that any living creature could dislike onions.

Homer was particularly fond of cider, which he mentioned frequently in his letters. Every fall he would order three barrels from Chelmsford, Massachusetts, where an exceptionally good grade was pressed. It was unpasteurized, and what part of it survived the winter was pretty heady by spring.

One March day Homer called in Will Googins to help him open the studio after one of his trips away from Prout's; when they rolled the last barrel of cider out from under the studio they found it frozen solid. "I know what I'll do," said Winslow. "I'll find a long bit tomorrow and we'll bore into the middle. It ought to be pretty good stuff." The next day the two drilled into the center of the barrel and drew off about three gallons of what they agreed was "a real potent brew." It should have been; this is, of course, the classic method of producing applejack, which has never been considered a suitable beverage for women, children, or timid males. The unfrozen center comes close to being pure alcohol, with a rich and zesty flavor highly appreciated by connoisseurs. What is left, naturally, is a flat and vinegary residue. Homer considered the drained barrel of still-frozen dregs, and said to Will, "This gives me an idea. About the time Arthur gets here it should be melted, and I'll give it to him." When Arthur arrived he accepted the barrel with thanks and hauled it, at some trouble and expense, to El Rancho. The next day he said to his brother, "Win, I don't know that I blame you much for giving away that cider. It's really not very good." Winslow never cracked a smile. "Is that so, Arthur?" he asked. "Will Googins and I drank some right out of the middle and we thought it was just fine."

Cider was not Homer's only drink; he was a good judge of choice liquors, but preferred Jamaica rum above all others, after the Medford variety was no longer to be had. In cold weather he would take a drink for warmth and stimulation, and often played host to his family, the tradespeople, and his many friends among the natives at Prout's. He could take enormous quantities without apparent effect; Mrs. Marguerite Downing Savage, who knew him during the last ten years of his life, was surprised to hear that he ever took a drink, for he had never once shown it as far as she was concerned. Most men of the day used hard liquor as a matter of course, so he was hardly exceptional. His Day Book shows payments to S. S. Pierce of Boston for liquor averaging about twenty dollars every two weeks, such checks outnumbering all others of his, yet his friends hardly ever noticed alcohol on his breath.

Mrs. Munroe recalled only one occasion when Homer took a little too much. One evening in the '90's he entertained some friends and apparently had one over the eight. When he went to bed he picked up a bucket of salt water, thinking it was the coal hod, and threw half of it on the fire before he could check himself. The place was thoroughly steamed up, and next morning furniture, walls, and floor were covered with a fine ash. Mrs. Munroe helped him clean the place up, and he was very contrite.

Mrs. Munroe, Mrs. Larrabee, Mrs. Vaill, Leonard Libby, Will Googins, and all the other friends Homer had at Prout's Neck grew to be very fond of him as they came to know him. His little foibles and eccentricities were ignored (perhaps, in private, chuckled at), for after all, they were no greater than the peculiarities to be found in most people. The Maine coast has always had its share of characters, and it is easy to imagine one of the natives of Prout's saying, "Win Homer peculiar? Why, you never knew my great-uncle — now, there was a character for you . . ." As far as Homer was concerned, they knew him to be honest, kind, helpful, dependable — the same kind of decent, good man they respected among themselves. True, his work was utterly different from theirs, but it was honest work and Homer paid attention to it. And, too, they understood his natural desire for privacy and freedom from interruption while he was working.

So, of course, did Homer's family. His nephew Charles gave me a very clear account of his famous uncle's relationship with the rest of the Homers. As he told me, Winslow had two personalities, one when he was working, another when he was off duty. When he put down his brush in the late afternoon, picked up his walking stick, whistled for Sam and went out, he was a polished, courteous, even genial gentleman. Relaxed and easy in his manner, he always greeted friends and acquaintances, often stopped to chat affably with them. Between jobs or at the end of the day he would unhesitatingly join his family or his friends in conversation, fishing, or a leisurely cup of tea — he was as friendly as any man in the colony when not engaged in the business of painting or working out in his mind something he would paint later. At his easel, on the other hand, he was intent on his business, keyed up, and when disturbed even testy. The family respected this desire to be left alone, and so did the people who worked for the Homers.

Even Lewis, of whom Homer was particularly fond, was careful to keep out of the studio during working hours; the artist used to hand him dirty dishes through the window so he would not have to come inside. The year-round residents at Prout's, too, took care not to disturb him at work.

Not so the summer people and the visiting artists. They were curious about watching the great man at work, and his determination to keep his sanctum private aroused an almost diabolical persistence in them. It became almost a game to bait him, and the battle of wills gave birth to many of the liveliest anecdotes about his short temper and odd ways. Actually, most episodes are exaggerated reports of Homer's characteristic brusqueness and firmness when he was busy. No matter how distinguished the visitors or how far they had come to "see the lion," it was almost certain that Homer would, sometimes courteously, sometimes testily, decline to see them. Yet, according to Downes, Mr. Ross Turner and his family from Salem, Massachusetts, who called on the artist in August 1896, were cordially received, entertained, and on leaving were presented with one of Homer's Gloucester watercolors.

But to Winslow, his studio was his sanctuary where he could paint, think, or putter. For his family he devised a system of identifying knocks. His older nephew, Arthur, was assigned one rap, repeated three times. The second, Charles, was known as "Two" and assigned a double rap, also three times repeated. When Homer heard one of the signal knocks he might or might not let the visitor in, depending on his mood or what he was doing. If he heard a rap not in the code, he could look out of his painting-room window and see who was there; strangers almost never were admitted, even if Homer happened to be free, unless he was in an unusually receptive mood.

Like many creative artists Homer was unusually sensitive, devoted to his work during painting hours to the exclusion of everything else, independent to the point of eccentricity. He did not like everybody and felt no particular need to pretend that he did. Through long habit (and perhaps partly in reaction to the teasing attempts to invade his working day) he came to make a fetish of privacy, even beyond his requirements for undisturbed working time.

When he found he could be seen in his living room from the Ark and from the road, he painted the upper portion of his window red and hung a Japanese screen over the lower part. His bedroom window he first painted, then sheathed over. Instead of having his mail come to the Prout's Neck or Oak Hill post office, he would let it accumulate at Scarboro station and send the four miles for it at his own expense. He wrote often to friends and to dealers, but discouraged them from writing him. Parties were one of his special dislikes. He found little to chat about with the other guests, nor did he enjoy spending time in idle politeness. Partly to escape his sister-in-law Mattie's "tea fights," as he called them, and partly to satisfy his brother Charles's desire for occasional privacy, Winslow built and gave him a duplicate of their cabin at the Tourilli Club, the foundation of which still stands in the Sanctuary. To make it authentic, he even hired a French Canadian carpenter named Laurence Archambault to build it out of local logs. Here the two brothers could retire for a smoke and a talk.

Though he was devoted to Mattie, she was rarely invited to his studio. He visited her in the Ark, of course, and usually ate his noonday meal there. Mrs. Munroe's blast on the dinner horn would generally bring him, although if hard at work he might ignore it, and the family would not see him until nightfall. Luncheon was at one, and afterward the family would invariably move to the closed-in porch to visit for an hour or so. Promptly at two-forty-five Mattie retired for her afternoon nap, and the guests were expected to depart. Unless engrossed in a painting project, Winslow almost always appeared for this meal, following protocol rigorously without complaint. But this concession, made for his family, he could drop in the fall, and he was always somewhat relieved to be able to get back to his work and his own hours.

Homer was most at ease with his own family and the year-round people of the Neck. He would drop in frequently on his friends among the local people, but he would usually make what New Englanders term a "dooryard call" — rather than go in, he would ask them to come outside to talk.

He did not feel comfortable with strangers, although he could, of course, be completely gracious and cordial. After all, he had been well brought up, traveled much, and was by nature a gentleman. But, considering most of the summer people as transients, he made little attempt to cultivate them. Those who had ability and worked hard he liked, but he had little use for idlers living on inherited wealth. He visited summer residents on the Neck only on very rare occasions, when he would make a formal call, dressed to the nines, and this was so unusual that his call was remembered as a momentous event. Unfortunately, these people were not used to such unconventional treatment, and being more articulate than the natives, spread tales of his surliness and bad temper. Even when they met Homer out on the cliffs he could be very short with them; they never considered that what for them was recreation — a walk along the shore — was to an artist an occasion of professional observation and an essential part of his work.

Being by nature a kind man, Homer's occasional bursts of temper and bad manners came almost invariably when he was disturbed in something that required his concentration. Frequently he regretted his anger as soon as it had passed, often hastening after the recent object of his wrath with an apology and even a gift of flowers. Ordinarily he was tactful, but if asked a question he invariably gave a straight answer, even at the cost of being blunt. On the other hand he always minded his own business and never volunteered advice or criticism unless invited to.

His refusals of invitations became a habit. He sold several lots to Mr. and Mrs. William B. Goodwin, who were adding to their property, and when he called to sign the deed, Mrs. Goodwin asked him to stay and have dinner. He replied, almost without thinking, "No thank you; I never dine out and I never accept invitations. I am perfectly satisfied with my own cooking." Then he paused, and added, "On second thought, the fish man didn't come today; I will stay." A few days later he made his courtesy call, dressed in his finest city clothes.

About the only kind of pie he enjoyed was sweet potato; Mrs. Munroe found this out and made one for him. He was so delighted that he left a vase of flowers and a fifty-cent piece on her kitchen table. But she once got in bad with him. She was out of ice and Homer stopped his work and took the time to go and get her some. Unfortunately, being a short man, he couldn't get it into the upper compartment of the icebox, and Mrs. Munroe, who was even shorter, but more experienced, took it from him and almost without effort put it in. Homer was furious. He flew into a rage, and said, "Your old icebox smells, anyway, and I'll never eat out of it again." He stamped out of the kitchen, but returned after a few days. Mrs. Munroe was out, so he couldn't apologize for his bad temper, but when she returned she found on the table a dollar bill, weighted down with a bottle of Homer's finest Canary wine, bearing a note: "Annie, the Belle of Prout's Neck."

In his biography, Downes tells of a priest who was unwise enough to knock on the studio door after Homer had retired, to ask for a contribution. The enraged Homer told him, among other things, "Even my brothers never disturb me this late at night." The priest replied, "I'm not your brother, I'm your father." Homer laughed and invited him in. When the priest left, he took with him a generous contribution toward the chapel which was being built at Scarboro.

Actually Homer liked people; he only disliked pretense. The children at Prout's were always welcome at his place unless he was busy; even then he would ask them in for a brief visit and then tactfully dismiss them. When he was free he would serve them crackers and Dundee marmalade, and he always had cheese for those who did not care for sweets. When they left he used to give them each a piece of candy "for the road"; they would have been amazed to hear that he was a formidable person. They knew that when he had a picture on his mind he was quiet and thoughtful, almost dreamy, and with the understanding and good sense that so many children have they left him alone because they did understand him — better, perhaps, than their elders.

Mrs. Larrabee remembers very well how he would even allow her to walk the cliffs with him and sit beside him as he sketched. He enjoyed her silent companionship and appreciated her little expressions of friendship, as when she would quietly present him with a tiny bouquet of wild flowers. Despite his relief when the vacation period was over, autumn was lonely for him once his family had gone for the season, and he would often ask the tradespeople in when they called, sometimes on the pretext of a question about something he was painting, but in reality, they knew, just to talk with someone for a few minutes. Mrs. Charlotte Stevens, whose friend Annie Libby sometimes looked after Sam during the winter, would go with her to return the dog in the spring. On these occasions Homer would invite them in and show them the drawings he had made during his winter in the South. During these quiet periods of the late fall or early spring, when the Neck was almost deserted, and even Homer felt the need for company, he often visited and ate meals with Zenas Seavey and his family on their nearby farm. In May, Mattie usually sent Thomas Roebuck, her English groom, and Parsons, her caretaker, to the Neck to open the Ark before the family came in June. Winslow would have them both over to the studio for dinners, and spent many evenings with them. He liked Len Libby, and used to bring flowers to Len's grandmother, Mrs. "Cap't Silas" Libby. Len recalled how Homer when alone was very impetuous; if something irritated him he would swear like a trooper, but if he realized Len, who was then only a boy, was within hearing, he would apologize to him. Like every old inhabitant at Prout's whom I met, Len appreciated Homer as an artist but even more as a fine and unusual man. He was more like them in many ways than were most of the summer people, but he never pretended to be a native. He was apart from both groups and was, primarily, himself. This they admired, and never tried to make him conform to a conservative social code as the summer people did. Above all, they did not think of him as a freak or as a famous person. In 1916, six years after his death, *The Gale* was sold to the Worcester Art Museum for $30,000. Not until the story appeared in the papers did many of them realize that they had had a famous man among them.

To an artist, people are part of the world he must study and observe, and Homer did this continually. Away from Prout's, particularly when he felt tired or stale, he would go to New York or Atlantic City and walk for hours just watching the crowds. He loved being among people, and sometimes, dreading the necessity for small talk and the publicity which his growing fame was bringing, he liked the anonymity of crowds. At other times he wanted to renew old friendships. When heading north he often stopped at the Parker House in Boston; if south, at the Seville House in New York. Here he would gather some of his old friends like John La Farge, and after a good meal they would talk shop for hours. Mattie and Charles had a home near Boston and she maintained a sumptuous apartment in New York; when Winslow was passing through she invited him for a visit, but if he got into a hot dispute with his cronies somewhere along the way, he might forget completely and never put in an appearance. These trips to New York and Atlantic City became annual events during his later life, as if he had to reacquaint himself with people after his long spells in the woods or at the ocean.

Although Homer was a lifelong bachelor, he was by no means a misogynist. He showed the respect and chivalry toward women normal to his time, and treated them continually in his work. As a young man he was attracted to girls but not wholly at ease with them; a man of great self-possession and decency, no slander was attached to his name, and with one exception no one ever hinted at any real romance.

The exception was Mattie; with her originated the story of his disappointment in love at an early age. Arthur's son Charles avowed that the story was pure invention. It only appeared at the end of Winslow's life, when he had become famous. Mattie was always addicted to romanticizing; after her husband's death she made of him a knight in shining armor. She apparently thought it necessary to concoct the tale to complete the "Winslow legend." She told it so convincingly to Robert Macbeth that he believed it; so too did many of the ladies at Prout's. Originally a simple story of a pretty but illiterate girl Homer had employed and with whom he fell in love, it grew with time and repeated telling. Finally she told how Winslow had sent the model off to be educated at his expense before they should be married, but that she had eloped with someone else, and that his bitterness affected his whole life and was the reason he never married. It is traditional that women hate to see a happily unmarried man, and a legend like this one both satisfies and delights them. Certainly Mattie's female acquaintances fostered and embroidered the story. Pretty little tales of this sort almost always spring up about famous artists, and this is no more fanciful than most. And, quite certainly, with no more basis in fact.

Mattie told another story to Mrs. Marguerite Downing Savage, to the effect that Winslow had as a young man been in love with a very lovely but delicate girl who had the misfortune to have "the vapors" once too often. She reported Homer as saying, "I'll not be a damned nursemaid all my life," and with that declaration he withdrew his attentions. Mrs. Savage agreed with Mattie's nephew Charles that this too was a figment of imagination, probably originating in the fact of Mattie's delicate constitution and Winslow's health and energy, for he really was quite intolerant of hypochondria or what he considered imagined illness. Some of his early female models look delicate, but this manner of delineation was more or less the style of the period in art; his later figures are almost always healthy, strapping young women. Mrs. Savage told me that Homer was extremely fond of a small, select circle of ladies, but that women as a whole he merely accepted.

His artistic interest in women was keen, and he shows them as very feminine but never seductive. He never painted a nude female figure. Middle-class Victorian America, above all New England, was hostile toward the nude in art, and not until the French influence in the '90's did the nude cease to be considered risqué if not salacious. The nearest thing to a nude model Homer ever used was a manikin, one of several wooden dolls he brought back from England, and these were always employed clothed. His approach to the whole subject of sex was normal to his time and his background — respectful, chivalrous, even tender, but reserved and diffident. With his associates he never showed any interest in discussing women romantically; when with guides, fishermen, hunters, or lumberjacks he would listen to and apparently enjoy a funny off-color story, but he never volunteered any himself. He was not a prude, and certainly never showed any sexually aberrant tendency. Why then did he never marry or become attached to any woman?

The truth is that Homer, like not a few other devoted creative artists, was married to his work. He discovered early in life that he had artistic ability; further, he believed that he had something important to say, and he directed his whole life toward the one aim of developing his technical and aesthetic powers to a point where he could use them to make an effective statement in his painting. To this end he would make any sacrifice. He braved the foulest weather, took long, hard trips, gave up the comfort and society of New York and the pleasant and valuable hours he might have spent with his professional associates — "the boys" as he called them. He stopped attending National Academy meetings, and avoided receptions, awards ceremonies, and openings of shows. He lived in Spartan simplicity in an almost barren frame house, often in freezing weather, on the primitive Maine coast, and even there sacrificed many hours of company with his friends and his family when his work required it. To an artist of Homer's caliber much is given, but if he is to put his great gift to its fullest use, much also is demanded. So much that there is little time left to share with a wife.

Within a few yards of Homer's studio was the small but attractive St. James's Episcopal church. He made sketches of the building and of the dedication ceremonies when it was consecrated, but he never went inside. Although not a member of this church, he often did helpful things for the sake of his father, who was a devoted communicant. Once when Mrs. Munroe baked a cake for the church he gave her a West Indies coconut to shred up for the frosting, supplied a handsome black lacquer tray and helped her arrange it artistically. At another time, he bought her some sweet peas at a church bazaar and gave the girl at the flower booth a check for a hundred dollars.

After his youth he never attended church or showed any particular interest in religion. Curiously, the only painting by another artist (except some of his mother's watercolors) that he owned was an engraving from Rubens's *The Elevation of the Cross* which Homer bought in France in 1867. Whether his interest in it was religious or artistic, he had it framed, and kept it hung on his studio wall until the end of his life. He never painted any religious pictures; in this he was typical of all the Impressionists after Manet. He respected religion, and wrote in one letter to his brother Charles, "I am so very thankful for all 'His mercies' that I now write to you. There is certainly some strange power that has some overlook on me directing my life." But quite probably his devotion to his art, which substituted for marriage, also took the place of religion, or at least of religious activity.

Perhaps to him works were greater than faith. Certainly he was generous and charitable — far more so than many more pious folk. In this, as with most other things, he took a direct and practical approach. When his Uncle Benson died and left his money to the African missions, Homer's pet joke was that "Uncle Benson had left his fortune to buy red flannel underwear for the African heathen." But Mrs. Vaill, an active Congregationalist, never appealed to him in vain for contributions. When the local doctor's horse broke its leg in the stable and had to be shot, Homer commissioned Harris Seavey to buy another and present it to the doctor. Alvin Brown's house burned down, and Homer and his father personally solicited funds from the summer people (a thing

Winslow hated doing) and raised enough money to build the Brown family an even better house than they had lost. One spring Homer returned from the West Indies to discover that Sam Libby had lost a leg in a hunting accident during the winter, and that his house had been struck by lightning and burned to the ground. The desperate family had been taken in by neighbors. Winslow lost no time in starting a subscription with a hundred dollars, and sent Harris Seavey out to solicit. Enough was raised to replace the house, which the neighbors built for Libby in about a week, thanks to Father Homer, who took the subscription list to Portland and persuaded a lumber firm to donate several hundred dollars' worth of building materials. Friends of the Libbys' held an old-fashioned "pound party" to which everyone was expected to bring a prescribed number of pounds of food, furniture, blankets, etc., and thus furnish the house well enough for the family to move in. This neighborly attitude made Homer seem, to the residents at the Neck, like one of themselves, and they reciprocated by many little kindnesses and favors, which he appreciated greatly.

Homer was, as we have mentioned, a real lover of animals, and though a great fisherman, he was not a hunter. He once, about 1890, bought a live duck for stewing purposes, but found himself unable to kill it. Instead the duck became a member of the family, and Homer had to board it out along with Sam during the winters at Annie Libby's house.

One summer while he was off in the Adirondacks for a few weeks, Mrs. Munroe was caring for Sam. The dog got hold of a chicken bone, and only with difficulty was she able to remove it from his throat, very probably saving his life. When Father Homer wrote of the occurrence, Winslow hurried back to Prout's; immediately he went to thank Mrs. Munroe and gave her twenty-five dollars. He loved Sam, and once told Mrs. Munroe that he did not know what he would do if anything ever happened to the dog.

Most of the friends of Homer's with whom I talked mentioned his sharp wit and sense of humor, which extended even to practical jokes. Many of his pictures show a feeling for fun — a number of the Civil War camp scenes, his *Bear Breaking Through a Canoe* (Fig. 51) and one called *Startled*, for example, as well as innumerable cartoons and sketches he would send to members of the family. He did a preliminary sketch for the *Bermuda Settlers* (now at Worcester) showing several razorbacks, one of whom faced the viewer with his prominent red snout. Homer would call a visitor's attention to the sketch, and later pull off the hog's nose (actually a red tin tag from a plug of Lucky Strike chewing tobacco) and move it over to the horizon. When the visitor looked at the picture again, the tag had become a scarlet setting sun. His few self-portraits are jocular caricatures, like the one called *Our Special* that shows him as a Civil War artist at the Front. Among friends he even laughed at his own baldness, about which he was ordinarily quite sensitive. He told Mrs. Larrabee that his father once got angry at him and skimmed a broken plate across the room at him, which shaved all his hair off.

He frequently laughed at himself, his pictures, and his family. The Homers on several occasions had group photographs taken, and one of these struck Winslow as a little pompous looking; he combined the picture with one of a *Winged Victory* from a magazine, flying with a palm branch in one hand and about to award the "Familia Homer" a laurel wreath with the other. Arthur is looking up, apparently at the figure, and Winslow was so delighted with the pseudo-classical paste-up that he had it framed, and hung it on his studio wall where it is still to be seen.

Even about the to him necessary business of being undisturbed, he sometimes had a little fun. When he was working near Cannon Rock (where nine of his greatest marines were conceived) he would post a small but boldly lettered sign at the head of the path which read: SNAKES! MICE! This was to discourage the curiosity of the "damned old women," as he called some of the more elderly lady summer people. When the scheme worked he was as delighted as a schoolboy.

Once Winslow put his ability at practical joking to therapeutic use. In 1895 Father Homer decided his time had come, so he had a bed set up in the Ark living room, where he lay all day, waited on by Mrs. Munroe and the newly arrived Lewis. His son Charles brought him champagne, and though the old man was an avowed advocate of the temperance movement, it was accepted as a medicine. All in all he found the situation much to his liking. His doctor told Winslow that although there was nothing organically wrong, his father really would die if he continued to languish in bed. Winslow replied, "I'll get him up."

He repaired to the studio and rigged himself up in a dressing gown, slippers, and his Zouave fez — all bright red. He had Lewis close both doors into the living room, and walked up and down the hall, sprinkling sulphur on a shovelful of burning coals. When the odor of "fire and brimstone" had filled the house, he held the embers so as to cast a weird light upward on his contorted face, and thrust his head through the door nearest the bed, muttering gibberish. The self-styled invalid made a phenomenal recovery and fled the room, long nightshirt flapping, shrieking that the Devil had come for him in person. Though this sounds like a boyish kind of psychotherapy, Winslow was fifty-nine at the time. He loved gags of this sort that fitted in with his sense of the dramatic.

His descriptive statements were often vivid, enhanced by his economy of words. Some of the residents at Prout's I talked with remembered things Homer had said to them half a century earlier. Like them, he spoke to the point. When the Reverend Stanley White and his two sons asked Homer's opinion of a board fence they were building, he measured it carefully with his eye and said, " 'Tain't plumb." And when Henry and Cyrus Merriam were helping their father paint a new fence, the General said to Winslow, "How's that for a nice bright color?" Winslow replied, briefly and honestly, "It's too damn' yeller."

When out walking, Homer usually carried a stick, which he used to express himself with as he talked. With men he had a colorful vocabulary, gained from his years of association with soldiers, fishermen, and woodsmen. In the presence of ladies or young people, however, he was scrupulously restrained in his language. His voice was mild and soft and very steady, with a slight hesitation in his speech, not enough to be a stammer, but just an occasional "er" or "ah."

He could not express himself fluently, as his brothers did, but he was exact, precise and forceful. Three consecutive sentences would be a long statement for him — but they would be loaded with meaning. He would mull an idea over in his mind until he knew precisely how he wanted to express it, then speak quickly and to the point. He was not afraid of long silences and was content to let others do the talking, unless someone made a false statement concerning something he knew about, particularly in the fields of art and nature. When Mrs. Larrabee was a girl she was out walking with Homer and mentioned that the ocean looked green. He paused, thought a while, and said, "No, Henrietta. Do you remember your mother's maple washing tubs? How they are painted blue? Well, the ocean is that same color." This is color analysis in terms a child can understand — and remember forever.

His precise and exact statements were the verbal indications of his phenomenal sense of orderliness in his life, his art, and his thinking. He worshipped punctuality, concentration on the job at hand, and hated above all things a piece of work left unfinished. More than once he would come across a sketch or painting begun fifteen years or more previously, and with his accumulated experience realize that now he could do what he had not been able to before. He would finish the work and sign and date it — as if he felt some compulsion to close this tiny paragraph in the voluminous book of his life's achievements. Though, like Titian, he often worked on several paintings at the same time, he never tired of one and jumped to another. He might notice a sky or sea effect and leave his work to capture it, but he always went back to what he had begun. With the close of the Civil War he returned to the ways of peace — but he completed every picture that he had conceived before Appomattox, as he did later all those inspired by Tynemouth.

His studio was austere, almost barren. An all-purpose tip-top deal table, four straight chairs, and a built-in hardwood settle by the fireplace were the only furniture. Nothing was upholstered, and he never owned an easy chair. The rustic settle which was the only place in the painting room where visitors could sit down was notorious for its uncomfortable wooden seat but effectively kept unwanted callers from delaying his work. His bedroom, formerly the old stable hayloft, was furnished with a hard bed, a single wooden chair, a washstand, and a pot-bellied stove. Today the studio (Fig. 4) is decorated with guns, spears, and souvenirs of outdoor life, but these were placed there after Winslow's death by his brother Charles, who was an omnivorous collector and filled his West Townsend house to overflowing. In his opinion they were needed to make the place look the way an artist's studio should. Winslow however made a fetish of cleanliness, and did the best he could in his own way, even during the winter, when water was scarce. When spring came he would have a huge cleaning session. He made two great mops from discarded suits of long winter underwear tied end-to-end. These fifteen-foot weapons he would wield in turn, one for soapy and one for clean water, swishing them around from his barefooted stance in the middle of the room.

His clothing was systematically arranged, as was all of his art gear, and every suitcase, trunk, and kit bag was plainly marked with his name and address. If he lent his brother a book or a grindstone, he made a note of the fact and checked it back in when it was returned. Len Libby remembered clearly this habitual neatness, and told me that the one departure would occur when Homer had finished a picture on which he had expended more than the usual time and effort — in such a case the artist would complete his signature and then scatter his brushes all over the table as if in relief.

Unlike most people of his day he detested the overcrowded Victorian parlors, and was always disturbed by things out of place or off balance. He was an inveterate picture-straightener, and Mrs. Munroe would often be amused to see him, almost unconsciously, adjust those in the Ark as he walked through, move a decanter a half inch to balance with its mate, or straighten the corner of a rug with his toe. His clothes were always in apple-pie order, his notes and records neat and clear, and his work schedule kept inviolate.

He extended the same respect for order to his real estate, of which he was fiercely jealous. The Putnams owned property next to his, and once started to put up a fence which Winslow believed to be several feet over his own line. He and Mrs. George Putnam, a strong-willed woman, had quite an argument, and Winslow left, muttering, "No damned woman is going to tell me where my property line is." He shortly returned to the field of battle with a surveyor's map of the whole Neck on which were carefully marked and numbered every lot. It was the original S. L. Stephenson survey, and proved Homer correct to the foot. But if Homer was outspoken about his rights, he seldom carried grudges. He and the Putnam family became good friends, and when he built his cottage above Kettle Cove adjoining their land, he set it far back from the shoreline out of respect for Mrs. Putnam's desire to have an unobstructed view of Eastern Point.

Homer put up a fence between himself and Dr. Charles Farr, his neighbor on the east, even though the two were perfectly friendly. Sharing his father's dislike of trespassing, he became very irritated at visitations from noisy young sightseers from nearby Saco. Once Dr. George Huntington (who later owned the house overlooking High Cliff) was brought from Gorham as a small boy for a picnic and fishing trip at Prout's. No sooner had the party tethered their horses and started down to the rocks than Winslow appeared, told them they were trespassing, and ordered them off. Huntington's father carefully explained why they were there, and asked if Homer could show them where they might hitch their horses on public land and get to the marginal way.

Before this politeness, Homer unbent and said, "Oh, let 'em alone, I didn't know you were decent people, I thought you were 'Saco-rats.' Come in and bring the boy."

In Homer's journals (Day Books), which he kept meticulously, he mentioned everything he did, the state of the weather, and many financial records. One of these, now in the Homer collection at Bowdoin College, covers the period from December 1, 1901, to January 9, 1903. It contains invaluable data about what pictures he was working on at specific dates, when they were finished and what he did with them, as well as data on weather conditions and identification of the models. When he sent paintings to dealers or buyers, he would include a thumbnail sketch in his Day Book for purposes of identification. Sometimes his original titles or his datings differ from those now used, the latter owing to his occasional errors as to when a sketch had been started, and to his habit of dating a work when he finished and signed it, even though it might have been begun several years before. He apparently discarded most of his Day Books, and it is a tragic loss, for many questions as to his work, his travels, and his daily life might be answered if they had survived. Unfortunately for historians, he had little interest in immortality, and when a portion of his Day Book had served its practical purpose, he tore whole sections of pages out and threw them away. When Downes expressed concern about his future fame he replied, in effect, that after he was dead he would not know or care.

Other entries of a minor nature, such as small sums paid his helpers, models, and the tradespeople were chalked on the studio walls, but his more important business affairs were conducted through the First National Bank of Portland, Maine, and he carefully preserved his canceled checks in yearly bundles. Through these, which his nephew Charles allowed me to examine, we can deduce much of his affairs and his whereabouts at any particular time.

He was addicted to buying favorite items in quantity; fruit and vegetables he would lay in by the case or the barrel, and once, when his brother Charles admired Winslow's new kerosene stove, he was taken out to the shed and shown five more just like it, still in their crates. Winslow told him, "When I find something I really like, and wear it out, all too often I go back for another and discover it is no longer manufactured." He added, with a grin, "Besides, these were a lot cheaper by the half-dozen." Once in the early '80's he arranged for the Libbys to board Sam for the winter and promised to send some food from New York. Shortly afterward, a hundred-pound wheel of dried pressed beef arrived. Len Libby stored it in his barn, where it froze solid, and he had to break pieces off with a sledge hammer. Unfortunately, Sam wouldn't touch it; the Libbys fed it to a sow and eventually raised a whole litter of pigs on it.

Actually, as long as he had enough money for his immediate wants, Homer was satisfied. Aside from his large wardrobe, he accumulated few possessions. He had, of course, a number of gold, silver, and bronze medals which had been awarded for his paintings, and these he would put in a cigar box when he left Prout's for the winter, and hide them under the lower branches of a juniper bush until spring.

Some of his financial habits were highly individual, but his affairs were in order and he paid his bills and his taxes promptly. He was a taxpayer and potential voter in Scarboro, but there is no record of his ever having voted or attended a town meeting there. He was not interested in politics, local or national, although he was a great admirer of dynamic Teddy Roosevelt. He was, nevertheless, civic-minded in his own way. He loved Prout's and was always ready to contribute to projects which would help improve the area.

A favorite swimming spot was the beach on Saco Bay which Homer called Biddey's Cove, but when the shifting sands spoiled it, the bathers moved to the surf beach east of the Neck. Homer saw the need for a bathhouse, and built one on the back stretch of the marginal way. This he rented until he had recovered the cost of construction, and then gave it to the Prout's Neck Association,

under whose supervision it is still in use. This was a purely altru-
istic gesture, since Homer never went swimming or beaching
himself. And it was this sort of generous, friendly act that endeared him to his friends at Prout's.

He certainly never made any pretension himself of being a
"great" man; he even avoided the natural occasions when Mattie
or others would have liked to lionize him. Once, at a social affair
at the Checkley House, he became embarrassed at all the praise
heaped on him by the ladies, and turning toward Charles said,
"You must remember that my brother here is quite as distinguished in his line of work as I am in mine."

This did not mean that he did not believe in his own ability and
in the quality of his work. He said in a moment of satisfaction
that *The West Wind* was "Damned good!" and over his signature
on a watercolor, *The Blue Boat,* he wrote "This will do the business!" Sometimes in letters to Charles he would say he had several
pictures in the making, "and very good pictures they are." His
confidence in his status as a painter was justified by the modest
but sufficient returns from sales, although he never reaped a fortune. Critical opinions ranged from high praise to harsh condem-
nation, but he neither despaired nor preened himself on reading
them. Medals and awards he accepted and was undoubtedly grat-
ified, but he never made any great to-do about them and rarely
went to public presentations to receive them. As far as we know,
he never speculated about becoming an immortal painter; he concentrated on the work at hand and left the future to take care of
itself. When in Paris he sent a few clippings to his mother, but
never saved any for himself during his whole life. Such eccentricity as he had never took the form of being a poseur.

The fact that people would try to see him just because he was
famous meant nothing to him; fame or no fame, he had work to
do, work he could not carry on when people were around. One
might think that once he had observed and learned a subject —
the sea, for example — he could have painted any number of
marines without further study, but this is the danger, the tempt-

ing danger that threatens every painter. A lazier man might have fallen into a formula of surf and rocks and turned out innumerable satisfying works — but a one-man show would be disastrous in the revealed monotony. As long as he lived Homer kept renewing his acquaintance with the sea in its myriad moods, and felt an absolute compulsion to paint the ocean's many faces as they appeared to him. In this way his paintings are as varied in mood as the sea itself. Reducing the sea and the shore to a formula would, to Homer, have been unthinkable.

Homer was never one to slide into the easy way of doing anything. He ground his own pigments, did the multitude of chores connected with the technical side of painting, and even much of the landscaping around his studio lawn. He loved his garden, puttered in it a great deal, and took huge delight in the flowers he grew. Oddly, except for his own work, he did not especially enjoy constructing things. Unlike his brother Arthur, he hired carpenters and masons to maintain his property at the Neck, and even had Zenas Seavey crate his paintings for shipment. He did build a wall — the stone wall at Kettle Cove — with his own hands, and was immensely proud of the job; he even had his picture taken in front of it. He used to install and take up his water pipe at the Neck in spring and fall, but fence-building and other long jobs he felt would rob him of valuable working hours, and so he hired them done, although he supervised and planned the work himself with shrewd Yankee practicality.

In painting, of course, he became a thorough master of his materials, but he never made technique in itself his end and aim. His was that supreme mastery that subordinates technical means to what they express. His methods and materials never called attention to themselves by slickness and cleverness, nor did they detract from his theme by their sloppiness. He was not out to paint a tour de force, but a carefully ordered visual impression of the world as he saw it, without any readily noticeable alteration of nature.

He had a flawless sense of design, but rather than distort the subject out of all reality for the sake of pattern, he could select in nature a grouping of objects which made a striking design, with but little help from him. It was the approach of the confirmed realist, combined with the boldness of essential Impressionism, and executed with the skill, sensitivity, and taste characteristic of Homer himself. For Homer, though he disclaimed relationship with all other artists, had learned much from them; and conversely, though he had gained many ideas and techniques and principles from the work of others, his way of painting remained distinctly his own.

When he went to a public gallery — and he did go, on occasion — names meant little to him. It was the picture itself that he considered. Wallace Gilchrist, a young Portland artist, told Alexander Bower of one of his visits with Homer. When he asked Winslow what he thought of the art of Whistler, Homer turned to his brother Arthur and in pretended ignorance asked, "Arthur, am I supposed to know anything about a fellow named Whistler?" Time and time again Homer claimed he never looked at paintings; as a young man he once said, "If you want to be a painter, never look at pictures." He later expressed it, "Look at nature, work independently, and solve your own problems." He hardly meant either statement literally; he was pointing out the weakness of so many of his contemporaries who were slavish imitators of European eclecticism. He expressed little curiosity about museums, old masters, or the history of art aside from technical points that came up in his work.

He knew many other artists, naturally. One of his relatives was the noted sculptor Augustus Saint-Gaudens, who married Augusta F. Homer and christened his son Homer Saint-Gaudens. But he never collected the work of others, and indeed, did not hoard his own as Turner and Degas did. Art was, to him, mostly a matter between himself and the nature he was painting. Consequently, he rarely discussed with other artists their theories of art or the prices they received for pictures. An exception was his old friend John La Farge. Another was Wallace Gilchrist, who used to bicycle out to Prout's and show Homer his watercolors, in which medium he was very capable. Winslow was exceptionally kind to him and gave him very specific and helpful criticisms.

It is probably important to recognize that Homer was not isolated in his seclusion, and by nature was alert to what was going on in the outside world. Leonard Libby asserted that throughout the time he served Homer as a houseboy and, later, did daily chores for him, the painter regularly subscribed to and assiduously read several daily newspapers and the *Illustrated London News*. For him to have remained alert and ignorant at the same time would have been not only contradictory but impossible. Thus, if Homer never asked advice or opinions from other artists, and after he moved to Prout's was almost wholly on his own, his independence was a matter of choice and circumstances. The only ones he could show his pictures to during intermediate stages were his family and his acquaintances at the Neck. None of them was a painter or a trained critic, but Homer frequently sought their opinions on practical matters. Particularly he would ask them if a local scene, an animal, or the activity of a model looked right to them, as he asked Elbridge Oliver about the crows in *The Fox Hunt*. He listened carefully to their comments, and in several cases made changes according to their recommendations.

To get the layman's reaction to a painting, he would strip the fireplace end of the Ark living room, roll up the rug, and display the work on the mantelpiece for Mrs. Munroe and Father Homer to view and criticize. He urged them to point out even the most minute faults, and assured them that he valued their ideas more than those of professionals. Often he would hang a painting from his balcony railing in glaring sunlight and study it from some fifteen yards away through the circle of his fingers. If the colors harmonized or balanced, if the piece had depth under these conditions, he believed the work would stand up in the softer light of a gallery. He never hesitated to make corrections, and spared no effort until the painting satisfied him perfectly. Mr. Bower believed that the layman's legend about painters not knowing when to stop is a fiction. Such judgment is merely one more of those critical faculties which a good painter must have. Homer had it, and never overpainted, but he also never stopped short of perfection. When he stopped work temporarily on any picture he would turn it to the wall, as Titian and Rubens did, so that when he went back to it he would have a fresh impression, but go back he did, always.

This pattern was one of the characteristics of his way of working. Unlike many painters who sit down before a subject with an empty canvas and never leave until it is completed, Homer customarily made rough sketches, studied and planned and built in his mind, and after sufficient observation, returned to his studio and only then began the actual painting. He had a phenomenal memory, not only for details of the subject but for the atmosphere and general mood of a scene. Sometimes he would do watercolors on the spot, but even these often served as intermediate studies for later oils. As has been discussed earlier in connection with *The Wreck*, a striking scene would be stored in his mind and brought to the forefront of his consciousness over and over until, perhaps years later and hundreds of miles away from it, he would be ready to set it down in a picture. Even with his intense physical and mental drive, he could avoid haste, and had the ability to suspend final action until he was perfectly sure — considering and sketching with infinite patience, then proceeding without hesitation, painting deftly and rapidly until he had achieved his purpose.

He was a man of contradictions, but in this he was hardly unique. From his father he inherited a dash and a buoyancy evident in his exuberance, keen wit, love of jokes, even his youthful and gay choice of clothes. From his gentle mother he inherited a calm unhurried nature, perfect self-control, kindly generosity, and incredible perseverance. He would spend hundreds of hours considering a subject and working out the laborious details of its execution, yet to "save time" he had a rubber stamp signature made and even signed his letters with it. He made a point of not mixing with other artists, professional and amateur, had practically no formal art training, and deprecated formal education, yet he offered to send one of the Gatchell boys, Lee, through school because he felt the boy showed promise as an artist.

He made a fetish of health, yet followed a regimen himself that would have killed anyone else. He was hard-working, punctual, temperate although not an abstainer, well-behaved and law-abiding. Yet he felt the greatest sympathy and friendliness toward his old model John Gatchell, who was shiftless, undependable, often drunk, and finally spent time in the State Penitentiary at Thomaston. When he went off to prison, Homer's only word of complaint was that he missed him, for he was a good model. The two men were on two utterly different social levels, yet in some strange way they were friends, and long after Homer's death, John still chuckled over the time he asked Homer why there were so many empty liquor bottles around the studio. Homer simply replied, "Don't know, John, I never bought an empty one in my life."

One of the greatest of American painters, his whole life devoted to painting, almost to the exclusion of every other thing, he had little or no concern for art in a philosophical sense as an impor-tant facet of civilization. By nature kind, gentle, and a real lover of people, he could for the sake of his work be ruthlessly seclu-sive, sarcastic, and even downright insulting, to such an extent that he gained a nationwide reputation as an ill-mannered hermit.

His whole life was a continuous study of nature, and he said over and over (and, I think, really believed) that he painted the world as it was, that the province of the artist was to look, and reproduce in his paintings what affected him most strongly.

To his young friend Wallace Gilchrist he once said, "Gilchrist, when you paint, try to put down exactly what you see. Whatever else you have to offer will come out anyway." Here, near the close of his long and distinguished career, Homer was reaffirming his allegiance to realism, and at the same time, perhaps uncon-sciously, explaining what he had been doing to pass beyond real-ism. His simple statement, it seems to me, is much more than just a piece of sound advice to a young painter. It is a characteristi-cally terse summing up of Homer's ultimate credo as an artist.

CHAPTER SIX

The Final Decade, 1900–1910

THE last ten years of Winslow Homer's life were the first ten years of the twentieth century. It began in his sixty-fourth year, and as if to signalize this event, Homer began to take more time off from his work to enjoy himself. In the photograph collection at the old studio, we find more and more pictures of Winslow relaxing, playing. One shows him with his brother Charles posing on Father Homer's Rock against High Cliff and the sea. Another is of the two standing on the lawn of the Ark, comparing catches of fish. Apparently they had been off on separate expeditions; Charles's flounders were generally caught from boats in Saco Bay, and Winslow's catch of tautog, an elusive and sporty game fish, was probably taken from the rocks, his favorite fishing spot.

He kept up his membership in the Century Club, which had moved in 1891 to its present location at 7 West 43rd Street. It was near Charles's New York apartment, and on Winslow's frequent visits to see his brother, the two Homers, or Winslow alone, would usually drop in at the club for lunch. Some of the older members remembered him long after he died — not as an effusive or clubby person, but as a reserved and pleasant one whose interesting and succinct comments they respected.

The most significant event of 1900 for both Winslow and Charles was the Exposition Universelle Internationale at Paris. Charles was honored by a bronze medal for his distinguished achievements in chemistry. Winslow was invited to serve on an

American jury of twenty artists to select the pictures which were to represent this country at the exposition's art show. The English-version catalogue of the American Fine Arts Exhibit was edited by H. Hobart Nichols, and in a biographical note it described Homer as a "pupil of the National Academy School and Frederick Kindel" (actually Frédéric Rondel). In his preface Nichols attributed the recent rise of an emancipated American school to the "fearless and dominating personalities" of George Inness, Homer Martin, and Alexander Wyant. Winslow Homer was not mentioned.

Each jury member was invited to exhibit some of his own work, and Homer showed *The Coast of Maine, The Fox Hunt, The Lookout — "All's Well,"* and *A Summer Night.* The last had hung for several years, on loan from the artist, in the Cumberland Club in Portland, Maine, without attracting a buyer. But when the French jury made its awards, the grand prizes went to Sargent and Whistler; gold medals were awarded Abbey, Alexander, Brush, Thayer, Chase, Cecilia Beaux, and Homer. And the picture of Homer's which impressed the French Ministry of Fine Arts most of all was *A Summer Night,* which they decided to purchase for the Luxembourg Palace Museum. They honored Homer on the same basis as his fellow Americans who were trained in the French schools, though he of all his countrymen showed the most independent American quality. Discerning European artists were beginning to recognize this originality, ability, and kindred spirit whenever they had an opportunity to observe his work. Walter Pach tells about a meeting with the French Impressionist Monet, when they talked of American painting, and of Winslow Homer, "whom he knew and admired through that painter's nocturne in the Luxembourg."

Homer did not go to Paris to accept his medal; he was in the Adirondacks when Mattie wrote to congratulate him. He was completely surprised, as he had thought the medals all awarded. When he returned to Scarboro, Mrs. Larrabee told me, her father, Zenas Seavey, took some mail to him, and among the parcels was one containing the medal. Mr. Seavey told his family that Winslow was very much moved by it.

One of the themes which he painted from a trip in June to the Adirondacks was *The Pioneer,* now in the Metropolitan Museum. This watercolor is an excellent illustration of Homer's skill in occult balance as a method of surface design, and in spatial organization from the foreground into the distance. The dark foreground pushes the eye into the second plane, and then by alternating passages of light and dark, to the far horizon. This is a baroque device which Homer used repeatedly; its application here is especially reminiscent of his middle period, and is very like the tonal-spatial organization of his *Shepherdess of Houghton Farm* of 1878.

The last decade of Homer's career saw no such outpouring of masterpieces as had the years of the 1890's, but there were still some great works remaining in his brush. Some have become famous "lasts" in one category or another; some brought to perfection subjects going back over many years. He had gained rich experience and developed a consummate skill, though, like an aging athlete, he found it necessary to wait for longer periods for his energy to well up and demand expression. But if he was getting a little tired, at least he never lost patience, nor the hard-earned deftness and experience which make his later painting so rich and satisfying. William Macbeth told Downes that "during his last years, Homer was in poor health and did little work." Actually, in view of his age, he kept at his painting with surprising regularity. After 1900, however, Homer had plenty of money for all his needs and painted more as an avocation than from necessity.

The few oils that he completed in 1900 are among his finest. During a summer squall that year a lumber schooner was driven in between Stratton's Island and the Neck, and Winslow followed her up along the shore until she cleared the rocks. He used the event as a theme for *On a Lee Shore* (1900). The rock formations are so similar to those in *Maine Coast* that a visitor at M. O'Brien

Fig. 72.   WEST POINT, PROUT'S NECK.
1900. Sterling and Francine Clark Art Institute.

and Son's Gallery in Chicago (where it was first shown) asked if it
was a replica. Homer replied that he had in his whole life made
but one replica, the watercolor *A Voice from the Cliffs,* which he
had based on *Hark! The Lark.* O'Brien sold the work to Dr. F. W.
Gunsaulus, president of the Armour Institute of Technology, who
sold it to the Rhode Island School of Design in 1901.

Near Checkley Point, Homer painted the brilliant *West Point,
Prout's Neck* (Fig. 72). Across the flat stretch of Saco Bay are the
distant beaches of Pine Point and Old Orchard and a sky illuminated by a flaming sunset. The technical bravura with which
Homer painted this oil is based upon a confidence that comes
with years of experience. The waves churning between the rocks
are rendered in conventions which he had evolved — amazingly
simplified impressions, yet perfectly convincing. Like the best of
the Japanese masters, Homer was able to sacrifice reality, even
physical possibility — as in the sinuously curling plume of spray
— for aesthetic effect, without seeming implausible. Our minds

[212]

may tell us a wave could not behave like this, but so delightful is the design that we unconsciously feel it ought to.

Homer's most famous piece of 1900 is the mighty oil *Eastern Point, Prout's Neck* (Fig. 74). In the dead center of the picture, surrounded by the creaming waves, is Black Rock, just offshore of the eastern extremity of the Neck, and the whole work is almost a portrait of that perpetually sea-washed ledge. William Hazeltine had done something similar with *Indian Rock* at Narragansett, and so had William T. Richards, N.A., a little-known painter who worked around Newport between 1879 and 1895. Richards was probably the first American painter to combine rocks and surf in the manner which Homer brought to full development. But neither he nor Hazeltine felt the power of the sea as Homer did. Their ocean was an element of calm beauty and gently breaking waves. Homer must have known the Hazeltine picture; Hunt's engraving of it appeared in *Appleton's Journal*, June 19, 1869, on the page facing the Homer picture *Artist in the Country*. Later Frederick Waugh gained a name for his rocks, but compared to Homer's they look geologically impossible, like papier-mâché rocks in a stage setting.

It was this painting that Downes's biography specifically mentioned as having been done in Homer's "portable painting house." I have already given my reasons and those of Winslow's nephew Charles for at least qualifying some of Downes's statements; the photograph (Fig. 73) demonstrates how impossible it would have been for any horse-drawn structure of this sort to be pulled along where this painting was made.

Winslow had acquired Eastern Point from his brother Arthur before 1900; few painters own the seashore subjects of their own masterpieces. But even before he had become a property owner at Eastern Point, Homer had seen its pictorial possibilities, particularly at high tide. One of his earliest watercolors done at Prout's was *Surf at Eastern Point;* though his favorite mares' tails are the only hint in that picture of the weight and power of the waves

Fig. 73. EASTERN POINT, PROUT'S NECK.
Photograph by Philip C. Beam, 1955.

which he was to bring to such racy and vigorous consummation in *Eastern Point, Prout's Neck*.

William Macbeth told Downes that Homer's Quebec watercolors, done over several years but mostly in 1895, marked "practically the end of his watercolor work." This is hardly fair to his output of the early years of the new century; some of these are among his best and most popular works. The years 1900 and 1901 saw some striking watercolors from his trips to southern waters. On his first trip to the Bahamas in 1885 he had made studies of the coral and rock formations there. *Glass Windows, Bahamas* was one of his earliest pieces depicting those islands; in 1898 he painted *Natural Bridge, Nassau* one of his most sweeping panoramas. In 1900 and 1901 he did the watercolors *Bermuda* and *Coral Formations*. These two titles, added to the pictures after Winslow's death by his brother Charles, are I am sure misnomers. The formations are not coral but stratified and water-eroded limestone (karst is the

Fig. 74. EASTERN POINT, PROUT'S NECK.
1900. Sterling and Francine Clark Art Institute.

geological term) common in Cuba, Yucatán, and the West Indies, but extremely rare in Bermuda; hence my guess that the *Bermuda* painting is actually probably the Bahamas. It is not surprising that with so many watercolors from his brush, many of them rather similar in theme and locale, some misnaming should have occurred. And particularly since he himself was occasionally guilty of mistitling, or of dating a picture when he finished and signed it, sometimes years after it had been started.

A picture listed in his Day Book in the Homer Collection as No. 9 of a watercolor group which he sent to Knoedler's in 1902 had been painted the year before, and Homer called it at that time *Bermuda Pigs*. In 1923 the *Revue de l'Art* reproduced it as *Dans le Jungle, Florida*. It is now in the Worcester Art Museum, and known as *Bermuda Settlers*. Several of his pictures are labeled "tornado," although they are actually hurricanes, the proper term for the water-born ocean "twister." Tornados, technically, are generated over land. Part of the confusion of dates and titles arises from his refusal to make, despite his brother Arthur's urging, any list of the whereabouts of his lesser-known pictures. He told Arthur, "During my lifetime I will know where they are, and after I am dead I won't care."

In 1885 he had begun to paint tropical island Negroes in their everyday activities, as he had previously painted plantation Negroes. Typically, his first studies were complex, like *Conch Divers* (Fig. 18). His later subjects became simpler, concentrating on the bodies of the natives, who seem as much at home in the water as on land, as in *The Sponge Diver* (Fig. 19), painted in 1889. None of these pictures gives the impression that the models were posed, but rather that Homer had caught them unselfconsciously at their accustomed tasks. Probably the most popular of the series is the famous 1898 work *Turtle Pound* (Fig. 69). A sketch of it with that title appears as No. 5 (in the same 1902 Day Book list as *Bermuda Pigs*), but for many years it was erroneously called "Turtle Pond." As in many other instances, Homer had his reasons for a particular title, and it is often essential to our understanding of a picture to know what it was.

In 1886, when Homer's tropical scenes were first exhibited in Boston, newspaper critics praised them for their tonal brilliance, but referred to his using primary colors at rather high intensity. Actually his effects are achieved principally by his skillful harmonizing of intensities and his use of large areas of high value, thus allowing the white paper to contribute to the brilliance. It was a technique the Impressionists knew well, one that Dodge MacKnight used effectively; Homer's tropical scenes show his continued use of the method throughout his later years.

It was, like most of Homer's techniques, conscious and carefully worked out. His old watercolor box from the studio at Prout's is now in the Homer Collection at Bowdoin College; in the mixing pans he wrote the names of the few tones which he used continually, making up a kind of permanent watercolor palette. All of this makes it a little difficult to understand why Kenyon Cox would say, "If Homer's color is not, like his workmanship, a positive injury to his expression, it seldom reaches the point of being a positive aid to it." And his statement, "A poor technician, an un-equal colorist, a powerful but untrained draughtsman, his faults might almost overbear his merits were he not a designer of the first rank," is made perfectly ridiculous by even a glance at *Turtle Pound*.

Homer's study of the southern natives is magnificently cli-maxed in two quite simple compositions, *The Bather* and *Rum Cay* (Fig. 68). The latter, under the title *Turtle Cay*, appears as sketch No. 6 in the Day Book entry for July 5, 1902. "Cay" like the Anglicized "key" is from the old native Taino word for island, and there is a Turtle Island off the coast of Georgia. This, or a similar location in the Bahamas, probably gave Homer his original title. He may have rechristened it later; or his brother Charles may have named it after Winslow's death, from Rum Cay, a small is-land east of Nassau.

In 1901 Homer was awarded another gold medal — this time from the Pan-American Exposition at Buffalo, for the watercolors he showed there. The same year he served on the jury for the Carnegie Institute's international exhibition, and during the whole decade honors of this sort came often.

In 1901, too, he had a new cottage built near the eastern end of the Neck. It overlooked Kettle Cove, and he called his new dwell-ing Kettle Cove. He built the stone wall himself, and on the back of a photograph of himself standing in front of it, he wrote proudly, "Photo of stone wall built by Winslow Homer, Scarboro, Me.," and signed it with his rubber-stamp signature. Although he told people he built the house "to die in," he rented it, and actually never lived in it himself. He realized that his career was tapering off, and perhaps because of this feeling began to think more about death.

The cottage was designed by John Calvin Stevens of Portland, whose brother, Henry Wingate Stevens, supervised the construc-tion; the same arrangement had been made when Charles L. Ho-mer and his brother Arthur P. Homer built cottages to rent in 1900. When John Stevens submitted his bill, he suggested as pay-

Fig. 75. THE COMING STORM.
1901. Mrs. Charles R. Henschel.

ment "Any production of Winslow Homer," having in mind one of
the Bermuda watercolors, which were selling in Boston for about
$300 at the time. His brother Henry did indeed get a watercolor
— but John was delighted to receive a magnificent oil, *The Artist's Studio in an Afternoon Fog* (Fig. 41), which the family later
sold to the Rochester Museum. The watercolor that went to Henry
was the delightful *Under the Coco Palm*, one of the Nassau series,
of a native seated under a palm tree drinking from a gourd. He
sold it to Knoedler sometime later and the proceeds were sufficient to put his son (now Dr. Theodore M. Stevens of Portland)
through medical school. Henry Stevens used to bicycle out to
Prout's, often starting before daybreak and stopping en route to
catch a mess of trout. His close friendship with Winslow, according to his nephew John Howard Stevens, dated from one morning
when he gave the artist a handsome fish; from then on they were
on cordial terms.

John Howard Stevens, according to Alexander Bower, was a

member of an amateur watercolor group, The Brush-Ins; he had become acquainted with Homer during the building of the cottage Kettle Cove, and he used to take the group to Prout's for painting trips after he had won the artist's friendship. Often Homer would show them good rock compositions, and would usually join them for a chat when their session was finished. He was affable and, of course, very helpful. He was still painting, although less and less. But if his output was less in quantity than it had been, there was no lowering of its quality.

The Coming Storm (Fig. 75), painted in 1901, is one of his most vigorously painted watercolors — almost the peak of his work in that medium. It is highly simplified, but every device of technique, tonal organization, and design strike the eye with maximum visual impact, paralleling the power of Vlaminck and the Fauves school of the early twentieth century in France.

Another superbly simple design is *Searchlight, Harbor Entrance, Santiago de Cuba* (Fig. 76), also painted in 1901 although Homer conceived it in 1885, when he first visited Cuba. At that time he made several sketches of the old guns at Morro

Fig. 76.   SEARCHLIGHT, HARBOR ENTRANCE,
SANTIAGO DE CUBA.
1901. The Metropolitan Museum of Art.

Castle, and in 1899, when the Spanish-American War made Santiago Harbor famous, he began work on the composition, and finished it in 1901. Perhaps the only really great painting to come out of that conflict, it is almost Mondrian-like in its strong interplay of straight lines and right angles. Homer was not in Cuba during the war, but built the design as he imagined it would have been with the searchlights of the American fleet probing the sky. It was his last experiment with moonlight and electric illumination and is quite haunting in its feeling. Considering the superb quality of this picture, one of the most unusual he ever painted, it is sad to note that Homer's professional experience with it was frustrating. As Goodrich points out, when it was first shown a number of critics quibbled in a most trivial way over whether it was "beautiful" or not, and it did not sell readily. Homer's sole Day Book entry for January 7, 1902, is a terse, "Wrote M. Knoedler net price $2200 for (Santiago)," but the next entry, January 9, reads impatiently, "Not hearing anything I have sent this tel. with regret — as I should have more money — and the doctors and lawyers must take the cake as the Artists are mostly D.F. — net price $2200." Knoedler, nevertheless, had to accept $2000 for it from George A. Hearn.

Since 1894 Homer had been studying the romantic and exciting logging activities on the upper reaches of the Hudson in the Adirondacks; the logjam in *Logging* and the rushing water in *The Rapids, Hudson River,* with its leaping trout, done in the same area, gave him excellent practice in watercolor rendition of different kinds of river scenes. In 1902 in *Hudson River* he varied his approach by using the log motif as the blind from behind which a lumberjack watches two deer.

If financial reward came slowly, honors were coming thick and fast. In 1902 the Pennsylvania Academy of the Fine Arts, the oldest art school in the country, awarded him its Temple gold medal for *Northeaster* (Fig. 55) and *Maine Coast,* which they exhibited. *Cannon Rock* (Fig. 53) won him another gold medal from the Charleston, South Carolina, Exposition, and now the critics were beginning to shower him with approving reviews. Frederick W. Morton, for example, began an article in *Brush and Pencil:* "Winslow Homer is unquestionably the most strictly national painter America has produced. . . . He is great because he has been loyal to himself, to his perceptions and convictions."

Mrs. Marguerite Downing Savage, a painter, met Homer at Prout's at this time, when she was twenty. Running out of yellow ochre while painting at the Neck, she ignored warnings about his unfriendliness, and knocked at Homer's door. To her delighted surprise, he gave her a large tube of ochre in his favorite Winsor & Newton brand, and they became very friendly. He showed great interest in her work, gave her many hints, and went out of his way to introduce her to people who might further her career. Once he brought John W. Beatty, then art director of the Carnegie Institute, to her studio to see her paintings.

From her hand we have the best portrait of him as he looked late in life. At an Ark tea party (perhaps to encourage her) he asked her to do a drawing of him, and after several sittings it was completed. According to his nephew Charles, Winslow liked it very much. When Mrs. Savage signed and dated it on September 6, 1902, Winslow paid her three twenty-dollar gold pieces for it.

This same year he finally finished a marine on which he had been working since 1900. At that time he decided that Chicago should be a good market, and arranged with his dealer there, O'Brien and Son, to do a marine especially for them to handle. For two years he made slow but steady progress, reporting to them periodically. At last what he had come to call "the O'Brien picture" or just "the O'B" was done; he titled it *Early Morning After a Storm at Sea* (Fig. 79), and his correspondence with O'Brien has been published by Downes. The letters are revealing, both of his process of painting and of his personality. He bragged a little in one letter — and then appended a sketch of "a man blowing his own horn."

Actually the picture culminated a project of study, observation, and work that had taken fifteen years. Soon after settling at

[221]

Fig. 77.   HIGH CLIFF, PROUT'S NECK.
Photograph by Robert Macbeth, 1936.

Prout's in 1883 Homer had found what is perhaps the most paint-able section of shoreline on the whole Neck (Fig. 77) and painted *Prout's Neck, Breakers* there. In 1887 he used the spot for *Break-ing Wave* (Fig. 78), and in 1894 returned to the subject from a slightly different viewpoint to do *Prout's Neck Surf*. Seven years later he turned at last to oil, and with this more "massive" me-dium captured in the "O'Brien picture" the thundering force of the great breakers.

Far more spectacular than the surf during a storm are these mighty waves which roll in from the sea for days afterward, and Homer caught them at their best, illuminated by the pale red sheen of early morning. It went off to O'Brien and Son on Novem-ber 14, 1902, and Homer was, as he said in a letter to them, "glad to get it out of my sight before I finish it too highly and spoil it." He was relieved to finish the two-year job, which he was satisfied represented all that he could have put into it. He told Mrs. Charles L. Homer that he considered it his finest marine.

On May 4, 1902, he had written to his brother Charles not to think of Prout's for two weeks — "you could not stand the cold" — and added a sketch on the envelope of frozen water pipes, burst by the cold. Again, on June 12, 1902, he wrote that he was

[222]

Fig. 78. BREAKING WAVE.
1887. Courtesy, Museum of Fine Arts, Boston.

Fig. 79. EARLY MORNING AFTER A STORM AT SEA.
1902. The Cleveland Museum of Art.

off the next week for Montreal to stay two days at the Windsor, then on down to Saratoga. There are many more letters to the family through 1902. The day before Christmas he sent a brief note from the Neck wishing Charles and Mattie a Happy New Year and Christmas, and including the terse comment: "I am very well; ten above zero."

One blessing that came with financial success was more time to fish. A photograph of 1903 and a watercolor that Boyas Gonzales painted for Mattie in 1904 show Winslow at his favorite sport. He liked to fish from the rocks. Arthur owned a small sailboat, *Texas*, and Charles a real yacht with several paid hands whom he boarded at the Checkley House. Laden with plenty of food and a hamper of liquor, he and Arthur would go out deep-sea fishing and stay for a week or more, and once in a while Winslow would go along, but he really cared little about sailing and detested line fishing as "sissy stuff." He never borrowed a boat from either, and rarely went sailing. He owned a small sloop, which he moored near his studio at Ferry Beach, but used the boat only as a model. No one at Prout's ever saw him sail it, and eventually it rotted at the mooring.

He loved the ocean but never swam; he loved boats but rarely sailed. His interest in them was pictorial — whether they were heavy Gloucester dories or Tynemouth fishing smacks — the lithe canoes of Canada and the Adirondacks, which he used for fishing, being the exception. The sleek schooners and sloops attracted his artist's eye on his first visit to the tropics in 1885, and he began painting them. The Canajoharie, N.Y., Art Gallery has a sparkling watercolor, *Sponge Fishing, Bahamas*, with a theme he repeated in *Sloop, Bermuda* (Fig. 67) in 1899 and in other similar watercolors, continually simplifying, reducing them more and more to their essential lines and masses.

In the spring and summer of 1903 he was in good health, good humor, and enjoyed his customary appetite, according to a letter to Charles dated May 11, inviting him to "come direct to my house — I will have pea soup English Mutton Chops and Native Dandelion Greens. Fresh lobsters for supper with Potato Salad

Bermuda Onions. . . . I am very well & enjoy this life here much better than bumming about in hotels." That season he allowed Charles Walker, the station agent, to photograph him. It was one of Walker's most artistic efforts, and Winslow humorously captioned it *In the Gloaming.* At the end of the year he wrote Arthur that he intended to go to Key West, adding, "I have an idea at present of doing some work but do not know how long that will last — at any rate I will once more have a good feed — goat flesh — & smoke some good cigars & catch some red Snappers. . . ."

At Key West, in 1903, he brought to completion his studies of the trim white local fishing boats at anchor in the harbor. Sometimes it was a cluster of boats, as in *Schooners at Anchor, Key West* and other watercolors, often with working crew members, occasionally with no figures at all. In other studies, like *Fishing Boats, Key West,* he did portraits of single boats, with the simplest of designs; a mere hint of modeling conveys the feeling of form, solidity, and distance. One of these, *Stowing Sail, Bahamas* (Fig. 80), is a study in washes of unsurpassed freshness. Three small

Fig. 80. STOWING SAIL, BAHAMAS.
1903. The Art Institute of Chicago.

Fig. 81.   WINSLOW HOMER AND GUIDES, HOMOSASSA
RIVER, FLORIDA.
Photograph taken about 1904. Homer Collection, Bowdoin Col-
lege Museum of Art.

touches of vivid red enliven the otherwise cool palette, and the
generally high key values convey the impression of airiness and
brilliance so characteristic of the tropics. Even in these simple,
apparently ingenuous watercolors, Homer's incredibly effective
use of color is undeniable evidence that he is one of the most
knowledgeable colorists in all modern art. After all, as Downes
notes in his biography, Homer's library included "a copy of Chevreul's book on color, which his elder brother had given him many
years before, and this copy was almost read to pieces, so worn was
it with use."

[226]

Fig. 82. PALM TREES, FLORIDA.
Photographed by Winslow Homer about 1904. Homer Collection,
Bowdoin College Museum of Art.

Stowing Sail, Bahamas is dated December 22, 1903, and Homer must have gone directly afterward to Homosassa, Florida, a fisherman's paradise on the central west coast about sixty miles north of Tampa, for he wrote Arthur from there in January 1904. He said he intended, when his guide left him for another engagement on the twentieth, to "take my own boat & work half the time & fish on my own hook. I have not done any business this fall so far & I shall only paint to see if I am up to it — & with a chance of paying my expenses." In the same letter from Homosassa he called the fishing there "the best in America" and listed some of

[227]

Fig. 83.   HOMOSASSA RIVER.
1904. The Brooklyn Museum.

Fig. 84.   THE TURKEY BUZZARD.
1904. Worcester Art Museum.

the fish that he was taking, several accompanied by sketches:
"Cavalle, yellow tail, silver body, Channel Bass   Look like a new
$20 gold piece. Trout, Black Bass, Sheepshead." The lack of a
guide and the weight of his almost seventy years could not keep
Homer from fishing, wherever he found himself. Like Lake Tourilli and Roberval in Canada, the combination of quiet isolation
(Homosassa must have had fewer than two hundred inhabitants
at that time) and excellent fishing delighted Homer, for his letters show him in an exuberant mood.

As to his painting, he was apparently up to it, for out of this
trip of 1904 to Homosassa came some of his finest watercolors.
Two photographs in the Homer Collection (Figs. 81 and 82)
taken with Homer's circular camera on one of his stays in Florida
show the appearance of the river areas around the turn of the
century. In the stern of one of these is Homer himself, rowed by
his Negro guides in one of the small skiffs characteristic of the
region. Both *Homosassa River* (Fig. 83) and *The Turkey Buzzard*

[229]

(Fig. 84) include similar boats and guides translated into watercolor but subordinated to the artist's perceptive simplification of the limpid waters and lush vegetation of the Florida scene.

Like the true sportsman, Homer not only enjoyed fishing but showed a real respect and even love for the game against which he pitted his skill and knowledge. He had a wide, almost scientific knowledge of innumerable species of fish, their habits and characteristics. He was fascinated by their grace and silvery beauty; to this he added an admiration for their strength and fighting qualities.

In a long series of paintings he paid tribute to the fisherman's art and saluted his worthy opponents, the fish themselves. Back in 1889 he had painted an impeccable watercolor, *Two Trout*, that is almost a still life. Far more often, though, he turned to the painting of fish in their natural habitats, and created in this way one of his real masterpieces, the delightful *The Mink Pond* of 1891 (Fig. 64). This gracious and engaging work is a perfect refutation of the contemporary comment that Homer was devoid of charm, as the words of Cox expressed: "He has no lyrical fervor; makes no attempt to express his own emotion or his mood."

Paul Klee, Jyaku-chu, Okyo Maruyama, Toko — these and many other artists have painted fish and fishing scenes down through the centuries, each capturing some significant detail of aquatic life, but none of them showing more observation, understanding, skill or enthusiasm than Homer does in his magnificent *Trout Breaking* of 1889 (Fig. 21), or in *Ouananiche Fishing* (Fig. 66), an 1897 painting from the Canadian salmon country, centered at Lake St. John in the Province of Quebec.

It was against the background of this long experience and enthusiasm that Homer finally brought this special subject to a climax. In 1904 at Homosassa he conceived a painting of the fish that to him resembled "a new $20 gold piece": *Channel Bass*, a watercolor that shows the hooked fish shooting through the turquoise water, over the bottle-littered river bottom. It was one of his finest works. Downes mentions these bottles as "a curious conceit," and quotes Homer as saying, "If anyone in Maine buys the picture, I will remove the bottles." Whether it was a distaste for litter or the Maine prohibitionists' unpleasant association of bottles with the demon rum, the picture was long unsold and in the possession of Charles L. Homer. It is now in the outstanding collection of Homer's work in the Metropolitan Museum in New York.

Another gold medal was bestowed on Homer in 1904 — this one from the Art Department of the Louisiana Purchase Exposition at St. Louis, for his exhibition there of two oils, *Early Morning* and *Weather-beaten,* and a watercolor, *Snake in the Grass.*

In October of that year he wrote a get-well note to Charles, who had been thrown from his Stanley Steamer when he tried to find out how fast it would go. Repeated public warnings from the Stanley twins did not prevent attempts of this sort, although the fact that a Stanley racer in 1907 attained (before it crashed) a speed of 100 m.p.h. proved how risky it could be. Fortunately Charles was only slightly injured. Winslow's letter shows his concern, although it was couched in playful terms.

> *Dear Charlie*
>
> *If you had hit your head in place of your shoulder it would have been a broken neck — That is all — !
> . . . if you are still impatient a club out of a chestnut tree might fetch you if you could be carried there in your convalescence — I am sincerely sorry for this accident*
>
>

Yours affectionately
> WINSLOW

A month later he wrote again to Charles, saying that he intended to stay until the snow was four inches deep and then get out. This letter he closes with the rather touching statement of how he felt about Prout's: "Football — Thanksgiving & other things will make no difference — this is the best place."

As Christmas approached, he wrote again, boasting of his good health, although many other residents of the Neck were sick:

Dec 17, 1904

> *Dear Charlie*
>
> *The snow is now deep & I am packing to leave soon*
> *Foss tumbled off a load of lumber hit his shoulder on the*
> *hard ground*
> *Googin's eyes played out laid up with blinders — every*
> *other man & all the women sick up & down the road*
> *with grippe*
> *I am very well*
>
>
>
> *Affectionately*
> **WINSLOW**
>

By 1904, Arthur's son, the "little Charlie" of a number of Homer's humorous letters and cartoons, was a graduate of the Massachusetts Institute of Technology and a grown young man. His Uncle Winslow immortalized him that year as the principal figure in his *Kissing the Moon* (Fig. 85), a wonderfully simple and natural yet unusual composition of a boat hidden in the trough of the waves.

One of the most disquieting reminders of advancing age is the sudden realization that one's friends are dying, one by one. In 1905 Homer's old friend Zenas Seavey died, and although Homer barely mentïoned the fact in a letter to Charles, he was deeply moved. Zenas's daughter Mrs. Larrabee told me that for the last two weeks of his life her father's physician had put him on a diet of whiskey and water. As soon as Winslow heard this, he ordered S. S. Pierce to send Mr. Seavey a five-gallon demijohn of the best whiskey available.

Still, life went on as the new century installed new mores and revealed the shape of things to come. About this time Mrs. Vaill's family, who owned the Southgate Hotel (now the Black Point

Fig. 85. KISSING THE MOON.
1904. Addison Gallery of American Art.

Inn) and its connected stable, went along with the new trend toward automobile transportation. After Harris Seavey's four-horse
coach accepted its fate, Homer reluctantly used cars, although
when leaving on a trip he would often send a note by Henry Lee to
Harry Kaler to come and take him and his luggage to the station,
sometimes ending, "A wagon will do."

In the spring of 1905 he went to the Adirondacks, but did only
a little sketching; most of the time he relaxed and fished. With
summer he joined his family at the Neck, but made no serious
attempt at work until the fall storms renewed his old zeal. In October there was one of those once-in-a-generation blows, and he
roamed the cliffs every afternoon during the storm and for some
time afterward.

On one of these days Mrs. Howard Larrabee walked with him
around the cliffs to the surf beach, where he gave her an enlight-

[233]

ening lecture on the surf and the proper way to observe it. He would indicate a distant wave, and then show her how to follow its course until it broke over the sixty-foot cliffs. That was the scientific observer in Homer, studying the inspiring and dynamic order in nature. Sometimes, Mrs. Larrabee added, he would be like a poet and watch in silence for long minutes.

In the Cooper Union Museum's unexcelled collection of Homer's drawings there are several sketches in which he set down impressions while they were still vivid, many of which he used in laying out finished paintings. One is of just such a storm as the one of 1905.

In an article on "Shipwrecks Along the New England Coast" in the *New England Magazine* Amy Woods wrote in 1904, "There is no more dangerous coastline in the world than that of New England, bristling with jagged rocks and hidden shoals, and many a gallant ship has weathered a storm at sea only to founder on this treacherous shore." Of the 273 Coast Guard lifesaving stations in operation on the entire American coast in 1903, she explained, 87 — nearly one-third — were needed for the New England coast alone. Portland has a safe, sheltered harbor, but the coastal area around Prout's often belied its beautiful appearance, as many ships found out to their sorrow. The two-masted schooner *Fanny Neadeth* was driven ashore just east of Prout's in 1901, and here, where Higgins Beach joins Prout's, are the barnacle-encrusted bones of another schooner, still visible at low tide. Roswell Goggins explained why so many sailing vessels piled up on Higgins Beach and in the vicinity of Cape Elizabeth at the entrance to Portland Harbor — several during the first decade of the 1900's.

Higgins Beach faces south and the water there is shallow, even quite far out. But a breakwater which ran from the end of the beach to a small island just offshore gave a certain amount of protection from the rocky cliffs of Cape Elizabeth and the stony eastern end of nearby Stratton's Island to the west, and during the fishing season many shallow-draft fishing sloops would run into this shelter to avoid the harbor duties at Portland. A larger

Fig. 86. THE WRECKED SCHOONER.
About 1908. City Art Museum of St. Louis.

schooner trying to claw off this lee shore in a bad blow had no
such refuge and could either attempt to clear the dangerous
Prout's Neck cliffs or equally formidable Stratton's Island and
gain the comparative shelter of Saco Bay on the west side or fight
her way east in the hope of rounding Cape Elizabeth and getting
to a safe mooring in Portland Harbor. Even under power, either
alternative is difficult; under sail alone it was often impossible. In
On a Lee Shore of 1900 Homer depicted a schooner which he had
seen on the way to safety. For one of his last and finest watercolors he painted a ship whose ending was tragic. It is entitled *The
Wrecked Schooner* (Fig. 86), and Goodrich has associated the
disaster represented with the loss of the *Washington B. Thomas*.
With some qualifications the deduction is logical, for both the
ship and her destruction were widely publicized and fit the circumstances of Homer's activity.

The *Washington B. Thomas* was built by the Washburn

brothers at the Watts shipyard in Thomaston, Maine, and launched in April 1903. At that time the builders of wooden ships along the New England coast and the masters and sailors who manned them were fighting for their lives against competition from metal steamships. To cope with this challenge, the Washburn brothers constructed a super-schooner, the *Washington B. Thomas*, launched her with considerable fanfare, and engaged a distinguished and famous master, Captain William J. Lermond, to sail her to Norfolk, Virginia, on her maiden voyage for a shipload of coal, a lucrative cargo at that time. En route back to her destination, Portland Harbor, she was becalmed in a dense fog near the harbor mouth on the night of June 11. When Captain Lermond could not obtain a harbor pilot at that hour, he unwittingly anchored in the foggy darkness close to the lee shore of Stratton's Island. During the night one of the most violent gales of the decade arose from the southeast without warning, tore the ship loose from both her anchors, drove her upon the jagged rocks at the southwest corner of the island, and began to batter her to pieces. Even the bare factual account in the Coast Guard records conveys the appalling plight of the crew throughout the night. So high were the mountainous seas that it was not until the following day that a Coast Guard surfboat from the Cape Elizabeth station was able to fight its way to the side of the ship and rescue the fourteen members of the crew, but Captain Lermond's bride of a few months had been torn from his grasp and carried out to sea. The captain, who had invested his life's savings in a third of the cargo but had no money left to insure his part, lost not only his wife but his entire fortune and died a broken man a few years later (1918) in a charity institution for seamen, the Snug Harbor home at New York.

The fate of the schooner was equally tragic. The gale continued to lash the ocean into a fury and tore the ship asunder until nothing was left except debris, which washed ashore at Old Orchard Beach throughout the following week.

Although the Coast Guard records list twelve shipwrecks in the area of the Cape Elizabeth station for the first decade of the century, the descriptions of none compare in character or importance with the doom of the *Washington B. Thomas* and the widespread attention given to the collapse of the ambitious hopes she carried. Goodrich is surely correct in believing that this calamity of 1903 provided the initial inspiration for *The Wrecked Schooner*. The actual painting of the finished watercolor may be reconstructed to some extent from the following evidence supplied by eyewitnesses of the tragedy.

Mrs. George Putnam stated that when the fog lifted on June 12, she watched the breakup of the helpless vessel on distant Stratton's Island from the cliffs below her cottage at Prout's along with other residents who had gathered on the cliffs. By that time the masts had been torn from the ship and only the hull was faintly visible in its position on the other side of the island. Leonard Libby, who was at that time working for Winslow Homer, said that he informed the artist of the catastrophe as soon as he heard the news and rushed with him to the cliffs. Homer, out of long habit, had grabbed a handy academy board on the way out of his studio, and on this he made, according to Mr. Libby, a simple sketch of the scene. He could do no more because even his keen eyesight could barely discern the outline of the hull. Both Mrs. Putnam and Mr. Libby stressed the point that Stratton's Island is six miles from the nearest point of observation on the cliffs at Prout's, and since the seas continued to run high, none but the Coast Guard rescue squad reached the ship before it was broken up. Homer's closest physical contact was through a few spars and the ship's wheel, which he collected from among the debris on Old Orchard Beach. The spars he arranged decoratively, Mrs. Putnam recalled, in a small garden he kept beside Duck Pond on his land at Eastern Point, where they remained until taken away by souvenir hunters a few years ago. The wheel of the ship he hung over the mantelpiece in the living room of his studio, where it can be seen today. After the passage of so many years, Mr. Libby could not remember the date of the destruction of the

Washington B. Thomas but was certain that it was the wreck he watched with the artist and which he saw him sketch. He recollected clearly that residents of Prout's went by boat to Stratton's Island after the storm subsided and salvaged enough coal from the rocks to last them through the following winter. She was, moreover, the only coal schooner to founder on those shores during that decade, a fact confirmed by the records of the Coast Guard service. Homer himself did not sign or date his watercolor of *The Wrecked Schooner* or identify the actual subject, to the consternation of his admirers and historians of art. Did he convert the sketch into the watercolor at once while details and impression were fresh in his memory? Or was the theme developed at a later date, and his final picture in that medium?

Charles L. Homer, a naval architect and himself a witness of the wreck, said that his uncle had regarded his original pencil or crayon sketch as a mere note because of the distance at which he had been forced to work, and that he had set the project aside until he had thought about it for several years. Exactly how much time Winslow took he did not recall.

The artist's sister-in-law, Martha Homer, was more positive about the dating of the picture. She maintained unequivocally until her death in 1936 that *The Wrecked Schooner* was the last watercolor Homer ever completed. In view of her keen interest in his work and her opportunity to follow it from a residence not more than a hundred feet from his studio, her opinion should not be lightly set aside. If, as she asserted, the picture was not finished until near the end of his life, the most plausible date would be some time late in 1908, when we know he was at Prout's and painting.

For all except antiquarians, the matter of dating may be of thin interest, but Homer's procedures and results are the interest of many. For him to jot a quick record of an event on the handiest piece of paper (sometimes the back of an old envelope) was second nature. To use it as the basis of a work of art brought to full development at a later time was equally consistent with his practice. It permitted him through a process of careful interpretation to transform a specific but limited incident into an artistic statement reflecting years of concern for the tragic aspects of life at sea and thus give it a larger meaning.

How much liberty he used in this case was pointed out specifically for me by Mr. James Harvie, naval architect for the noted shipbuilding firm at Bath, Maine (the Bath Iron Works), who indicated the extent to which Homer had departed from his source. To his expert eyes there were numerous differences to be found in old photographs between the size, proportions, and design of the five-masted, 290-foot, 2639-ton *Washington B. Thomas,* the largest schooner ever built at Thomaston, and the relatively small two-master in *The Wrecked Schooner,* which Mr. Harvie estimated would not have exceeded a thousand tons or one hundred and fifty feet in length. By the time Homer completed his translation of actuality into art, the *Washington B. Thomas* had been altered beyond recognition, at least as the source of his inspiration.

Here again Homer had simply employed freely his gift for dramatization of a concept to the benefit of the picture's power as a work of art instead of a mere record. Formal and dramatic elements were combined by him in any way he thought advisable to give his composition the fullest possible clarity and vividness of effect. It is fitting that this watercolor of a subject so close to his interests emerged as one of his strongest. How far he had progressed since 1880 can be seen by comparing it with the beautifully luminous but tame *Wreck Near Gloucester,* painted before he went to Tynemouth or settled at Prout's.

Another great marine of his final period is *Diamond Shoal* (Fig. 87), of 1905, the last important watercolor Homer signed and dated, and one of his most impressive. It may not have been the last he did — Mattie asserted firmly that *The Wrecked Schooner* was completed later, and it may have been. The probably insoluble matter is not all-important, as both were certainly painted about the same time, and both are equally powerful. Homer showed wonderful originality in *Diamond Shoal* in emphasizing

Fig. 87.   DIAMOND SHOAL.
1905. International Business Machines Corporation.

the headlong, lifting surge of the schooner by opposing it at right angles to the distant, bobbing lightship. This interplay of conflicting attitudes not only gives the composition striking interest and vitality but creates a feeling of dramatic tension. A lifetime of painting in watercolor was joined in this work to Homer's years of intense study of boats and the sea. The two paintings mark a magnificent crowning achievement of a career in which skill, energy, and inspiration were maintained to the end.

The winter of 1905 was a bitter one, and Homer in December commented on the weather in a letter to Arthur: "All work here has been stopped since Tuesday night big snow storm high drifts. Cannot see church steps." It was too much even for him. That month he left for Atlantic City, and from the Hotel Rudolf addressed a letter on December 23 to his nephew Charles which shows some of his sentiments about his family: "After seeing a tramp steamer burn up this morning (out at sea) I had a quiet half hour to think of my relations knowing they were not on board

& I made a draft of my impression of things in the way of a Christmas greeting to them." A little later he went farther south for the winter. In February he wrote Charles from the Monticello at Norfolk, Virginia, and in the letter gave evidence that he was not particularly happy at having achieved his three-score years and ten: "I do not consider this 70th much of a subject of congratulation."

He returned to Prout's for the summer and lived quietly in the studio. Yet 1906 was the first year of his long career in which he did no painting to speak of. On arriving at Scarboro, according to Downes, he found a letter which had been waiting for him since the previous November. It was from Mrs. Grace K. Curtis, who told him that she had been born on the coast of Maine, loved it still, and admired his work, particularly as she knew so many of the scenes he had painted. She added that she was an invalid, and would cherish some simple sketch from his own hand. He replied immediately, explaining his delay in answering her letter, and sent three sketches of the Maine coast, saying he was "quite through with them."

It was in 1906 that *The Gulf Stream* was finally purchased by the Metropolitan for $4500, the highest price he had ever received, in spite of some caustic and ridiculing comments about it, and that Homer wrote his sharp note in reply to some of the sillier criticisms. His irritation was only passing, however, for the late Harold T. Pulsifer of Brunswick, Maine, called on Charles and Mattie at the Ark during that summer and spent nearly two hours with Winslow in his studio, finding him in a good frame of mind.

From the summer into October of that year he seems to have had a serious illness, the first of his adult life, and he hated it. In a letter to Charles written October 18 he shows bitter resentment that he could be afflicted like ordinary mortals, saying, "I have entirely recovered my health — I am now an ordinary old man — No doubt about either of the above facts . . ." By December he was feeling healthy enough to invite Arthur to Christmas dinner, and by the middle of January 1907 was his old buoyant self. He wrote to Charles commiserating with him on his suffering of the past two years and on a recent trip to the dentist; of himself he said, "I am not any too bad considering my age."

Early in February he went to Atlantic City as usual and on to Norfolk as he had done for the past five or six years, but in May he was back at Scarboro. He wrote to Charles that he was reopening his "factory" (the old painting room in the studio) after two years. Actually he had done a little work during 1905, and under the pressure of inspiration had painted *Diamond Shoal*, but he had followed nothing like his old prolific program.

As Winslow and his two brothers were growing old, the next generation, rather disconcertingly to him, was growing up. "Little Arthur" was already married, and his brother Charles ("Two") was to be married to Mary George Clark on June 8, 1907. Winslow attended the wedding on his way to Saratoga and the Adirondacks. He was impeccably groomed, and rivaled his more cosmopolitan older brother in the graciousness and charm of his behavior.

Charles L. Homer himself told me that when he brought his bride to the Neck for the first time when his uncle was there, he warned her not to disturb Uncle Winslow, and she had not gone near him. After about ten days Winslow appeared at El Rancho and said, "I just want to inquire about the state of your combined healths. Incidentally, I want to see if my nephew is being properly fed, for it is my understanding that no bride can cook a decent meal." He held out two baskets and said, "Will you accept these with my compliments?" In his studio fireplace he had prepared two broiled chickens, some beets, and some potatoes boiled in their jackets. At the insistence of Georgie, as she was called by the family, he finally agreed to stay and eat with them; after that he and Georgie were friends, and she was granted the almost unique privilege of visiting him in his studio by the hour.

That Thanksgiving, Homer entertained his brother Arthur and young Charles and his bride at the Parker House in Boston.

Charles recalled that the mantelpiece was lined from end to end with Manhattans. The young couple each had one — Arthur and Winslow took care of the rest, and he vividly remembered Winslow's saying, "You and Georgie are too young." Sherry with the soup, a Moselle with the fish, Burgundy with the turkey, and brandy and coffee were topped off with a thimbleful of Kirschwasser — yet the seventy-one-year-old Homer was apparently unaffected when he bade his guests good-night.

After Thanksgiving, Homer returned to Scarboro, and had recovered sufficiently from his illness of the previous year to set to work in the reopened "factory," for on November 30 he wrote his brother Charles that he had finished "that picture, by letting well enough alone . . . which is the rule for grown artists *only*. This picture will not be new to you as it is the two girls and old pilot that have been hanging in my studio so long. Only I have made a new thing representing evening — It is now a *very fine picture*." He concluded by chiding Charles, "You are rather well. That would not do for me — I am A No 1 in health. I regret that I must leave here soon — it is so cold," explaining, "frost on the windows this morning . . . mop frozen stiff in the other room."

The painting is *Early Evening* now in the Freer Gallery. Soon after his return from Tynemouth he had started an oil of the subject from a sketch, or a series of sketches, of the north coast girls and an old weatherbeaten fisherman. The cliffs, however, are those of Prout's, and by introducing the quality of evening light in 1907, when he finished the work, he made it a very impressive piece indeed. The effect of dusk gives it a lovely mood of quietness surrounding the dignified, sculpturesque figures. It was Homer's final salute to Tynemouth, where more than a quarter of a century before he had found in the atmosphere and the people of that North Sea port exactly what he needed to make his stay there the crucial turning point of his career.

Actually the unfinished canvas had never been ignored; occasionally, to amuse visitors, Homer had a trick of touching the right corner of the ancient fisherman's eye with a stick of chalk, and instead of looking out to sea the old salt would have the appearance of leering at the two girls.

Through December he wrote cheerful and informative letters to his two brothers in spite of references to frigid weather, giving every evidence that he was in good health and high spirits and (for a man of his age) quite active, saying in one letter to Charles, "I am enjoying every minute of my life here, busy outdoors, & in."

During the early months of 1908 he did no painting of any consequence. He traveled, wrote a good many letters, and busied himself with matters of real estate at Prout's. The first three months of the year he spent in Florida. When he returned to Prout's at the end of March he found that thieves had broken into his studio and ransacked the place; he was particularly upset by the loss of a watch which had been given him by his mother. He did more dabbling with real estate; he had his own house shingled; he plowed over and grassed in what had been his flower garden, as it required too much attention, and made plans to go to the Adirondacks as soon as Charles had arrived at the Neck for the summer.

The spring of 1908 brought Homer a significant honor — one of the most important events of his artistic life. The Carnegie Institute, under the direction of Homer's old friend John Beatty, made a special feature of his work at its twelfth annual exhibition. Twenty-two oils, the finest of his whole career, were borrowed from public and private collections and given the best possible hanging in their own gallery. Downes is very perceptive in his comments on the event:

> One of the most remarkable things about this [exhibition] is that it was so largely made up of pictures owned by the public art museums of America. Eight museums were represented by no less than eleven pictures — just one half of the entire collection. In the history of the art of painting in America it would be quite impossible to find another living

artist with such a large number of his works in public collections. The exhibition in Pittsburgh constituted the first serious attempt to give an adequate idea of what the man stood for in art, and it was an overwhelming demonstration of his originality, power, and distinction.

Unfortunately the opinion of so distinguished an institution as the Carnegie, and the warm public reaction to the show, failed to win over several critics who continued to voice their scorn for Homer's work until his death. The most virulent of these was Miss Leila Mechlin, whose article "Winslow Homer" in the *International Studio* of June 1908 demonstrates an almost incredible facility for inept judgment. A few excerpts are typical of the venom in which she dipped her pen. "There is none who, from the technical standpoint, commonly paints more hatefully than he. . . . Apparently the mode of delivery does not concern him . . . In his method of rendering Mr. Homer outrages the strongest convictions of perhaps nine-tenths of the present-day painters."

The patent injustice of her attack irritated and shocked Homer's many admirers, and may well have been a reason why Downes decided, at that time, to undertake a biography of the painter. However, when he wrote to Homer to enlist his aid in the project, Homer replied, in a letter dated August 1908:

> It may seem ungrateful to you that after your twenty-five years of hard work in booming my pictures I should not agree with you in regard to that proposed sketch of my life. But I think it would probably kill me to have such a thing appear, and, as the most interesting part of my life is of no concern to the public, I must decline to give you any particulars in regard to it.

Homer's attitude toward adverse criticism came as near as that of any modern artist to turning the other cheek. He rarely bothered to answer his critics, but maintained his composure with dignity and the confidence that his work would speak for him. Time has shown that he could have chosen no better spokesman.

Late in May of that year, Homer suffered a cerebral hemorrhage, and Arthur, who had already arrived at Prout's, persuaded
him to come to El Rancho where he could be properly cared for.
He only stayed about two weeks; when Arthur went into his bedroom one morning it was empty. There was a note on the living
room desk: "I am well and have quit. Winslow."

He was far from well, for the stroke had left him with some
muscular impairment and had seriously affected his eyesight. He
would, of course, firmly deny any such thing, and during the next
few days while he remained at the studio and gathered his
strength, he would not admit any incapacity. Harvey Urquahart,
Homer's favorite local butcher, told Charles L. Homer about de-
livering an order to his uncle after his eyesight had been affected
by one of his illnesses: "I stopped to give Winslow his meat, and
he came out to the cart, which was like old Bart Pillsbury's with
the back that raised up rather than a door. Well, Winnie came
around and gave his head a hard bump, and he blasted Hell out of
me. I said, 'Now look here, you got no business going 'round when
you can't see.' Then Winslow said, nicely, 'Come in, Harvey.' We
sat and drank for a while, and then Winnie said, 'Now, dammit,
you can't see either. Go out and bump your damned cart your-
self.' "

When Winslow wrote to his older brother he made no attempt
to disguise his condition, but tried to treat it lightly. In his first
attempt to write (on June 2) he said, "only think I shall shave
tomorrow — & if I do I shall call myself well all but tying my
neck tie — Thank Heaven — Dear Mattie — thank you for the
flowers." Two days later he wrote again.

June 4th 1908

Dear Charlie

   I can tie my neck tie very well now & shall be able to
shave very soon —
   I received the canvas just now but wish to tackle the

[246]

job without it some time providing I can paint as well
as ever — I think my pictures better from having one
eye in the pot & one eye up the chimney
  A new departure in the world
  I am very well tell Dr. Bartlett —

Love to Mattie

W

Only nineteen days after he had begun to recover from the stroke, Homer was at the Worden Hotel in Saratoga Springs, New York, and there he wrote to Arthur. This was on June 23, and by July 3 he was at the North Woods Club in the Adirondacks. Apparently he was not aware that he had had a shock, for in a letter written on that day to Charles, he closes, "Try and find out what was the matter with me — Affectionately, Bro Winslow." He still could not tie his tie as he used to, in a sailor's knot, even though he tried every few days to do so, but he reassured his brother that: "As you see I now can write plain enough — & in all other matters everything is all right."

As had become his practice, he left the North Woods Club late in July, spent a night at Saratoga, and went on to Montreal and the old cabin in Canada. He returned in August to Prout's, and judging from his letters during the fall, one would think illness had never touched him. He was well enough to catch some smelts on Sunday afternoon (October 5), clean them and salt them lightly, and on Monday he sent a mess to Charles and Mattie with directions for cooking them, finishing with "I am very well" underlined three times. On December 8 he wrote them that he was planning to stay at Prout's until January, when he would go to New York for about three days, then directly south to Homosassa. In this letter he says, "I am painting when it is light enough on a most surprising picture but the days are short & sometimes very dark."

Fig. 88. RIGHT AND LEFT.
1909. National Gallery of Art, Washington, D.C. Gift of the Avalon Foundation.

The "surprising picture," which he finished on January 7, is the popular duck-hunting scene *Right and Left* (Fig. 88). Homer's long association with guides and sportsmen, and his keenly observant interest in every sport, had made him thoroughly familiar with all the activities of field and stream. In the Cooper Union Museum is a superb drawing of a wild duck in flight which Homer did when preparing to paint his familiar canvas *Wild Geese*. This piece shows three wild geese flying over the sand dunes, and at the foot of the picture two birds apparently shot down by an unseen hunter. But Mrs. Roland C. Lincoln, the first owner of the painting, asserted, according to Downes, that the work was originally titled *At the Foot of the Lighthouse,* and the two birds may well have been killed when they flew into the structure, a not uncommon occurrence. Although more complex, it is reminiscent of Okyo Maruyama's *Flying Wild Geese.*

Right and Left, painted eleven years later, seems to be Homer's simplified and even more striking solution to the same problem that had engaged both artists. Charles L. Homer told me how his

[248]

uncle came to get the idea for the painting. Winslow's good friend Phineas W. Sprague from Boston summered at the Neck, and often stayed on for the fall duck-hunting. In October or November of 1908 he bagged several ducks, and hung a brace of them on Homer's studio door. When Winslow saw them his imagination was set at work and he soon conceived the design for *Right and Left*. A hunter at the instant of firing is a static and almost wooden figure; Homer decided, by putting him into the far distance, barely suggested by the sketchiest of strokes and half-hidden behind the left-hand bird, to reduce the man and his boat to almost nothing. By doing this he takes us out to where the ducks are, makes us experience the target end of the event, as if we ourselves are the hunted and feel the impact of the hit. It is a complete reversal of the approach of Eakins and of most other painters of sporting scenes.

To see what a shotgun blast looked like to someone under fire, Homer hired Will Googins to row offshore in a boat and fire blank charges up toward the cliff where he stood watching. So accurate is his interpretation of the scene that a sportsman who saw the untitled canvas at its first showing (at the Knoedler Galleries in 1909) instantly exclaimed, "Right and left!" — the hunter's term for knocking down a bird with each barrel. And *Right and Left* the painting was titled. Long owned by Mrs. Randal Morgan of Philadelphia, who knew Homer for many summers at Prout's, the work is now in the National Gallery.

Homer spent the Christmas season of 1909 at the Neck, and as usual wrote to all the Homer clan, sending them greetings, telling of his good health, his work, and even sending Arthur a present of twenty-five dollars, "to be used for Christmas cheer in form of strange grub, & all the English illustrated Papers *for your family.*"

For years Homer had been threatening to give up painting, but 1909 found him still at his easel. Compared with his efforts of the decade before, his output was small, but it was significant. Most of what he was doing seems to be the realization of old ideas which he had "thought of painting someday," or the last perfect-

Fig. 89.   CAPE TRINITY, SAGUENAY RIVER.
1904. Guennol Collection, New York City.

ing touches to a few unfinished works. It was almost as if he knew
that "someday" was here, and was tying up all the loose ends of
his artistic life.

In 1883 he had painted in watercolor a panorama which he
had called *Marine View with Mountains*, a not particularly impressive study. Twelve years later, on a visit to Canada in 1895,
he explored the theme again in *Wolfe's Cove* (Fig. 48), just before or after a trip up the Saguenay. He came to love that wild and
silent section of Quebec, and in 1904 indicated in a letter to
Charles that he was working on a picture of the Cape Trinity
country. The Cooper Union Museum has a small sketch of Homer's which he had squared off for transfer to canvas. It was the
prototype of his *Cape Trinity, Saguenay River* (Fig. 89) which he
completed (according to the date on the back of the stretcher) in
June 1909.

The painting is less concerned with the details of nature than
with its magnificence and its almost forbidding grandeur. From
the painter's low viewpoint at the level of the river the mountains
tower into the clouds, their massive and timeworn silhouettes

looming up like symbols of eternity. This thoughtful, brooding work was Homer's last tribute to the mysterious, transforming power of moonlight.

A whole chapter in Homer's painted "book of North America" is concerned with the exciting and colorful activity along the American and Canadian rivers. His fascination with the fishermen and their boats at Tynemouth and on the Maine coast was paralleled by a keen interest in the north-woods guides and their primitive but exceedingly practical canoes. What his horse was to the Westerner, the canoe is to the woodsman, and whether gliding silently over a glassy lake or plunging dangerously through the creaming white water of a rushing torrent, the man becomes almost part of his craft. Homer saw the beauty of this relationship even in the '70's and '80's, but only set about depicting it seriously with several studies in the last decade of the nineteenth century. Early experiments are *The Guide* (1895), *The North Woods* of 1894 (Fig. 38), and *The Portage* (1897).

On the Saguenay he did *Entering the First Rapid* and *Saguenay River, Lower Rapids* in 1897, and *Saguenay River, Grand Discharge, St. Johns, P. Q.* in 1902, playing around the theme of swiftly moving water. This is no easy task, and requires a nice balance between order and turbulence to avoid making the water look chaotic on the one hand or frozen on the other. The Japanese, of course, were masters of the process. Kano Motonobu's *Rapids*, Hiroshige's *Whirlpool at Naruta* and Maruyama Okyo's *Hozu River* are classic examples of successful handling of this difficult problem, and there is more than a slight similarity to their conventions in Homer's method of simplifying and stylizing fast-moving water. He related this natural phenomenon to human life by using it as a background for fishing scenes, as in *Casting*, in which the fisherman is, I feel sure, his brother Charles. But he needed more excitement, a closer relationship between the man and the setting, and even a sense of danger to give the theme the dramatic quality he had been able to capture when dealing with men and the sea. He found his drama in the tricky and dangerous

Fig. 90.   SHOOTING THE RAPIDS AT GRAND
DISCHARGE.
1902. The Brooklyn Museum.

work of the guides shooting the rapids of the wild Canadian
rivers.

When he began to study the possibilities, in 1895, he made a
series of photographs which were rather dull but provided some
useful records of the theme; that year he painted *Trip to Chicoutimi*. Two years later he tried again with *Shooting the Rapids,
Canoe in the Rapids* (Fig. 65) and the similar *Ile Marlin, P. Q.*,
(probably a mistitling of Ile Maligne at the Southern end of Lake
St. John). By 1902 he was ready to do the dashing watercolor
Shooting the Rapids at Grand Discharge (Fig. 90), a painting
whose distilled intensity is a culmination of the whole series in
watercolor, but he was to go even further in oil.

Downes wrote that Homer sent the group to Doll and Richards
in Boston, but in July 1904 asked that they be returned, as he
proposed painting another picture. Apparently he wanted to review them in preparation for his oil *Shooting the Rapids, Sague-*

Fig. 91.   SHOOTING THE RAPIDS, SAGUENAY RIVER.
1905. The Metropolitan Museum of Art.

nay River (Fig. 91). I had the story of the painting's conception from Homer's nephew Charles.

On Winslow's first visit to Lake St. John in Quebec Province, he and his brother Charles had four very capable guides, and at the end of their stay the two Homers showed their appreciation by giving each guide a pint of good whiskey — a literal "pourboire." With quite understandable concern lest the bottles be broken on the downstream trip, they foresightedly drank them on the spot. According to reports from the Homer brothers, the cruise was a memorable one. From his own canoe Winslow could watch his brother's guides paddling with a wild and alcoholic disregard for either hell or high water, while Charles hung to the gunwales in sheer terror. Winslow recorded the scene in the oil which critics call an unfinished work; I agree, however, with his nephew's opinion that the painter considered it completed. He could have "finished" it any time from 1905 on, and had he wished to do so, I feel that he would have by 1907, when he was doing just that to other partly painted works. He often spoke of "letting well enough alone," and many of his later paintings are nearly if not just as sketchy as this one. As his nephew said to me, "The impression-istic quality gained by stopping short of detailed final touches or slickness is perfectly appropriate to this subject."

Homer stayed at Prout's through most of 1909, painting occa-sionally and putting his economic affairs in order. He had con-cluded a most formal agreement with Arthur over the removal of a barn that spring. Like the good Yankee that he was, he was very businesslike in such matters, even with his brothers.

He wrote to Arthur the middle of November, declining an invi-tation for Thanksgiving, and was apparently busy: "I breakfast at 7 every day. I have little time for anything   many letters unan-swered & work unfinished. *I am painting*. I am at last through work at 3:30 — Cannot give you any more time — W. Homer."

The canvas on which he was working was to be the last oil painting that he would finish, the magnificent picture entitled *Driftwood* (Fig. 92). The figure in this wonderfully conceived de-sign is that of a fisherman in oilskins and sou'wester trying to salvage a huge log or spar driven inshore by a fall storm — the same old interplay of man and the elements that had become the theme of Homer's philosophy. The scene is plainly that at Kettle Cove, which Homer had come to love so deeply that he had built his house "to die in" there, and where, thirty-four years previ-ously, when he visited his newly married brother, he had made his first drawing (*The Honeymoon of Mr. and Mrs. Arthur B. Ho-mer*) at Prout's Neck. After he had finished painting *Driftwood*, he knew that he would never paint again. He took his palette, deliberately messed it up, and hung it with his maulstick on the wall of his studio. That was his way of saying "Finis."

During the opening weeks of 1910 he felt his strength failing, but admitted it reluctantly. A letter to Arthur, written from the Hotel Seville in New York on January 18 tells of his medical treat-ments and that "there has been no particular change in my case

Fig. 92.   DRIFTWOOD.
1909. Dr. and Mrs. Samuel Emlen Stokes.

. . . it is only an acid stomach — all the other machines are in perfect order."

He returned to Prout's when summer came. William Macbeth visited him there late in August, and took a photograph of his old friend (the last, as far as we know), who obligingly removed his hat to pose. Homer was, as always, immaculately dressed and held himself erect, but his face is old, lined, and tired. Ill as he was, he insisted on roaming the Neck with Macbeth, who wrote a moving account of the visit which Downes recounts. In it he tells how Homer would stop here and there, saying, " 'From this point I painted *The Fox Hunt,* from over there *The Undertow'* and so on, pointing to the scene of many a familiar canvas." After luncheon they looked over a portfolio of charcoal sketches and watercolors, which they had often done before. Homer tried to find something new to show his friend, but finally closed the cover saying, "No, you have had them all . . ." There was nothing new, and there would not be.

Charles told me of his uncle's last few days. By September the artist was visibly ill and could hardly see, but stayed in his studio and refused help from anyone until he finally was persuaded to go to Arthur's cottage, but he stayed there only a week and then returned to the studio. Dr. B. F. Wentworth of Scarboro diagnosed his illness as a severe hemorrhage of the stomach and put him to bed; he refused to have a woman attend him, and the family obtained the services of a male nurse from Boston. Stubborn as ever, he refused to die "until he was good and ready," and about the middle of September sat up and asked how soon he could have a drink and a smoke. During the next two weeks he chatted cheerfully with his brothers about some of the escapades of their boyhood in Cambridge. On the morning of the 29th of September he took a sudden change for the worse, and died at half-past one that afternoon.

On October 3 his body was carried to Cambridge, and after a brief ceremony was cremated in accordance with his wishes. His ashes were buried in the family lot at Mount Auburn cemetery between the graves of his parents. His estate, appraised by his old friend Mr. Frank Coolbroth, was valued at about seventy thousand dollars. The rest he had spent or given away.

As with many famous men, his death did what even the persuasiveness of his art had not — it silenced the last few abusive critics, and there was no word of dissent from the praises that were printed in honor of his great talent, honesty, and indomitable spirit. But if he could have read his obituary in the Portland *Daily Press* he would undoubtedly have been dismayed. Worshipping youth as he did all his life, when he grew old he deter-

mined to outlive the eighty-nine years granted to both his father
and grandfather — and he did live to be seventy-four and was
immensely proud of it. But the headline in the Portland paper
reported his age at death as a mere sixty-three. Could the outspoken Homer have seen it, I wonder what profane and peppery
comment he would have made . . .

Homer was born in 1836 and died in 1910; in a very real sense,
the span of his life comprised the true nineteenth century. His
personality suited that time well, and even the one great tragic,
disturbing event of his period, the American Civil War, came
when he was young and adaptable, and enlarged rather than upset his outlook and his fortunes. True, he found some of the superficial aspects of his era distasteful, but he was fundamentally
in harmony with the society of which he was a part. In many
respects his period was a good one in which to live, and after a
full and satisfying life, he died before the First World War and
the Jazz Age overwhelmed the kind of life he had known. Many
great artists have outlived their happiest days. Fate was kinder to
Winslow Homer.

Appendix

THIS appendix furnishes the names of owners of pictures by Winslow Homer which are mentioned in the text, insofar as the ownership is known to the author. Pictures reproduced as figures are excepted, since the legends and list of illustrations supply the owners' names. Former ownership by Charles L. Homer is indicated because of the unquestionable authenticity and historic interest of pictures in his collection. The collection may be said to have comprised the Homer family collection and often to have represented special favorites of the artist. He gave them over a period of years to his two brothers, who bequeathed them to Charles.

Adirondack Lake. Museum of Fine Arts, Boston, Massachusetts.
Adirondack Scene. Cooper Union Museum, New York City.
Adirondacks. Fogg Art Museum, Cambridge, Massachusetts.
Adolescence. Homer Collection, Bowdoin College Museum of Art, Brunswick, Me. Given to Bowdoin recently by Mrs. Homer.
After the Hunt. Los Angeles County Museum, Los Angeles, California.
Afterglow. Museum of Fine Arts, Boston, Massachusetts.
Artist in the Country. *Appleton's Journal,* June 19, 1869.
Backrush. Mr. and Mrs. Charles Shipman Payson.
Bass Fishing, Florida. Formerly Charles L. Homer.
Bather. Metropolitan Museum, New York City.

Below Zero. F. P. Moore.
Bermuda. Metropolitan Museum, New York City.
Bermuda Pigs. Worcester Art Museum, Worcester, Massachusetts.
Big Pines. Formerly Charles L. Homer.
Blue Boat. Museum of Fine Arts, Boston, Massachusetts.
Boatman. Brooklyn Museum, Brooklyn, New York
Boats of the Devonshire Coast. Museum of Fine Arts, Boston, Massachusetts.
Boy Fishing. Dr. Anthony T. Ladd.
Breakers Near Rocks, Prout's Neck. Philadelphia Museum of Art, Philadelphia, Pennsylvania.
Breaking Storm, Maine Coast. Art Institute of Chicago, Chicago, Illinois.
Breaking Wave on a Shore Line. Worcester Art Museum, Worcester, Massachusetts.
Breezing Up. National Gallery of Art, Washington, D. C.
Buccaneers. Cleveland Museum of Art, Cleveland, Ohio.
Bungalow, Bermuda. Metropolitan Museum, New York City.
Burnt Mountain. Mrs. Charles R. Henschel.
Camp Fire. Metropolitan Museum, New York City.
Casting. Addison Gallery of American Art, Andover, Massachusetts.
Channel Bass. Metropolitan Museum, New York City; formerly Charles L. Homer.
Coast in Winter. Worcester Art Museum, Worcester, Massachusetts.
Coast of Maine. Art Institute of Chicago, Chicago, Illinois.
Coral Formations. Worcester Art Museum, Worcester, Massachusetts.
Croquet Scene. Art Institute of Chicago, Chicago, Illinois.
Danger Ahead. Appleton's Journal, April 30, 1870.
Deer Drinking. Mr. and Mrs. Courtlandt P. Dixon.
Derelict and Sharks. Frank L. Babbott.
Dory. Museum of Fine Arts, Boston, Massachusetts.
Early Morning. Freer Gallery, Washington, D. C.
Eastern Point, Prout's Neck (Prang chromolithograph). Metropolitan Museum, New York City.
End of the Day. Art Institute of Chicago, Chicago, Illinois.
Entering the First Rapid. James J. Storrow.
Fallen Deer. Museum of Fine Arts, Boston, Massachusetts.
Farmhouse. Homer Collection, Bowdoin College Museum of Art, Brunswick, Maine.
Fisher Girl, The. Museum of Art, Amherst College, Amherst, Massachusetts.
Fisher Girl. Museum of Fine Arts, Boston, Massachusetts.
Fisher Girl on the Beach. Brooklyn Museum, Brooklyn, New York.
Fisherman's Holiday. Freer Gallery, Washington, D. C.
Fishermen Beaching a Boat. Cooper Union Museum, New York City.
Fishing Boats, Key West. Metropolitan Museum, New York City.
Fishing in the Adirondacks. Fogg Art Museum, Cambridge, Massachusetts.
Fishing Off Scarboro. Art Institute of Chicago, Chicago, Illinois.
Fishwives. Currier Gallery of Art.
Flamborough Head, England. Art Institute of Chicago, Chicago, Illinois.
Florida Jungle. Worcester Art Museum, Worcester, Massachusetts.
Flower Garden. Metropolitan Museum, New York City.

Glass Windows, Bahamas. Brooklyn Museum, Brooklyn, New York.

Governor's Palace, Havana. Formerly Charles L. Homer.

Governor's Wife, Bahama Islands. Rhode Island School of Design, Providence, Rhode Island.

Guide. Mr. and Mrs. Charles Shipman Payson.

Guide Carrying a Deer. Mr. and Mrs. Charles Shipman Payson.

Gulf Stream (study). Cooper Union Museum, New York City.

Hark! The Lark. Layton Art Gallery, Milwaukee, Wisconsin.

Heavy Surf, Prout's. White House Collection, Washington, D. C.; formerly Charles L. Homer.

Honeymoon of Mr. and Mrs. Arthur B. Homer. Mrs. Alice Homer Willauer; formerly Charles L. Homer.

Hound and Hunter. National Gallery of Art, Washington, D. C.

House and Trees in Nassau. Brooklyn Museum, Brooklyn, New York.

Hudson River. Museum of Fine Arts, Boston, Massachusetts.

Hunting Dog Among Dead Trees. Museum of Fine Arts, Boston, Massachusetts.

Huntsman and Dogs. Philadelphia Museum of Art, Philadelphia, Pennsylvania.

Ile Marlin, P.Q. Mrs. Charles R. Henschel.

Incoming Tide, Scarborough, Maine. Mrs. Charles R. Henschel.

Indian Camp, Montagnis Indians, Pointe Bleue, Quebec. Museum of Fine Arts, Boston, Massachusetts.

Indian Camp, Roberval, P. Q. Cleveland Museum of Art, Cleveland, Ohio; formerly Charles L. Homer.

Inside the Bar. Metropolitan Museum, New York City.

In the Jungle, Florida. Brooklyn Museum, Brooklyn, New York.

Light Blue Sea at Prout's. Formerly Charles L. Homer.

Light on the Sea. Corcoran Gallery of Art, Washington, D. C.

Logging. Corcoran Gallery of Art, Washington, D. C.

Logging. Mrs. Edwin S. Webster.

Long Branch, New Jersey. Museum of Fine Arts, Boston, Massachusetts.

Lookout. Fogg Art Museum, Cambridge, Massachusetts.

Maine Coast. Metropolitan Museum, New York City.

Mending the Nets. Mr. and Mrs. Solton Engel.

Moonlight. Canajoharie Art Gallery, Canajoharie, New York.

Mountains and Palms, Cuba. Mrs. Charles L. Homer; formerly Charles L. Homer.

Musicians. Metropolitan Museum, New York City.

Nassau, N. P. Bahamas. Formerly Charles L. Homer.

Natural Bridge, Nassau. Metropolitan Museum, New York City.

North Woods (Prang chromolithograph). Addison Gallery of American Art, Andover, Massachusetts, and Clark Art Institute, Williamstown, Massachusetts.

North Woods Club. Art Institute of Chicago, Chicago, Illinois.

Nursemaid. Mrs. Norman B. Woolworth.

Old Friends. Worcester Art Museum, Worcester, Massachusetts.

Old Settlers, Adirondacks. Museum of Fine Arts, Boston, Massachusetts.

On a Lee Shore. Rhode Island School of Design, Providence, Rhode Island.

On the Cliff. Addison Gallery of American Art, Andover, Massachusetts.
Oranges on a Branch. Formerly Charles L. Homer.
Palm Tree, Nassau. Metropolitan Museum, New York City.
Palm Trees, Nassau. Toledo Art Museum; formerly Charles L. Homer.
Palm Trees, St. John's River, Florida. Formerly Charles L. Homer.
Parliament Buildings. Joseph H. Hirshhorn; formerly Charles L. Homer.
Perils of the Sea. Clark Art Institute, Williamstown, Massachusetts.
Pioneer. Metropolitan Museum, New York City.
Portage. Mrs. Richard de Wolfe Brixey.
Portrait of Captain Smith. Fine Arts Gallery of San Diego, San Diego, California.
Prisoners from the Front. Metropolitan Museum, New York City.
Prout's Neck, Breakers. Art Institute of Chicago, Chicago, Illinois.
Prout's Neck, Evening. Art Institute of Chicago, Chicago, Illinois.
Prout's Neck, Looking Toward Old Orchard. Addison Gallery of American Art, Andover, Massachusetts.
Prout's Neck Surf. Philadelphia Museum of Art, Philadelphia, Pennsylvania.
Rainy Day in Camp. Metropolitan Museum, New York City.
Rapids, Hudson River. Art Institute of Chicago, Chicago, Illinois.
Road in Nassau. Mrs. F. M. Blake.
Rowing Homeward. Phillips Gallery, Washington, D. C.
Royal Palms, Cuba. Cooper Union Museum, New York City.
Saguenay River, Grand Discharge, St. Johns, P. Q. Mrs. Frederica Frelinghuysen Emert.
Saguenay River, Lower Rapids. Mr. James J. Storrow.
Sailing the Catboat. Mr. and Mrs. Arturo Peralta-Ramos; formerly Charles L. Homer.
Salt Kettle. Fogg Art Museum, Cambridge, Massachusetts.
Schooner at Anchor. Clark Art Institute, Williamstown, Massachusetts.
Schooner on Saco Bay. Formerly Charles L. Homer.
Schooners at Anchor, Key West. Mrs. Richard de Wolfe Brixey.
Schooners in the Moonlight. Formerly Charles L. Homer.
Scotch Mist. Marion Kooler McNay Art Institute, San Antonio, Texas.
Shark Fishing. Laurence S. Rockefeller.
Shepherdess of Houghton Farm. Pulsifer Collection, Colby College, Waterville, Maine.
Shore and Surf. Metropolitan Museum, New York City.
Shore and Trees at Nassau. Brooklyn Museum, Brooklyn, New York.
Signal of Distress. Mrs. Charles F. Williams.
Signal of Distress (study). Cooper Union Museum, New York City.
Skating in Central Park. City Art Museum of St. Louis, St. Louis, Missouri.
Sketch of a Soldier. Cooper Union Museum, New York City.
Small Sloop, Saco Bay. Formerly Charles L. Homer.
Snake in the Grass. J. C. Nicoll.
Spanish Flag. Philadelphia Museum of Art, Philadelphia, Pennsylvania.
Startled. Philadelphia Museum of Art.
Storm on the English Coast. Mrs. Roger S. Warner.
Sunday Morning in Virginia. Cincinnati Art Museum, Cincinnati, Ohio.

Sunset Over Saco Bay. Formerly Charles L. Homer.

Sunshine and Shadow, Prout's Neck. Art Institute of Chicago, Chicago, Illinois.

Surf at Eastern Point. Mrs. Charles Cheney Hyde.

Taking an Observation. Mr. and Mrs. Charles Shipman Payson.

Three Girls. Mrs. Roger S. Warner.

Three Men in a Canoe. Knoedler Galleries, New York City; formerly Charles L. Homer.

Till Death Do Us Part (etching of *Undertow*) sketches. Clark Art Institute, Williamstown, Massachusetts.

Town in Bermuda. Formerly Charles L. Homer.

Trip to Chicoutimi. Mrs. Edwin S. Webster.

Two Figures by the Sea. Denver Art Museum, Denver, Colorado.

Two Men in a Canoe. Mr. and Mrs. Charles Shipman Payson; formerly Charles L. Homer.

Two Trout. International Business Machines Corporation; formerly Charles L. Homer.

Under the Coco Palm. Fogg Art Museum, Cambridge, Massachusetts.

Undertow. Clark Art Institute, Williamstown, Massachusetts.

Visit from the Old Mistress. National Collection of Fine Arts, Smithsonian Institution, Washington, D. C.

Voice from the Cliffs. Mr. and Mrs. Stavos Niarchos.

Wall, Nassau. Metropolitan Museum, New York City.

Watching a Storm on the English Coast. Mrs. Jacob H. Rand.

Watching the Breakers. Art Institute of Chicago, Chicago, Illinois.

Weather-Beaten. Mr. and Mrs. Charles Shipman Payson.

White Rowboat, Florida. Formerly Charles L. Homer.

Wild Geese. Mr. and Mrs. Charles Shipman Payson.

Windstorm, Bahamas. Mrs. Richard de Wolfe Brixey.

Woodman and Fallen Tree. Museum of Fine Arts, Boston, Massachusetts.

Wreck Near Gloucester. Museum of Art, Carnegie Institute.

Wreck of the Atlantic. Harper's Weekly, April 26, 1873.

Wreck of the Iron Crown. Mr. and Mrs. Carleton Mitchell.

Young Ducks. Mr. and Mrs. Charles Shipman Payson.

Selected Bibliography

American Landscape: The Private Collection of the Late Burton Mansfield. New York: Privately Printed, 1933.

American Paintings Belonging to William T. Evans. Catalogue. New York: American Art Galleries, 1900.

An Introduction to Homer. Exhibition Catalogue. New York: Macbeth Gallery, 1936.

Annual Reports of the United States Life-Saving Service. Washington, Government Printing Office. 1900–1910.

Atwood, Wallace W. *The Physiographic Provinces of North America.* Boston and New York: Ginn and Company, 1940.

Barker, Virgil. *American Painting: History and Interpretation.* New York: The Macmillan Company, 1950.

Beam, Philip C. *The Language of Art.* New York: The Ronald Press Company, 1958.

Beatty, John W. "American Art at Paris." *American Review of Reviews* (New York), November 1923.

Benjamin, Samuel Greene Wheeler. *Art in America: A Critical and Historical Sketch.* New York: Harper & Brothers, 1880.

Bolton, Theodore. "The Art of Winslow Homer: An Estimate in 1932." *Fine Arts* (New York), February 1932.

———. "Watercolors by Winslow Homer: Critique and Catalogue." *Fine Arts* (New York), April 1932.

Boswell, Peyton, Jr. *Modern American Painting.* New York: Dodd, Mead and Company, 1939.

Brief Account of the Family of Homer or de Homere, of Ettingshall, County Stafford, England, and Boston, Massachusetts. Albany, New York: Joel Munsells Sons, 1889.

Brinton, Christian. "Winslow Homer." *Scribner's Magazine* (New York), January 1911.

Buchanan, Charles L. "Inness and Winslow Homer." *Bookman* (New York), July 1918.

Burroughs, Alan. *Limners and Likenesses.* Cambridge: Harvard University Press, 1936.

Caffin, Charles H. *American Masters of Painting.* New York: Doubleday, Page and Company, 1902.

———. "American Painters of the Sea." *Critic* (New York), December 1903.

———. "A Note on the Art of Winslow Homer." *Bulletin of the Metropolitan Museum of Art* (New York), March 1911.

———. *Story of American Painting.* New York: Doubleday, Page and Company, 1907.

Cahill, Holger, and Alfred H. Barr, Jr., *Art in America in Modern Times.* New York: Reynal and Hitchcock, 1934.

Carnegie Institute, Pittsburgh. *Watercolors by Homer and Sargent.* 1917.

Chase, J. Eastman. "Some Recollections of Winslow Homer." *Harper's Weekly* (New York), October 22, 1910.

Church, William C. "A Midwinter Resort, with Engravings of Winslow Homer's Water-color Studies in Nassau." *Century Magazine* (New York), February 1887.

Clemens, Samuel Langhorn. *The Gilded Age: A Tale of Today.* Hartford: American Publishing Company, 1874.

Clifford, Henry. "Winslow Homer Oils, Watercolors and Drawings in a Centenary Exhibit Current in Philadelphia." *Art News* (New York), May 9, 1936.

Coburn, F. W. "Winslow Homer's 'Fog Warning'." *New England Magazine,* new series, vol. 38 (New York), July 1908.

Coffin, William A. "A Painter of the Sea." *Century Magazine* (New York), September 1899.

Cole, Walter W. "Crayon Studies by Winslow Homer." *Brush and Pencil* (New York), January 1903.

Cook, Clarence. *Art and Artists of Our Time.* Vol. 3. New York: S. Hess. 1888.

Cortissoz, Royal. *John La Farge: A Memoir and a Study.* Boston: Houghton Mifflin Company, 1911.

———. Foreword, *Catalogue of an Exhibition of Watercolors by Winslow Homer.* Carnegie Institute, Pittsburgh. September 9–October 23, 1923.

Cox, Kenyon. "The Art of Winslow Homer." *Scribner's Magazine* (New York), September 1914.

———. "Three Pictures by Winslow Homer in the Metropolitan Museum." *Burlington Magazine* (London), November 1907.

———. "Watercolors of Winslow Homer." *Art in America* (New York), October 1914.

———. *Winslow Homer.* New York: Privately Printed, 1914.

Davidson, Martha. "A Final Word on Winslow Homer." *Art News* (New York), December 19, 1936.

Dezarrois, André. "Une exposition de l'art americaine." *Revue de l'art ancien et moderne* (Paris), July 1923.

Downes, William Howe. "American Painters of the Sea." *American Magazine of Art* (New York), November 1931.

——. "American Paintings in the Boston Art Museum." *Brush and Pencil* (New York), August 1900.

——. *The Life and Works of Winslow Homer.* Boston: Houghton Mifflin Company, 1911.

——. *Twelve Great Artists.* Boston: Little, Brown and Company, 1900.

——. "Winslow Homer." *Dictionary of American Biography.* Vol. 9. New York: Charles Scribner's Sons, 1932.

——, and F. T. Robinson. "Later American Masters." *New England Magazine* (Boston), April 1896.

——, and F. T. Robinson. "Winslow Homer." *Art Interchange* (New York), May 1894.

duBois, Guy Pène. "Two Exhibitions by Winslow Homer." *Magazine of Art* (New York), January 1937.

Eliot, Alexander. *Three Hundred Years of American Painting.* New York: Time, Inc., 1957.

Encyclopaedia Britannica. Fourteenth Edition. Chicago and New York: Encyclopaedia Britannica, Inc., 1937.

Flexner, James Thomas. *American Painting: First Flowers of Our Wilderness.* Boston: Houghton Mifflin Company, 1947.

——. *A Short History of American Painting.* Boston: Houghton Mifflin Company, 1950.

——. *That Wilder Image.* Boston: Little, Brown and Company, 1962.

Fowler, Frank. "An Exponent of Design in Painting." *Scribner's Magazine* (New York), May 1903.

Freund, Frank E. W. "Winslow Homer." *Sketch Book Magazine* (New York), August 1926.

Gabriel, Ralph Henry. *The Lure of the Frontier.* Pageant of America Series. Vol. 2. New Haven: Yale University Press, 1929.

——. *Toilers of Land and Sea.* Pageant of America Series. Vol. 3. New Haven: Yale University Press, 1929.

Gallatin, A. E. *American Water-Colourists.* New York: E. P. Dutton and Company, 1922.

——. "Winslow Homer Memorial Exhibition." *Art and Progress* (New York), April 1911.

Gardner, Albert Ten Eyck. Introduction, *Winslow Homer: A Retrospective Exhibition.* National Gallery of Art, November 1958–January 1959; Metropolitan Museum of Art, January–March 1959; Museum of Fine Arts, Boston, March–May 1959.

——. *Winslow Homer, American Artist: His World and His Work.* New York: Clarkson N. Potter, 1961.

Gentner, Philip J. "Winslow Homer and His Work." *Bulletin of the Worcester Art Museum* (Worcester, Mass.), October 1911; January 1912.

Goodrich, Lloyd. *A Century of American Landscape Painting, 1800–1900.* Pittsburgh: Carnegie Institute, 1939. New York: Whitney Museum of American Art, 1938.

————. "A 'Lost' Winslow Homer." *Worcester Art Museum Annual*. Worcester, Mass.: 1937–1938.

————. *American Watercolor and Winslow Homer*. Minneapolis: The Walker Art Center, 1945.

————. *Winslow Homer*. New York: Witney Museum of American Art and Macmillan Company, 1944.

————. *Winslow Homer*. New York: George Braziller, Inc., 1959.

————. Foreword, *Winslow Homer Centenary Exhibition*. New York: Whitney Museum of American Art, 1937.

Goodyear, William H., *Watercolors of Winslow Homer*. New York: Brooklyn Museum Quarterly, October 1915.

————. "Watercolors by Winslow Homer." *Brooklyn Museum Quarterly* (New York), October 1915.

Graham, Lois Homer. "An Intimate Glimpse of Winslow Homer's Art." *Vassar Journal of Undergraduate Studies* (Poughkeepsie, New York), May 1936.

"A Great American Painter." *Outlook* (New York), February 18, 1911.

"A Great Painter of the Ocean." *Current Literature* (New York), July 1908.

Hagen, Oskar. *The Birth of the American Tradition in Art*. New York and London: Charles Scribner's Sons, 1940.

Hartley, Marsden. *Adventures in the Arts*. New York: Boni and Liverwright, Inc., 1921.

Hartmann, Sadakichi. *History of American Art*. Vol. 1. Boston: L. C. Page and Company, 1902.

Hathaway, Calvin S. "Drawings by Winslow Homer in the Museum's Collections." *Chronicle of the Museum for the Arts of Decoration of Cooper Union* (New York), April 1936.

Hind, C. Lewis, "American Paintings in Germany." *International Studio* (New York), September 1910.

Hitchcock, Ripley. *The Art of the World: World's Columbian Exposition*. (Chicago, 1893). New York: D. Appleton and Company, 1894.

Hoeber, Arthur. "Winslow Homer, A Painter of the Sea." *World's Work* (New York), February 1911.

"Homer, Artist and Man, Revealed at a Show in His Old Studio." *Art Digest* (New York), August 1936.

"Homer Memorial Exhibit." *American Art News* (New York), February 11, 1911.

Howard, W. Stanton. "Winslow Homer's 'Northeaster'." *Harper's Magazine* (New York), March 1910.

Ingalls, Hunter. "Elements in the Development of Winslow Homer." *Art Journal* XXIV: 1, Fall 1964.

Isham, Samuel. *History of American Painting*. New York: Macmillan Company, 1927.

Katz, Leslie. "The Modernity of Winslow Homer." *Arts* (New York), February 1959.

King, Daisy B. "An Exceptional Case." *Corcoran Art Journal* (Washington, D. C.), November 1893.

Knauff, C. W. "Winslow Homer, Art Amateur." *Churchman* (New York), July 23, 1898.

————. "Winslow Homer." *Churchman* (New York), November 23, 1898.

Krout, John Allen. *Annals of American Sport*. Pageant of America Series. Vol. 15. New Haven: Yale University Press, 1929.

La Farge, John. *Considerations on Painting*. New York and London: Macmillan Company, 1895.

La Follette, Suzanne. *Art in America*. New York: Harper and Brothers, 1929.

Lane, James W. "Winslow Homer, Artist." *Commonweal* (New York), April 3, 1936.

Larkin, Oliver W. *Art and Life in America*. New York: Rinehart and Company, 1949.

"The Late Winslow Homer." *Fine Arts Journal* (Chicago), November 1910.

Libbey, Dorothy Shaw. *Scarborough Becomes a Town*. Freeport, Maine: Bond Wheelwright, 1955.

Lowell, Orson. "Water Colors by Winslow Homer." *Brush and Pencil* (Chicago), June 1898.

Macbeth, Robert W. Foreword, *Centenary Loan Exhibition*. Prout's Neck, Maine: Prout's Neck Association, 1936.

————. *Winslow Homer*. New York: Living American Art, 1936.

Mather, Frank Jewett, Jr. "The Art of Winslow Homer." *Nation* (New York), March 2, 1911.

————. *Estimates in Art*. Series II. New York: Henry Holt and Company, 1931.

————. Foreword, *Homer-Ryder-Eakins Exhibition*. New York: Museum of Modern Art, 1930.

————. "Winslow Homer as a Book Illustrator." *Princeton University Library Chronicle* (Princeton, N. J.), November 1939.

————, Charles Rufus Morey and William James Henderson. *The American Spirit in Art*. Pageant of America Series. Vol. 12. New Haven: Yale University Press, 1929.

McCausland, Elizabeth and Hermann Warner Williams, Jr. *American Processional*. 1492–1900. Washington, D. C. The Corcoran Gallery of Art, 1950.

————. "Winslow Homer — Graphic Artist." *Prints*. New York. April 1937.

McSpadden, J. Walker. *Famous Painters of America*. New York: Thomas Y. Crowell & Company, 1907.

Mechlin, Leila. "Winslow Homer." *International Studio* (New York), June 1908.

Metropolitan Museum of Art. *Winslow Homer Memorial Exhibition*. New York: February 1911.

Michel, André. *Histoire de l'Art*. Vol. 8. Paris: A. Colin, 1929.

Montignani, John B. "Winslow Homer, Artist-Correspondent." *Bulletin of the Metropolitan Museum of Art* (New York), June 1942.

Morton, Frederick W. "Winslow Homer, Artist." *Brush and Pencil* (Chicago), April 1902.

Moulton, Augustus F. *Old Prout's Neck*. Portland, Maine: Marks, 1924.

Mumford, Lewis. *The Brown Decades*. New York: Harcourt, Brace and Company, 1931.
Muther, Richard. *History of Modern Painting*. Vol. 3. London: J. M. Dent, and New York: E. P. Dutton, 1896.

National Cyclopedia of American Biography. Vol. 11. New York: J. T. White and Company, 1901.
Neuhaus, Eugen. *History and Ideals of American Art*. Palo Alto: Stanford University Press, 1931.
Nichols, H. Hobart. *Catalogue of the Fine Arts Exhibit of the United States of America, Paris Exposition, 1900*. Boston: Noyes, Platt and Company, 1900.

O'Connor, John, Jr. "A Footnote to 'The Wreck.'" *Carnegie Magazine* (Pittsburgh), February 1937.

Pach, Walter. *Queer Thing, Painting:Forty Years in the World of Art*. New York and London: Harper and Brothers, 1938.
————. "Winslow Homer et la signification de son oeuvre." *L'Art et les Artistes* (Paris), November 1912.
Pattison, James William. *Painters Since Leonardo*. Chicago: Herbert S. Stone and Company, 1904.
Phillips, Duncan. *Brief Estimates of the Painters in a Collection in the Making*. Phillips Publications, No. 5. New York: E. Weyhe, 1926.
Pope, Arthur. *The Language of Drawing and Painting*. Cambridge: Harvard University Press, 1949.
————. *The Painter's Terms*. Cambridge: Harvard University Press, 1929.
————. "Water-colours by Winslow Homer." *Fogg Art Museum Notes* (Cambridge), June 1926.
Pousette-Dart, Nathaniel. *Winslow Homer*. New York: Frederick A. Stokes Company, 1923.
Private Art Collection of Thomas B. Clarke. Catalogue. New York: American Art Galleries, 1899.
Pulsifer, Harold Trowbridge. "Winslow Homer's Paintings Shown at Prout's Neck." *Portland Evening Express* (Portland, Maine), July 23, 1936.

Reuterdahl, Henry. "Winslow Homer: An Appreciation from a Seagoing Viewpoint." *Craftsman* (New York), April 1911.
Richardson, Edgar Preston. *American Romantic Painting*. New York: E. Weyhe, 1944.
————. *Painting in America: The Story of 350 Years*. New York: Thomas Crowell Company, 1956.
————. *The Way of Western Art*. Cambridge: Harvard University Press, 1939.
————. "Three Early Works by Winslow Homer." *Bulletin of the Detroit Institute of Arts* (Detroit), 1951–1952.
Robinson, Francis W. "Works by Winslow Homer in Cincinnati Collections." *Bulletin of the Cincinnati Art Museum* (Cincinnati), January 1937.
Rowe, L. Earle. "Winslow Homer." *Bulletin of the Rhode Island School of Design* (Providence), July 1917.

Saint-Gaudens, Homer. *The American Artist and His Times.* New York: Dodd, Mead and Company, 1941.

————. *Survey of American Painting.* Pittsburgh: Department of Fine Arts, Carnegie Institute, 1940.

————. "Winslow Homer." *Carnegie Magazine* (Pittsburgh), February 1937.

————. "Winslow Homer." *The Critic* (New York), April 1905.

————. *Winslow Homer Centenary Exhibition: 1836–1936.* Pittsburgh: Carnegie Institute, 1936.

Sanborn, Ashton. "Winslow Homer's 'Adirondack Guide.'" *Bulletin of the Museum of Fine Arts* (Boston), June 1948.

Schlesinger, Arthur Meier. *The Rise of the City, 1878–1898.* New York: Macmillan Company, 1933.

Sheldon, George W. *American Painters.* New York: D. Appleton and Company, 1879.

Sherman, Frederick Fairchild. *American Painters of Yesterday and Today.* New York: Privately Printed, 1919.

Soby, James Thrall, and Dorothy C. Miller. *Romantic Painting in America.* New York: Museum of Modern Art, 1943.

Stanton, Howard. "Winslow Homer's 'Northeaster.'" *Harper's Magazine* (New York), March 1910.

Stonehouse, Augustus. "Winslow Homer." *Art Review* (New York), February 1887.

Tyrell, Henry. "American Aquarellists — Homer to Marin." *International Studio* (New York), September 1921.

"Unsuspected Art of Winslow Homer." *Literary Digest* (New York), October 22, 1910.

Van Dyke, John C. *American Painting and Its Tradition.* New York: Charles Scribner's Sons, 1919.

Van Rensselaer, M. G. "An American Painter in England." *Century Magazine* (New York), November 1883.

Van Rensselaer, Mrs. Schuyler. *Six Portraits.* Boston and New York: Houghton Mifflin Company, 1889.

Walker, John, and James Macgill. *Great American Paintings from Smibert to Bellows, 1729–1924.* New York: Oxford University Press. 1943.

Ware, Moses Weld. *Beacon Lights in the History of Prout's Neck.* Scarborough, Maine: The Prout's Neck Association, n.d.

Washburn, Gordon Bailey. "American Classics of the Nineteenth Century." *Carnegie Magazine,* October 1957.

"Watercolors by Winslow Homer." *Art and Progress* (New York), December 1915.

Watson, Forbes. "Ryder, Eakins, Homer: Museum of Modern Art Exhibition." *The Arts* (New York), May 1930.

————. "Winslow Homer." *American Magazine of Art* (New York), October 1936.

————. *Winslow Homer.* New York: Crown Publishers, 1942.

Wheelwright, John. "Remington and Winslow Homer." *Hound and Horn* (New York), July–September, 1933.

White, C. Langdon, and Edwin J. F. Foscue. *Regional Geography of America.* New York: Prentice-Hall, 1943.

"Winslow Homer." *Nation* (New York), October 6, 1910.

"Winslow Homer." *Outlook* (New York), October 15, 1910.

Winslow Homer. Exhibition Catalogue. Philadelphia: Pennsylvania Museum of Art, 1936.

Winslow Homer, Artist. Exhibition Catalogue. New York: M. Knoedler and Company, 1936.

"Winslow Homer's Rank in American Painting." *American Review of Reviews* (New York), July 1908.

Winslow Homer Watercolors and Drawings. Exhibition Catalogue. New York: Wildenstein Galleries, Summer 1948.

Winslow Homer Water Colors and Early Oils from the Estate of Mrs. Charles S. Homer and Other Sources. Exhibition Catalogue. New York: Macbeth Gallery, May–June 1938.

Woods, Amy, "Shipwrecks Along the New England Coast." *New England Magazine,* November 1904.

Wright, Willard Huntington. "Modern American Painters — and Winslow Homer." *Forum* (New York), December 1915.

Young, J. W. "The Art of Winslow Homer." *Fine Arts Journal* (Chicago), February 1908.

Index

Italic figures denote illustrations in the text.

ABBEY, EDWIN A., 210
Adams, Edward D., 80
Adams, Henry, 162
Addison Gallery of American Art, 98
Adirondack Lake, 163
Adirondack Preserve Association, 86, 98
Adirondack Scene, 104
Adirondacks, 101
Adirondacks, 3, 13, 25, 42, 50, 86, 96, 106, 118, 124, 126, 127, 130, 178, 195, 210, 220, 224, 233, 242, 244, 247
Adolescence, 5
Afterglow, 54
After the Hunt, 106
After the Tornado, Bahamas, 162
Alexander, John W., 210
Alma-Tadema, Sir Lawrence, 113
American, New York, 170
American Art News, 171
American Fine Arts Exhibit, Exposition Universelle, Paris, 210
American House, Boston, 45, 73, 140
American Spirit in Art (Frank J. Mather), 147
American Watercolor Society, 11, 55, 59, 79
Amherst College, 117
Appleton's Journal, 10, 213
Appomattox, 199
Archambault, Laurence, 187
Ark, the, Prout's Neck, 31, 36, 40, 42, 45, 49, 51, 60, 65, 88, 89, 95, 110, 121, 143, 153, 163, 179, 181, 182, 187, 200, 206, 209, 221, 241
Arles, France, 80
Armour Institute of Technology, Chicago, 212
Army of the Potomac, 7
Artist's Studio in an Afternoon Fog, 121, *123,* 217

At the Foot of the Lighthouse (Wild Geese), 248
Atlantic City, 64, 80, 191, 240, 242
Atwood, Charles B., 111

Bachelor Homes — Prout's Neck, Winter of 1897-1898, 154
Backrush, 92
Bahamas, 74, 86, 88, 159, 214, 215, 217
Ballou's Pictorial, 5, 6
Bamboo in the Wind (Wu Chên), *160, 161,* 162
Bar Harbor, Maine, 29
Baroque art, 121
Barrie Co., George, 114
Barye, Antoine Jean, 134
Bass Fishing, Florida, 87
Bath, Maine, 239
Bath Iron Works, 239
Bather, 217
Bear Breaking Through a Canoe, 133, *134,* 196
Beatty, John W., 119, 154, 221
Beaux, Cecilia, 151, 210
Beaux Arts, École de, 113
Believe It-or-Not, Robert Ripley, 156
Belmont, Mass., 38, 74, 154
Below Zero, 116
Bensell, Eugene B., 10
Bermuda, 74, 86, 166, 214, 215, 218
Bermuda Pigs (Bermuda Settlers), 215
Bermuda Settlers, 196, 215
Bertin's brokerage house, Paris, 33
Biddey's Cove, 202
Big Pines, 124
Bixbee, William J., 135
Black Point, Prout's Neck, 28
Black Point Inn (Southgate Inn), 29, 232, 233

[273]

Black Rock, Eastern Point, Prout's Neck, 213
Blown Away, 144, 145
Blue Boat, 100, 203
Blum, Robert, 152
Boatman, 106
Bolton, Theodore, 20, 73, 98, 99
Boston, Mass., 4, 6, 18, 25, 36, 44, 73, 108, 127, 140, 145, 152, 153, 155, 158, 179, 191, 216, 218, 249, 252, 256
Boudin, Eugène, 9
Bowdoin College, 74, 115
Bower, Alexander, 69, 89, 154, 205, 206, 218
Boy Fishing, 104, 105
Boynton, Captain Thomas, 143
Breakers Near Rocks, Prout's Neck, 120
Breaking Storm, Maine Coast, 120
Breaking Wave, 222, 223
Breaking Wave on a Shore Line, 91
Breakwater, Tynemouth, 56
Breezing Up, 11
Brooklyn Museum, 50
Brooks Brothers, N.Y., 180
Brown, Alvin, 154, 194
Brown, J. G., 172
Brueghel, Pieter the elder, 95
Brunswick, Maine, 241
Brush, George de Forest, 210
Brush and Pencil, magazine, 221
Brush-Ins, the, 219
Buccaneers, 77
Bucksport, Maine, 5
Bufford, John H., 5, 25, 48
Bulletin, New York, 170
Bungalow, Bermuda, 160
Burnham, Daniel H., 111
Burnt Mountain, 107

Calling the Worshippers. See Alma-Tadema, Sir Lawrence
Cambridge, Mass., 5, 256
Cammock House, Prout's Neck, 29, 69
Camp Fire, Adirondacks, 13, 14, 100
Campaign Sketches, 118
Canada, 3, 106, 126, 127, 130, 132, 134, 178, 224, 247, 250
Canaday John, 4
Canajoharie Art Gallery, N.Y., 224
Cannon Rock, Prout's Neck, 117, *137,* 139, 140, 196, 220
Canoe in the Rapids, 164, 165, 252
Cape Elizabeth, Maine, 60, 65, 69, 234, 235, 236, 237

Cape Trinity, Saguenay River, 250
Captains Courageous, 13, 72
Carnegie Institute, Museum of Art, 153, 154, 158, 159, 217, 221, 244
Carter, Hattie, 54
Casanova, Giovanni Jacopo, 175
Casting, 251
Catalonia, steamship, 24
Central Park in Winter, 111
Century Club, N.Y., 209
Cézanne, Paul, 33, 77, 152, 171, 172
Channel Bass, 230
Charleston, South Carolina, Exposition, 220
Chase, William Merritt, 210
Chase Gallery, J. Eastman, Boston, 58, 59
Checkley House, Prout's Neck, 29, 34, 143, 154, 203, 224
Checkley Point, Prout's Neck, 142, 143, 212
Chelmsford, Mass., cider, 183
Chevreul, Michel Eugene, 226
Chicago, Illinois, 111, 116, 221
Chicoutimi, Saguenay River, P.Q., 127
Chinese painting, 164
Chronological bronze medal, 150
City Art Museum, St. Louis, 6
Civil War, 8, 9, 16, 53, 54, 86, 108, 179, 196, 256
Clarke, Thomas B., 82, 98, 107, 112, 147, 149, 150, 157, 158, 159
Clarke Collection, 108
Cloud Shadows, 89
Coast Guard service, United States, 234, 236, 237, 238
Coast in Winter, 107
Coast of Maine, 121, 210
Cohling, tailor, Portland, Maine, 180
Columbia University, N.Y., 52
Coming Storm, 218, 219
Conch Divers, 77, 78, 216
Conrad, Joseph, 147
Constable, John, 107
Converse Gold Medal, 142
Coolbroth, Frank, 158, 256
Cooper Union Museum, 64, 104, 234, 250
Copley, John Singleton, 4
Coral Formations, 214
Corcoran Art Journal, 175, 176
Corcoran Gallery, Washington, D.C., 153
Courbet, Gustave, 7, 95, 110
Cox, Kenyon, 68, 171, 216, 217, 230
Cuba, 3, 215, 219, 220

Index

Cullercoates, England, 18
Cumberland Club, Portland, 210
Cumberland County, Maine, 74
Cummings, Professor Thomas Seir, 6
Cunard steamship line, 24, 147
Cupid and Psyche (Lionel Royer), 113
Currier and Ives, 13, 111
Curtis, Mrs. Grace K., 241

Daily Advertiser, Boston, 59
Daily Press, Portland, 256, 257
Dana, Richard Henry, 147
Danger Ahead, 10
Dans le Jungle, Florida (Bermuda Pigs, also *Bermuda Settlers*), 215
Davis, Samuel, 155
Day Book, Homer Collection, Bowdoin College, 56, 74, 103, 162, 184, 201, 215, 216, 217, 220
Deer Drinking, 133
Degas, Edgar, 9, 33, 75, 145, 205
Delacroix, Eugene, 134
Derelict and Sharks, 169
Diamond Shoal, 239, *240*, 242
Disaster (Walter Langley), 113
Disasters of War (Francisco Goya), 8
Dispatch, Pittsburgh, 151
Doll and Richards Gallery, 58, 69, 73, 74, 79, 108, 110, 147, 252
Doré, Gustave, 20
Dory, 68
Dougherty, Paul, 170
Downes, William Howe, 18, 59, 64, 80, 81, 89, 119, 135, 145, 155, 156, 171, 177, 186, 189, 201, 211, 213, 214, 221, 226, 230, 241, 244, 245, 248, 252, 255
Driftwood, 254, 255
Dubufe, Guillaume, 113
Duck Pond, Eastern Point, Prout's Neck, 237
Duran, Carolus, 151
Durand-Ruel, Georges, 33

EAKINS, THOMAS, 4, 16, 249
Early Evening, 243
Early Morning After a Storm at Sea, 93, 221, 223, 231
Eastern Point, 34, 57, 95, 141, 156, 157, 200
Eastern Point, Prout's Neck, 158, 213, *214*
Eastman Kodak No. 1, 75
Eight Bells, *81*, 82, 85, 103, 108, 147

El Greco (Domenikos Theotocopoulos), 171
El Rancho, cottage, 28, 41, 50, 184, 242, 246
Elevation of the Cross. See Rubens, Peter Paul
Ellis, Carrie (Mrs. John Gatchell), 103
End of the Day, 163
End of the Hunt, *106*, 107
England, 8, 16, 23, 24, 25, 54, 56, 80, 193
Enjoying the Breeze, 56
Entering the First Rapids, 251
Ernesta (Cecilia Beaux), 151
Europe, 14, 16, 75, 96
Evening Post, New York, 95, 170
Exceptional Case, An, 175
Exposition Universelle Internationale, Paris, 209

Fallen Deer, 133
Falmouth Hotel, Portland, Maine, 73
Faneuil Hall, Boston, 4
Fanny Neadeth, schooner, 234
Farmhouse, 5
Farr, Dr. Charles, 200
"Father Homer's Rock," 42, 209
Fauves, French school, 219
Fearns, Annie Jane (Mrs. William H. Munroe), 40
Ferry Beach, 33, 91, 121, 156, 224
First National Bank, Portland, Maine, 201
Fisher Girl on the Beach, 55, 112, 117
Fishermen Beaching a Boat, 148
Fishermen's Holiday, 163
Fishing Boats, Key West, 225
Fishing in the Adirondacks, 163
Fishing Off Scarboro, 23
Fishwives, 55, 112
Fitzgerald, Riter, 170, 171
Flamborough Head, England, 24, 168
Flanagan, Michael, 52
Florida, 42, 74, 86, 87, 89, 152, 229, 230, 244
Florida Bobolinks, 152
Florida Jungle, 77
Flower Garden, 160
Flying Wild Geese (Maruyama Okyo), 248
Flynn, Michael "Farmer," 103
Fog Warning, 69, 70, 71, 72, 73, 85, 125, 147
Fogg Art Museum, Harvard University, 101

Foss, Joseph, 57, 58, 232
Fountains at Night — World's Columbian Exposition, 115
Fox Hunt, 109, 111, 206, 210, 256
France, 8, 194
Freer Gallery of Art, Smithsonian Institution, Washington, D.C., 243
Friend Street, Boston, 4

Gale, 111, 176, 191
Galveston, Texas, 28, 53, 162
Gardner, Albert Ten Eyck, 111
Gatchell, John, 82, 100, *102,* 103, 106, 145, 149, 154, 182, 208
Gatchell, Lee, 208
Gatchell, Wiley, 100, 103, 105, 106, 107
Gauguin, Paul, 33, 80, 152
Gilbert Rocks, Prout's Neck, 122
Gilchrist, Wallace, 205, 208
Gilded Age, 114
Girl and Sheep, 57
Girl in a Fog (Fisher Girl), 117
Girls, Pine Point, 56
Gladiolas (Mrs. Charles S. Homer, Sr.), 36
Glass Windows, Bahamas, 214
Gloucester, Mass., 11, 12, 17, 18, 19, 21, 57, 66, 72, 91, 148, 224
Godey's Lady's Book, 10
Gonzales, Boyas, 224
Goodrich, Lloyd, 56, 99, 159, 177, 220, 235, 237
Goodwin, Mr. and Mrs. William B., 188
Googins, Alonzo, 30
Googins, Helen, 180
Googins, Roswell, 66, 68, 182, 234
Googins, William, 183, 184, 185, 232, 249
Governor's Palace, Havana, 74
Governor's Wife, Bahama Islands, 74
Goya, Francisco, 8
Grand Banks, Newfoundland, 72
Grand Concourse, World's Columbian Exposition, 111, 115
Great Massacre Pond, Prout's Neck, 101
Great Wave (Katsushika Hokusai), 108
Guide, 106, 251
Guide Carrying a Deer, 99
Guide Hiding a Canoe, 107
Gulf Stream, 168, 169, 170, 171, 172, 179, 241
Gunsaulus, Dr. F. W., 212

Halibut Fishing, 70, 72
Hamilton, Miss Mary, 40, 65

Hamilton Place, Boston, 58
Harding, Charles, 118
Harding, Mrs. Charles (Ida Meserve), 54, 57, 117, 153
Hark! the Lark, 56, 212
Harper's Weekly, 6, 7, 8, 11, 12
Harvard College, 5
Harvie, James, 239
Haul of Herring, 68
Hazeltine, William T., 213
Hearn, George A., 220
Heavy Surf, Prout's, 61
Herald, Boston, 125
Herald, New York, 170
Herring Net, 66, *67,* 68, 69, 70, 72, 85
Herter, Albert, 172
Higgins Beach, Maine, 65, 149, 234
High Cliff, Coast of Maine, 122, *125*
High Cliff, Prout's Neck, 97, 122, *124,* 154, 200, 209
Hiroshige, Ando, 9, 66
Hirshhorn, Joseph H., 17
History of Modern Painting. See Muther, Richard
Hokusai, Katsushika, 107, 108, 140
Holt, Harvey, 102, 103,
Homer, Arthur Benson, 27-28, 39, 41, 53, 65, 81, 82, 141, 157, 162, 184, 191, 204, 205, 215, 224, 225, 227, 232, 240, 241, 242, 243, 246, 247, 249, 254-255, 256
Homer, Mrs. Arthur Benson (Alice Patch), 27, 108
Homer, Arthur Patch, 27, 47, 186, 217
Homer, Augusta F., 205
Homer, Charles Lowell, 27, 28, 34, 38, 39, 47, 53, 61, 74, 79, 81, 88, 90, 92, 95, 97, 98, 99, 100, 112, 139, 140, 145, 156, 162, 178, 179, 180, 185, 186, 201, 213, 217, 221, 231, 238, 240, 242-243, 246, 248
Homer, Mrs. Charles Lowell (Doris Piper), 34, 70
Homer, Mrs. Charles Lowell (Mary George Clark), "Georgie," 222, 242, 243
Homer, Charles Savage, Jr., 28, 30, 38, 41, 42, 46, 47, 49, 50-51, 52, 53, 65, 74, 84, 88, 95, 96, 106, 115, 116, 119, 121, 126-127, 133, 138, 141, 143, 149, 150, 152-153, 154, 156, 157, 181, 187, 191, 192, 197, 199, 202, 203, 209, 214, 217, 222, 224, 231, 232, 241, 242, 243, 244, 246, 247, 251
Homer, Mrs. Charles Savage, Jr. (Martha E. French, "Mattie"), 36, 45, 49, 51,

53, 96, 98, 115, 138, 141, 154, 157, 181, 187, 191-192, 203, 210, 224, 238, 239, 241, 246, 247
Homer, Charles Savage, Sr., 5, 28, 36, 38-41, 44-47, 49, 54, 65, 110, 135, 140, 150, 152, 157, 181, 195, 196, 197, 206, 207, 253
Homer, Mrs. Charles Savage, Sr. (Henrietta Maria Benson), 5, 34, 36, 51, 65
Homer Collection, Bowdoin College, 201, 216, 229
Homer's Cabin, Tourilli Club, Province of Quebec, 133
Homosassa, Florida, 227, 229-230, 247
Homosassa River, 229, 229
Honeymoon of Mr. and Mrs. Arthur B. Homer, 254
"Hotel de Wiggin," Prout's Neck, 154, 155
Hotel Rudolf, Atlantic City, 152, 240
Hotel Seville, New York City, 254
Houghton Farm, Cornwall, N.Y., 57
Hound and Hunter, 107, 133
House and Trees in Nassau, 166
How We Went up the Mountain (Eugene B. Bensell), 10
Hozu River (Maruyama Okyo), 251
Hudson River, N.Y., 57, 130, 220
Hudson River Logging, 130, 164
Hunting Dog Among Dead Trees, 124
Huntington, Daniel, 12
Huntington, Dr. George, 200
Huntsman and Dogs, 99, 108
Hyde, Mrs. James Nevin, 60, 84

Ile Marlin, P.Q., 252
Illustrated London News, 206
Impressionism, French, 9, 26, 75, 194, 216
In the Gloaming (photograph, Charles Walker), 225
In the Jungle, Florida, 77
Incoming Tide, 55, 61
India Wharf Station, Portland, Maine, 134
Indian Camp, Montagnis Indians, Pointe Bleue, 132
Indian Camp, Roberval, P.Q., 132
Indian Rock, Narragansett (William T. Hazeltine), 213
Inness, George, 110, 157, 159, 210
Inside the Bar, 55
International Exhibition, Carnegie Institute, 150, 217
International Exposition, Paris, 8

International Studio, 245
Isles of Shoals, Maine, 27
Item, Philadelphia, 170

JAMAICA RUM, 184
Japan, 162
Japanese art, 9, 66, 91, 110, 111, 145, 162, 164, 212, 251
Jordan, Charles, 149, 156
Jyaku-chu, 230

KALER, HARRY, 233
Kaler, Mrs. Harry, 182
Kappes, Alfred, 152
Keenan, Sergeant Joseph, 154
Keene Valley, New York, 102
Kelsey, Albert, 8
Kendall, Sergeant, 172
Kettle Cove, Prout's Neck, 44, 122, 200, 204, 217, 219, 254
Key West, Florida, 225
King, Daisy B., 176
Kipling, Rudyard, 13, 72, 147
Kissing the Moon, 232, 233
Kittery, Maine, 27
Klackner, C., galleries, N.Y., 82, 96, 119
Klee, Paul, 230
Knoedler Galleries, N.Y., 169, 215, 218, 220, 249
Kuniyoshi, Utagawa, 95
Kurtz, Charles M., 114

LA FARGE, JOHN, 97, 108, 162, 191, 205
Ladd, Anthony, T., 104
Lady in Brown (Sir John Lavery), 151
Lamb, Mrs. Ella Condie, 172
Land and Sea (Paul Dougherty), 170
Langley, Walter, 113
Larrabee, Mrs. Howard C. (Marie Annie Seavey), 54, 88, 99, 100, 184, 190, 196, 198, 232, 233, 234
Latin Quarter, Paris, 180
Lavery, Sir John, 151
Lawrence, William Witherle, 52
Lawrence Scientific School, Cambridge, Mass., 49
Lee, Henry, 64, 65, 69, 73, 81, 103, 182, 233
Lermond, Captain William J., 236
Levitt, Christopher, 66
Libby, Mrs. Allen (Maude Googins), 89, 91, 142
Libby, Annie, 190, 195
Libby, Benaiah, 28, 29

Libby, Isa May, 80
Libby, Leonard, 65, 80, 99, 180, 183, 185, 190, 199, 202, 206, 237
Libby, Louise, 28, 29, 30
Libby, Minerva, 28, 29
Libby, Nehemiah, 28
Libby, Samuel, 195
Libby, Captain Silas, 29
Libby, Mrs. Silas, 190
Libby, Captain Thomas, 28, 29
Libby's Neck (Prout's Neck), Maine, 28
Life Line, 62, *63*, 64, 96, 108, 149
Light Blue Sea at Prout's, 61
Light on the Sea, 153, 154, 170
Lincoln, Mrs. Roland C., 248
"Little Arthur" (Arthur Patch Homer), 242
"Little Charlie" (Charles Lowell Homer), 232
Logging, 220
London, England, 17, 151
Long Branch, New Jersey, 9
Longfellow, Henry Wadsworth, 12
Lookout, 54
Lookout—"All's Well," 145, *146*, 147, 153, 159, 210
Lotos Club, New York, 142
Louisiana Purchase Exposition, St. Louis, 231
Louvre, Paris, 8, 9
Lowell, Mass., 65
Luxembourg Palace Museum, Paris, 210

MACBETH, ROBERT, 140, 192
Macbeth, William, 211, 214, 255
MacKnight, Dodge, 216
MacMonnies, Frederick, 111, 115
Ma Yuan, 105
Maine Coast, 139, 211, 220
"Maine Law," prohibition, 134
Manet, Edouard, 9, 33, 121, 172, 194, 210
Mansfield, Burton, 117
Marine View with Mountains, 250
Martin, Homer, 210
Martinique, island of, 80
Maruyama Okyo. *See* Okyo, Maruyama
Massachusetts Institute of Technology, 232
Mather, Professor Frank Jewett, Jr., 147
Mattie, yacht, 106
McClellan, General George B., 7
McKim, Charles Follen, 111
Mead, William R., 111
Means, Professor Thomas, 117

Mechlin, Miss Leila, 245
Medford rum, 184
Medici, Lorenzo de, 159
Melcher, Gari, 151
Melville, Herman, 147
Mending the Nets, 57, 58
Mending the Tears, 142
Merriam, Cyrus, 51, 197
Merriam, Henry, 197
Merrick, J. Vaughan, 46
Merrick, Thomas B., 46
Metropolitan Museum of Art, N.Y., 50, 111, 121, 161, 170, 211, 231, 241
Millet, Jean François, 9, 59
Ministry of Fine Arts, French, 210
Mink Pond, 164, 230
Minneapolis, Minn., 75
Mondrian, Piet, 220
Monet, Claude, 163
Monticello Hotel, Norfolk, Va., 241
Montreal, Province of Quebec, 224, 247
Moonlight, 91
Moonlight, Wood's Island Light, 120
Morgan, Mrs. Randal, 249
Morro Castle, Santiago de Cuba, 219, 220
Morse, Samuel Finley Breese, 75
Morton, Frederick W., 221
Motonobu, Kano, 251
Moulton, Augustus F., 73
Mount Auburn Cemetery, Cambridge, Mass., 157, 256
Mountains and Palms, Cuba, 161
Munroe, William H., 33
Munroe, Mrs. William H. (Annie Jane Fearns), 40, 42, 47, 99, 109, 134, 143, 153, 179, 184-185, 187, 189, 193, 195, 197, 200, 206
Murger, Henri, 180
Musée National d'Art Moderne, Paris, 90
Museum of Fine Arts, Boston, 55, 111, 125, 159
Musicians, 9
Muther, Richard, 151-152
Muybridge, Eadweard, 75

NASSAU, BAHAMAS, 74, 168, 169, 218
Nassau, N.P., Bahamas, 160
Nation, 171
National Academy of Design, N.Y., 6, 7, 64, 69, 79, 80, 108, 169-170, 193, 210
National Gallery of Art, 111, 249
Natural Bridge, Nassau, 214

Index

New England, 29, 71, 79, 192, 193
New England Magazine, 234
New Orleans, La., 65
New York City, 6, 18, 24, 25-26, 32, 52, 55, 74, 80, 96, 97, 151, 154, 158, 175, 177, 191, 193, 202, 247
Newhall, Beaumont, 75
News, Indianapolis, 172
Nichols, H. Hobart, 210
Night Watch (Rembrandt), 13
Norcross, Grenville, 73, 125
Norcross, Miss Laura, 125
Norfolk, Va., 236, 241, 242
North Sea, 16, 17, 19, 21, 24, 72, 243
North Woods, 118, *119,* 251
North Woods Club, Adirondacks, 107, 133
North Woods Club, Minerva, Essex County, N.Y., 50, 86, 107, 247
Northeaster, 93, *139,* 140, 220
Notre Dame (Jean-François Raffaelli), 151
Nursemaid, 9

OAK HILL STATION, Scarborough township, 65, 155, 187
O'Brien and Son's Gallery, Chicago, 116, 211, 212, 221, 222
"O'Brien picture;" "O'B" (*Early Morning After a Storm at Sea*), 221, 222, *223*
O'Keeffe, Georgia, 36
Okyo, Maruyama, 230, 248, 251
Old Friends, 124
Old Orchard, Maine, 33, 65, 212, 236
Old Prout's Neck, 73
Old Settlers, Adirondacks, 107, 124
Old Town, Maine, 100
Oliver, Elbridge, 65, 109, 158, 206
On a Lee Shore, 211, 235
On the Cliff, 117
Oranges on a Branch, 183
Orient, 79
Oriental art, 162
Ouananiche Fishing, 164, *165,* 230
Our Special, 196

PACH, WALTER, 210
Pacific Mills, Lawrence, Mass., 49
Painter's Terms, The (Arthur Pope), 171
Palm Tree, Nassau, 161, 162
Palm Trees, St. John's River, Florida, 88
Pan-American Exposition, Buffalo, 217
Paris, France, 8, 9, 14, 33, 203, 210

Parker House, Boston, 191
Parliament Buildings, 17
Payson, Mr. and Mrs. Charles Shipman, 122
Peabodeau, Alphonse. *See* Flanagan, Michael
Pennsylvania Academy of the Fine Arts, 122, 142, 220
"Perpetual Youth," 47
Perry, Commodore Matthew C., 9
Persian painting, 164
Phelps, Orson "Mountain," 102
Philadelphia, Pa., 114, 249
Philadelphia Centennial, 111
Picasso, Pablo, 147
Pillsbury, Bartlett, 158, 246
Pine Point, Maine, 117, 212
Pioneer, 211
Pissarro, Camille, 75, 152
Pittsburgh, Pa., 245
Plains of Abraham, Quebec, 131
Poe, Edgar Allan, 175
Pope, Arthur, 171
"Portable Painting House," 155
Portage, 251
Portland Art Museum, Portland, Maine, 69
Portland, Maine, 27, 65, 73, 135, 177, 179, 195, 218, 234, 236
Portrait of Captain Smith, 66
Prang Company, N.Y., 118, 121
Prisoners from the Front, 7, 8
Prout, Timothy, 28
Prout's Neck, Breakers, 222
Prout's Neck, Breaking Wave, 61, *62*
Prout's Neck, Evening, 120
Prout's Neck, Looking Toward Old Orchard, 66
Prout's Neck, Rocky Shore, 61, *62,* 140
Prout's Neck Association, 29, 84, 202
Prout's Neck Surf, 222
Puccini, Giacomo, 180
Pulsifer, Harold T., 241
Putnam, Mr. and Mrs. George, 200, 237

QUEBEC, CITY OF, 126, 127, 131, 134
Quebec, Province of, 42, 126, 158, 214

RAFFAELLI, JEAN-FRANÇOIS, 151
Rainy Day in Camp, 7
Rapids, Hudson River, 220
Rapids (Kano Motonobu), 251
Reichard, Gustav, gallery, N.Y., 79, 97
Rembrandt van Rijn, 15, 16, 83, 175

Remington, Frederic, 75
Renoir, Auguste, 33
Revue de l'art, 215
Rhode Island School of Design, 212
Richards, William T., 213
Richardson, Mrs. Loring C. (Sadie Sylvester), 54
Right and Left, 248
Road in Nassau, 76
Roberval, Lake St. John, P.Q., 126, 229
Rochester Memorial Art Museum, University of Rochester, 218
Roebuck, Thomas, 52, 190
Rondel, Frédéric, 6, 210
Roosevelt, Theodore, 202
Rowing Homeward, 87
Royal Academy, London, 56
Royal Palms, Cuba, 161
Royer, Lionel, 113
Rubens, Peter Paul, 207
Rum Cay (Turtle Cay), 78, *167*, 168, 217
Ryder, Albert, 4

SACO BAY, MAINE, 27, 33, 54, 65, 73, 142, 202, 209, 212, 235
Saco River, Maine, 66
Saguenay River, Grand Discharge, St. Johns, P.Q., 251
Saguenay River, Lower Rapids, 251
Saguenay River, Province of Quebec, 127
Sailing a Dory, 57
Sailing the Catboat, 11, 18
Sailing Vessel in a Storm (Sesson), 145
Saint-Gaudens, Augustus, 111, 205
Saint-Gaudens, Homer, 205
St. James Episcopal Church, Prout's Neck, 41, 46, 193
St. John, Lake, P.Q., 126, 127, 164, 230, 253
St. John's River, Florida, 86
St. Lawrence River, Canada, 131
St. Raymond, Province of Quebec, 126
Sainte Anne River, Province of Quebec, 127
Salem, Mass., 186
Salt Kettle, 160
Sam, 54, 116, 152, 178, 185, 195
Sanborn, Benjamin Franklin, 33, 57, 89, 142, 154
Sanborn, Cora Googins, 56, 91, 142
Sanctuary, Prout's Neck, 84, 101, 187
Santiago de Cuba, 74, 160
Santiago Harbor, Cuba, 44, 220
Saratoga Springs, N.Y., 224, 242

Sargent, John Singer, 4, 210
Savage, Mrs. Maxwell (Marguerite Downing), 184, 192, 221
Saved, 64
Scarboro (Scarborough), England, 23
Scarboro station, 187
Scarboro; also Scarborough township, Cumberland County, Maine, 28, 57, 65, 106, 109, 116, 150, 152, 154, 158, 182, 189, 210, 241, 242, 243, 256
Scarborough River, Maine, 66
Schooner at Anchor, 68
Schooner at Anchor, Key West, 225
Schooner on Saco Bay, 66
Schooners in the Moonlight, 66
Scotch Mist, 148
Searchlight, Harbor Entrance, Santiago de Cuba, 219
Seavey, Benjamin Franklin, 179
Seavey, Harris, 65, 100, 194, 195
Seavey, Winslow, 179
Seavey, Zenas, 88, 179, 190, 204, 232
Sesson, Shūkei, 145
Seville House, N.Y., 191
Shark Fishing, 169
Sheeler, Charles, 75
Shepherdess of Houghton Farm, 211
Shipbuilder (Gari Melcher), 151
Ship's Boat, 60, 61, 149
"Shipwrecks Along the New England Coast" (Amy Woods), 234
Shooting the Rapids, 252
Shooting the Rapids, Saguenay River, 252, 253
Shooting the Rapids at Grand Discharge, 252
Shore and Surf, 166
Shore at Nassau, 160, 166
Signal of Distress, 95, 96, 149
Skating in Central Park, 6
Sketch of a Soldier, 7
Slave Ship (J. M. W. Turner), 170
Sloop, Bermuda, 166, 224
Small Sloop, Saco Bay, 66
"Smiling Sharks" (*Gulf Stream*), 170
Snake in the Grass, 231
Snug Harbor home, N.Y., 236
Society of American Artists, 153
Solitary Angler, 105
South Sea Islands, 162
Southgate Inn, Prout's Neck, 30, 54, 232, 233
Spanish-American War, 220
Spanish Flag, 76

Spanish fleet, 44
Sponge Diver, Bahamas, 78, *79,* 168, 216
Sponge Fishing, Bahamas, 224
Sprague, Phineas W., 249
S. S. Pierce Company, Boston, 41, 184
Stanley Steamer, 231
Startled, 196
Stephenson, S. L., 29, 44, 200
Stephenson, Mrs. S. L., 44
Stevens, Mrs. Albert (Charlotte Googins), 103, 109, 180, 190
Stevens, Henry Wingate, 217
Stevens, John Calvin, 217
Stevens, John Howard, 218
Stevens, Dr. Theodore M., 218
Stewart, Julius, L., 113
Storm-Beaten (Weather-Beaten), 122
Storm on the English Coast, 148
Stowing Sail, Bahamas, 225, 227
Stratton's Island, Maine, 66, 211, 234-237
Street Scene, Santiago de Cuba, 76
Study (for *Gulf Stream*), 169
Study (for *Herring Net*), 68
Study (for *The Wreck*), 148
Sullivan, Louis, 111
Sumac (Mrs. Charles S. Homer, Sr.), 36
Summer Night, 89, *90,* 91, 95, 96, 110, 115, 120, 142, 145, 210
Summer Squall, 143, *144,* 145
Sun, New York, 170
Sunday Morning in Virginia, 152
Sung (dynasty) painting, Chinese, 130
Sunlight on the Coast, 92, 93, 95
Sunset, Saco Bay, 142, 153
Sunset over Saco Bay, 121
Sunshine and Shadow, 120
Surf at Eastern Point, 213
Surf at Prout's, 61
Sylvester, Sadie (Mrs. Loring C. Richardson), 57

TAIT, A. F., 13
Taking an Observation, 81
Tampa, Florida, 227
Tarbell, Edmund C., 154
Telegraph, Philadelphia, 108
Temple gold medal, 220
Tenth Street Studios, N.Y., 26
Texas, sailboat, 81, 224
Thames River (England), 17, 121
Thayer, Abbott, 210
Thomaston, Maine, 236
Thoreau, Henry David, 105
Thornton, James, 155

Three Men in a Canoe, 129, 130
Tidal Wave (Hokusai), 140
Till Death Do Us Part, 80
Times, New York, 59, 170
Titian, Tiziano Vecelli, 198, 207
Toko, Hideyoshi, 230
Tornado, Bahamas, 161, 162
Toulouse-Lautrec, Henri de, 152
Tourilli, Lake, Province of Quebec, 126, 127, 229
Tourilli Club, Lake Tourilli, P.Q., 50, 126, 133, 187
Town in Bermuda, 74
Transcript, Boston, 58, 95, 108, 110, 171
Trip to Chicoutimi, 252
Trout Breaking, 86, *87,* 230
Trout Fishing, Lake St. John, Province of Quebec, 129, 130
Turkey Buzzard, 229, 230
Turner, J. M. W., 17, 19, 134, 140, 170, 205
Turner, Ross, 186
Turtle Cay (Rum Cay), 217
Turtle Island, Bahamas, 217
Turtle Island, Georgia, 217
Turtle Pond (Turtle Pound), 78, *167,* 168, 216, 217
Two Figures by the Sea, 55
Two Men in a Canoe, 130
Tyne, River, 17
Tynemouth, England, 8, 15-21, 23, 25, 27, 28, 31, 54, 55, 56, 57, 58, 59, 60, 61, 62, 64, 66, 72, 80, 81, 83, 85, 96, 102, 112, 117, 145, 147, 148, 199, 224, 239, 243, 250

UKIYOE PRINTS, Japanese, 145
Uncle Tom's Cabin, 152
Under the Coco Palm, 218
Undertow, 80, 149, 256
Union League Club, N.Y., 153, 157
Urquahart, Harvey, 158, 246

VAILL, MRS. EDWARD G. (Addie Kaler), 52, 99, 103, 121, 182, 185, 194, 232
Valentine Company, Brooklyn, N.Y., 49
Valley Forge, Pa., 158
Van Gogh, Vincent, 33, 80, 171, 174
View Near Naples (Mrs. Charles S. Homer, Sr.), 34
Virginia, state of, 11
Visit from the Old Mistress, 107
Vlaminck, Maurice, 219
Voice from the Cliffs, 55, 56, 59, 212

Voyage into New England. See **Levitt,** Christopher, 66

WALKER, CHARLES, 158, 225
Wallace, Rufus, 102
War Department, U.S., 44
Washburn Brothers, shipbuilders, 235, 236
Washington B. Thomas, schooner, 235-239
Watching a Storm on the English Coast, 112
Watching the Breakers, 96
Watching the Tempest, 22, 23, 148
Waterfall in the Adirondacks, 163
Watts shipyard, Thomaston, Maine, 236
Waugh, Frederick, 213
Weather-Beaten (Storm-Beaten), 122, 125, 231
Weir, J. Alden, 26
Wentworth, Dr. B. F., 256
West Indies, 42, 195, 215
West Point, Prout's Neck, 29, 54, *212*
West Townsend, Mass., 51, 52, 57, 139, 199
West Wind, 48, 96, 97, 107, 121, 149, 203
Whirlpool at Naruto (Ando Hiroshige), 251
Whistler, James Abbott McNeill, 17, 121, 205, 210
White, Reverend Stanley, 197
White, Stanford, 111
"White City" (World's Columbian Exposition, Chicago), 111
White Ribbon Society, Maine, 44, 135
White Rowboat, Florida, 88
Wiggin, "Captain" John, 154, 155
Wiggin, Joseph, 155

Wild Geese, 248
Willows Hotel, Prout's Neck, 27, 29
Windsor Hotel, Montreal, 224
Windstorm, Bahamas, 162
Winslow Homer Road, 39
Winsor and Newton, art supplies, 221
Winter, Prout's Neck, 93, 95
Winter Coast, 94, 95, 123
Winter Street studio, Boston, 25
Wolfe's Cove, Province of Quebec, 131, 250
Women on the Rocks, 117
Woodbine (Mrs. Charles S. Homer, Sr.), 36
Woodman and Fallen Tree, 100, 124
Woods, Amy, 234
Wood's Island Light, Maine, 65, 91
Worcester Art Museum, 191, 196, 215
Worden Hotel, Saratoga Springs, N.Y., 247
World, New York, 170, 171
World's Columbian Exposition, 111, 114, 176
Wreck, 148, 149-151, 207
Wreck Near Gloucester, 239
Wreck of the Atlantic, 12
Wreck of the Hesperus (Daniel E. Huntington), 12
Wreck of the Iron Crown, 148
Wrecked Schooner, 235, 237-239
Wright, Lewis, 42, 45-47, 135, 136-139, 186, 197
Wu Chên, 161

Yachting (Julius L. Stewart), 113
Young, Mahonri, 9, 98, 99
Young Ducks, 105
Yucatan, 215